THE ARCHAEOLOGY OF CANTERBURY

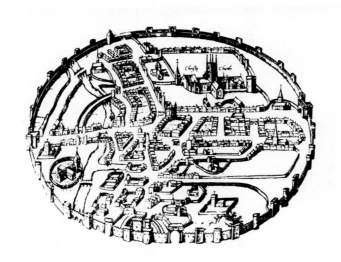

Frontispiece. Aerial view of the bombed area of Canterbury, looking north

THE ARCHAEOLOGY OF CANTERBURY

General Editors: A.P. Detsicas, M.A., F.S.A., and T.W.T. Tatton-Brown, B.A.

VOLUME VII

EXCAVATIONS IN THE ST. GEORGE'S STREET AND BURGATE STREET AREAS

By

S.S. Frere, C.B.E., M.A., Litt.D., D.Litt., F.B.A., F.S.A., and Sally Stow, M.A.

WITH CONTRIBUTIONS BY

A. Brocklebank, P. Bennett, B.A., P. Blockley, B.Sc., G.C. Dunning, B.SC., D.Lit., F.S.A.,
I.P. Garrard, B.J. Marples, M.A., M.Sc., D.F. Roberts, M.A., D.Phil., Sc.D.,
L. Sellwood, B.A., T.W.T. Tatton-Brown, B.A., and M.G. Wilson, F.S.A.

Published for the
Canterbury Archaeological Trust
by the
Kent Archaeological Society
Maidstone
1983

Published with the aid of a grant from the Department of the Environment

ISBN 0 906746 04 3

Printed in Great Britain by
Redwood Burn Limited, Trowbridge, Wiltshire,

CONTENTS

PART II: THE FINDS

PREFACE

Much of the south-eastern part of Canterbury was devastated by air-raids in 1942 (*Frontispiece*), and for almost a decade lay in ruins, devoid of reconstruction. The cellars along the street-frontages were indeed soon emptied of rubble because of the lurking danger of unexploded bombs; behind the frontages wild vegetation, dominated by buddleia and elder bushes, gradually became rampant. There was evidently an opportunity for archaeological exploration in the interval before rebuilding could take place.*

The situation was unprecedented in British archaeology. Under the wise guidance of the late Canon R.U. Potts, of B.H. St. J. O'Neil (at that time Chief Inspector of Ancient Monuments at the Office of Works), and of Major F.W. Tomlinson, a Canterbury Excavation Committee was set up; the members were fortunate to persuade Major Tomlinson to become their Hon. Secretary. The success of the project was in very large measure due to his local knowledge, organising ability and enthusiasm; a tradition of keen activity was quickly established and was later ably maintained by his successor John Boyle (at that time Town Clerk of Canterbury). Excavations, which lasted 6–10 weeks each year during holiday periods and were carried out by a varying force of volunteer diggers some 10–20 strong, began under the late Audrey Williams (later Mrs. W.F. Grimes) in 1944, and were thus the first of the post-war urban excavations to get under way. In 1946, when Audrey Williams was appointed Curator of the Verulamium Museum, she was succeeded as Director of Excavations by the present writer, under whom work continued on the same basis until 1955, after which two shorter seasons of 3–4 weeks were undertaken in 1956 and 1957. In 1960 two seasons of work were undertaken at the site of the Simon Langton School; these were supervised by John Wacher and Miss M.G. Wilson, respectively.

Until 1948 the work-force was entirely volunteer and the digging entirely manual, taking place in the cellars exposed by bombing. In that year a public appeal was made for funds, after which a slightly more ambitious programme was undertaken which allowed preparation of some trenches by machine in areas lacking cellars and which involved the hire of one permanent workman and even, occasionally, a small gang of contract labour.

In these days of professional units, substantial funding and extensive back-up facilities, it is salutary to remember the necessarily small scale of this early work. Government funding was limited to paying the subsistence of the director. The virtual absence of other comparable excavations at the time assured us of the services of a large and friendly pool of volunteers, many of whom returned again and again, not a few becoming excavators of great skill. The

---

* for the situation see *Antiquity*, xxiii (1949), 153–60.

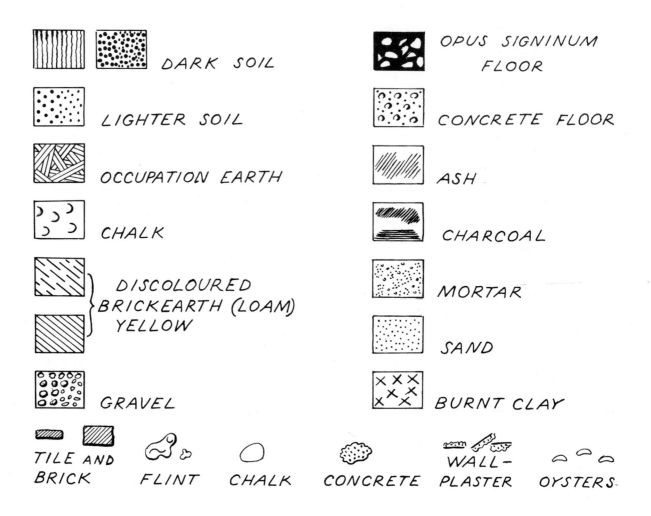

Fig. A.   Key to Sections

help given by Miss M.G. Wilson and Mr. J.S. Wacher as site-supervisors is gratefully acknowledged; Miss Wilson's contribution to the success of the excavations was outstanding, and she later drew much of the pottery and many of the small finds on a purely 'expenses' basis.

Many years were to pass after the end of this first series of excavations in Canterbury before the facilities enjoyed as a matter of course by almost all modern excavations were made possible by an input of Government funds commensurate with the demands of the work. At the time of the Canterbury excavations the present writer was not a full-time archaeologist; the digging took place during school holidays, at the end of which there were often two or three tea-chests of finds to be sorted and drawn during the term, in addition to the preparation of final plans and sections.

For some years reports on the work appeared regularly in *Archaeologia Cantiana*; but the momentum could not be maintained. Space earmarked for Canterbury in *Arch. Cant.* was needed for the reports on excavations undertaken independently by Dr. F. Jenkins. Then, as post-war archaeology expanded in Kent, the editors let it be known that less space could be devoted to Canterbury. At the same time the pattern of excavation in the city made it sometimes inevitable that adjoining sites should be dug on widely separated occasions; a prompt report on one would be rendered out of date by later work.

This realization, together with the mounting backlog of finds and the heavy burden of plan- and section-drawing at a time of decreasing personal leisure, led to a break in the momentum of publication. The break was greatly prolonged by the intervention of the writer's Verulamium excavations of 1955–61 and their aftermath, which made large inroads into the time of both Miss Wilson and myself.

Work was resumed when Miss Wilson became free to undertake the final drawing of many of the sections; and in 1977 the Department of the Environment provided funds for the employment of Miss Sally Stow as research assistant at Oxford to prepare a full draft report in association with myself. Her archaeological understanding, industry and ability have greatly lightened the burden of producing the present work. Little major rewriting has been required, and the task of reaching an agreed text has been both speedy and agreeable. Some of the site plans are also the work of Miss Stow. Finally the writer's debt to Mrs. Lynda Smithson must be acknowledged. Her faultless and critical typing of a difficult manuscript and speedy retyping of revised drafts has been a great encouragement.

The establishment of the Canterbury Archaeological Trust in 1975 inaugurated a new series of excavations in the city on a much larger scale than those of the Canterbury Excavation Committee. Rarely were the old excavations able to explore areas sufficiently large for recovery of full plans of buildings, although a few Belgic, Roman and Saxon structures were adequately observed; in general they relied on trenches and sections rather than upon area excavation, and were able to establish a stratigraphic sequence which in turn built up a series of approximately-dated pottery types. Nevertheless in 32 seasons of work a good and comparatively reliable picture of the development of the city since pre-Roman times was achieved.

Much of the work took place in areas of the city which have since been more fully explored by the Trust. Reports on the earlier work have been written and will be incorporated in the reports of the Trust's work, as has been done in Volume I of this series. The present volume records excavations in the neighbourhood of St. George's Street, Burgate Street, Canterbury Lane and St. George's Lane (the last now replaced by the Bus Station). These are areas of the city which were among the first to be rebuilt, during the fifties, and in which the Trust has consequently had no opportunity to excavate. The information in the present report is therefore unlikely to be superseded for some time. A well-preserved Roman bath-building, part of a Roman town house and streets, together with some important late Saxon remains are among the significant discoveries. Opportunity is taken to include some groups of post-medieval pottery, the first from Canterbury to be published; and an Appendix records some additional details of the plan of the Butchery Lane building which have come to light since the original publication in *Archaeologia Cantiana*, lxi (1948).

S.S. FRERE

LIST OF FIGURES

LIST OF PLATES

ABBREVIATIONS

Antiq. Journ.   *The Antiquaries Journal.* Society of Antiquaries of London.

Arch. Ael.[1], [4]   *Archaeologia Aeliana*, first or fourth series. Society of Antiquaries of Newcastle-upon-Tyne.

Arch. Cant.   *Archaeologia Cantiana.* Transactions of the Kent Archaeological Society, Maidstone.

Arch. Newsletter   *The Archaeological News Letter*, London (*seriatim* 1948–1965)

BB1, BB2   Black-burnished ware of Categories 1 and 2 (see Gillam, below).

Callender   M.H. Callender, *Roman Amphorae* (Oxford, 1965).

Chautard   J. Chautard, *Imitations des monnaies au type esterlin frappées en Europe pendant le XIIIe et le XIVe siècles* (Nancy, 1871).

C.H.K.   R.A.G. Carson, P.V. Hill and J.P.C. Kent, *Late Roman Bronze Coinage* (London, 1960).

Ciani   P. Ciani, *Les monnaies françaises de la Révolution à la fin du Premier Empire* (Paris, 1931).

Crummy   N. Crummy, 'A Chronology of Bone Pins', *Britannia* x (1979), 157–63.

Gillam   J.P. Gillam, 'Types of Roman Coarse Pottery Vessels in Northern Britain', *Arch. Ael.,*[4] xxxv (1957), 1–72.

Gose   E. Gose, *Gefässtypen der römischen Keramik in Rheinland*, Beiheft der *Bonner Jahrbücher*, 1950.

Hurst (1964)   J.G. Hurst, 'Stoneware Jugs' in B. Cunliffe, *Winchester Excavations 1949–1960*, i (Winchester, 1964).

Hurst (1977)   J.G. Hurst in M.R. Apted *et al.* (eds.), *Ancient Monuments and their Interpretation* (London, 1977) 219–38.

JBAA   *Journal of the British Archaeological Association.*

Medieval Arch.	*Medieval Archaeology.* Journal of the Society for Medieval Archaeology, London.
Newstead	J. Curle, *A Roman Frontier Post and its People: The Fort of Newstead . . .* (Glasgow, 1911).
Northampton	J.H. Williams, *St. Peter's Street, Northampton, Excavations 1973–76* (Northampton, 1979).
Num. Chron.	*The Numismatic Chronicle.* Journal of the Royal Numismatic Society, London.
O.R.L.	*Der Obergermanisch-Raetische Limes des Römerreiches*, Lieferung 32, Kastell Zugmantel.
Plymouth	Cynthia Gaskell Brown (ed.), *Plymouth Excavations: Castle Street, the Pottery.* Plymouth Museum Archaeological Series, i (1979).
Proc. Cambridge Ant. Soc.	*Proceedings of the Cambridge Antiquarian Society*, Cambridge.
Proc. Soc. Antiq.	*Proceedings of the Society of Antiquaries of London.*
R.I.C.	H. Mattingly, E.A. Sydenham, C.H.V. Sutherland and R.A.G. Carson (eds.), *Roman Imperial Coinage*, London.
Richborough iii	J.P. Bushe-Fox, *Third Report on the Excavations of the Roman Fort at Richborough.* Reports of the Research Committee of the Society of Antiquaries of London, No. X (Oxford, 1932).
Southampton	C. Platt and R. Coleman-Smith, *Excavations in medieval Southampton 1953–1969*, vol. ii (Leicester, 1975).
Steinzeug	Gisela Reineking-von Bock (ed.), *Steinzeug*, Katalogue des Kunstgewerbemuseums Köln, iv (1976).
V.C.H.	*The Victoria County History* (London).
Verulamium	S.S. Frere, *Verulamium Excavations* i. Reports of the Society of Antiquaries of London, No. XXVIII (Oxford, 1972). Vol. ii (1983); vol. iii (forthcoming).
Williamson	G.C. Williamson, *Trade Tokens in the Seventeenth Century*, i (London, 1889).
Wroxeter iii	J.P. Bushe-Fox, *Third Report on the Excavations on the site of the Roman Town at Wroxeter, Shropshire 1914.* Reports of the Research Committee of the Society of Antiquaries of London, No. IV (Oxford, 1916).
Young	C.J. Young, *Oxfordshire Roman Pottery*, British Archaeological Reports, No. 43 (Oxford, 1977).

BIBLIOGRAPHY

M. Biddle   'Excavations at Winchester, 1962–3', *Antiq. Journ.*, xliv (1964), 188 ff.

M. Biddle   'Excavations at Winchester, 1965', *Antiq. Journ.*, xlvi (1966), 308 ff.

M. Biddle   'Excavations at Winchester, 1967', *Antiq. Journ.*, xlviii (1968), 250 ff.

M. Biddle   'Excavations at Winchester, 1969', *Antiq. Journ.*, l (1970), 277 ff.

M. Biddle   'Winchester: the development of an early capital', in H. Jankulin *et al.* (eds.), *Vor- und Frühformen der europäischen Stadt im Mittelalter* (Göttingen, 1974), 229 ff.

G.C. Boon   'The Roman Temple at Brean Down, Somerset, and the dating of minimissimi', *Num. Chron.*, Ser. 7, Vol. i (1961), 179

G.C. Boon   *Silchester: The Roman Town of Calleva*, 2nd ed. (1974)

P.D.C. Brown   'The Church at Richborough', *Britannia*, ii (1971), 225 ff.

P. Corder (ed.)   *The Roman Town and Villa at Great Casterton, Rutland, Third Report for the Years 1954–1958,* (University of Nottingham, 1961)

S.S. Frere   *Verulamium Excavations,* vol. i. Reports of the Research Committee of the Society of Antiquaries of London, No. XXVIII (Oxford, 1972)

S.S. Frere   *Verulamium Excavations,* vol. ii (London, 1983)

F. Jenkins   'Canterbury: Excavations in Burgate Street, 1946–8', *Arch. Cant.*, lxiii (1950), 82 ff.

F. Jenkins   'The Post-Roman Submergence of the Land Surface at Canterbury, Kent', *Archaeological News Letter* June 1954, 34–5

J.P.C. Kent   'Barbarous Copies of Roman Coins: Their Significance for the British Historian and Archaeologist' in *Limes-Studien*, Basle (1959), 65 (Report of the third International Congress of Frontier Studies)

J.P.C. Kent in P. Corder   *Great Casterton,* iii (1961), 28–9

B.H. St. J. O'Neil	'Some Minimissimi found at Canterbury and their Significance', *Num. Chron.*, viii (1948), 226–9
J. Pilbrow	'Discoveries made during Excavations at Canterbury in 1868'. In a letter from James Pilbrow, Esq., F.S.A. to Earl Stanhope, P.S.A., *Archaeologia* xliii (London, 1871), 151 ff.
H.G. Richardson and G.O. Sayles, (ed.)	*Select Cases of Procedure Without Writ under Henry III*, Seldon Society, vol. 60 (1941)
C.H.V. Sutherland	'The Canterbury Minimissimi Again', *Num. Chron.*, ix (1949), 242–4
W. Urry	*Canterbury Under the Angevin Kings* (London, 1967)
R.E.M. Wheeler	*London in Roman Times*, London Museum, 1930
A. Williams	'Canterbury Excavations in 1945', *Arch. Cant.*, lx (1947), 68 ff.
A. Williams and S.S. Frere	'Canterbury Excavations, Christmas 1945 and Easter 1946', *Arch. Cant.*, lxi (1948), 1 ff.

INTRODUCTION

Five large and twelve small sites were excavated in the St. George's Street-Burgate Street area between 1947 and 1957[1] (Fig. 1). This part of Canterbury had suffered extensive bomb damage in 1942 (*Frontispiece*), but the excavations were for the most part carried out in very restricted areas in advance of redevelopment and without the resources for large-scale clearance; hence it was usually the street frontages, often occupied by cellars, that had to be examined first. Small-scale trial-trenching by hand in areas behind the cellars was usually found to be unrewarding because of extensive pit-digging in the Middle Ages.

Chapters I–III describe sites along St. George's Street. Here a well-preserved bath-building (Fig. 1, Site 2) was found on the north side of the street (Chapter I). Built in the first half of the third century it was extensively renovated and altered *c.* A.D. 355–60, and was burnt down not long afterwards. A large group of *minimissimi* was found in one of the rooms. The building had hypocausts of varying height which offer interesting evidence on heat-control. Further east, opposite St. George's Church, part of a large Roman house with apsidal east end (Fig. 1 Site 3) was excavated (Chapter II). At the end of the second century a timber-framed building had been placed on the site and was occupied for half a century. About 240–250 the masonry house replaced this building and continued in use until late in the fourth century. Chapter III describes the remaining minor sites near St. George's Street.

In two areas, C XV R (Fig. 1, Site 4) and C XVII Y (Fig. 1, Site 6), especially the first, it was possible to clear a considerable area of superficial deposits by mechanical excavation. At both sites considerable stretches of Roman street-metalling were encountered, which proved very useful in helping to determine the Roman street plan. An east—west street seemed to be aligned on the West Gate, but did not pass through the Burgate. If the road from Richborough did enter the city through a predecessor of the Burgate (of which a trace was found under 68, Burgate) it will have continued its oblique line to join the street-grid some 325 ft. (99 m.) within the defences. Both the east—west street and the north—south one found on Area R had been laid down at an early date, probably in the early fifties of the first century, if not earlier; they had been frequently re-metalled, and the metalling was in consequence built up to a final thickness of almost 1.5 m. Towards the middle of the second century additions were made to the street-grid; an east—west street ran eastwards from Area R, and a narrow metalled lane was constructed southwards from Area Y. The latter went out of use and was

---

1. In this area Audrey Williams had excavated three cellars on the south side of Burgate Street west of Iron Bar Lane in 1945 (Fig. 1, Site 7); the report on this work appeared in *Arch. Cant.*, lx (1947), 68 ff. The Roman buildings in Butchery Lane (Fig. 1, Site 1) were excavated in 1945 and 1946 by Audrey Williams and S.S. Frere and reported in *Arch. Cant.*, lxi (1948), 1 ff.

built over after a century's use. In Area R itself part of a house with walls of brickearth was recognised in Canterbury for the first time, and nearby a timber-framed structure probably of fifth-century date was built on the surface of a street. In the same area a post-medieval cellar was examined which yielded an interesting group of pottery of late sixteenth- to early seventeenth-century date. These sites are discussed in Chapters IV and VI.

On the east side of Canterbury Lane (Fig. 1, Site 8) a continuous sequence of structures and deposits extending from the pre-Roman period to the destruction-levels of 1942 was examined. Here a sequence of Roman buildings was recovered, of which the most interesting was a house with walls of brickearth which spanned the third century, at the end of which it was destroyed by fire. Above the scanty remains of a successor lay a thick deposit of dark soil, taken to represent Dark-Age cultivation. It was sealed by an extensive area of cobbling, which was covered by a substantial late Saxon occupation-layer. The fortunate presence of some sherds of Badorf-type ware (imports from the Rhineland) enables the extensive associated pottery, mainly local in origin, to be dated to the period c. A.D. 850–950. The site also contained a fourteenth-century well at the bottom of which were found almost 100 pitchers and jugs, most of which seem to have been lost when in turn they became detached from the hook of the well-pulley. This excavation is described in Chapter V.

Finally, Chapter VII discusses a site east of St. George's Lane and south of St. George's Street (Fig. 55), where later the Bus Station was built. Here the area examined was greatly disturbed by pits and wells, many of them of recent date; nevertheless, important groups of post-Roman and particularly of post-medieval pottery were recovered.

Each season of work received a consecutive code-number (C (= Canterbury) XV, XXII, etc.), which is followed by a letter code for the individual site. Thus C XX C IV 8 stands for layer 8 in Trench IV on Site C in the twentieth season at Canterbury. These codes are identified in the report on each site and are used on the section-drawings and plans.

In referring to certain types of medieval pottery from Canterbury it has been found convenient to use the classification of groups discussed in *Arch. Cant.*, lxviii (1954), 128 ff. The dating of these is now considered to be as follows:

Group I	c.	975–1025
Group II	c.	1050–1100
Group III	c.	1080–1150
Group IV	c.	1250–1300

The authors desire to express their gratitude to Mr J.G. Hurst, Dr. Richard Hodges, Miss Maureen Mellor and Mr R. Symonds for help and advice in connection with the sources of some of the pottery and to B.R. and K.F. Hartley for identifying the samian and *mortaria*, respectively.

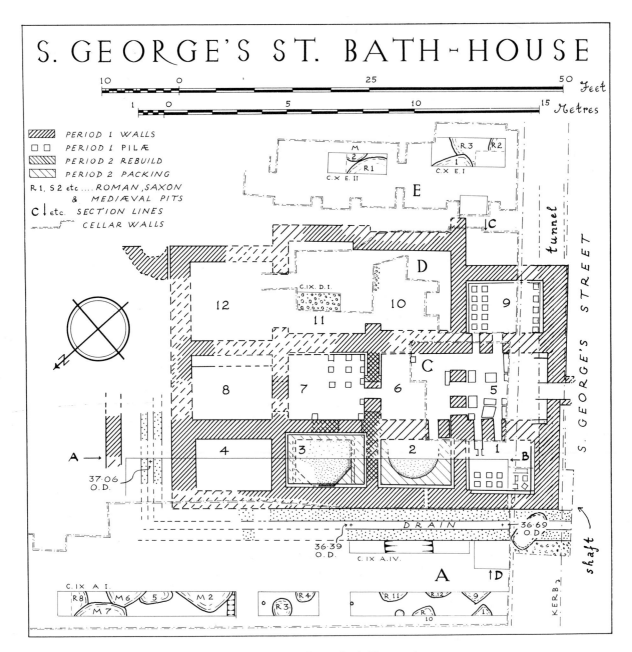

Fig. 2. St. George's Street Bath-House: plan

PART I. THE EXCAVATED SITES

I. ST. GEORGE'S STREET BATH-BUILDING

In 1947 four cellars on the north side of St. George's Street (Fig. 1, Site 2; Fig. 2, Cellars A, C, D and E) were investigated; further work was done on the NE corner of the building in 1949,[2] and finally in 1982 the south-west side of the building was briefly examined before its destruction in a sewer-tunnel. The 1982 work is recorded by Paul Bennett in Appendix IX below.

In 1947 a long trench was first cut close to the NW side of Cellar A.[3] This produced a series of Roman and medieval pits cut into Roman layers of grey or yellow loam. During the progress of this work it was noticed that the lower courses of the SE wall of the cellar were of different material from its upper courses, and appeared to be Roman. Further clearance proved this to be true (Pl. I) and that the eighteenth-century cellar-diggers, encountering the outer wall of the bath-building, had used its outer face as the inner face of their cellar, though this meant creating a cellar 4 ft. narrower than their frontage. A cold-bath floor could be seen protruding from below the cellar stairs (Pl. I). The party-wall of the shop itself (running just south-west of Section A-B) rested on a very deep footing which had cut into the Roman building below: between this footing and the Roman wall a narrow belt of stratified floors and other layers remained (Fig. 3, Section A-B, Pl. II).

Cellar C was smaller but deeper than A: it had cut through the hypocaust of the second Roman period and used as its floor the tiled basis of the hypocaust which covered the blocked remains of its predecessor of Period 1. Cellar D, of irregular shape, had re-employed the *opus signinum* floor of Room 9, but continual shovelling of coal had worn down the Roman concrete; here and there holes had appeared (Pl. XIII), leading to our discovery of modern coal in the hypocaust below. North-east of Cellars C and D excavation from the surface produced substantial remains of walling in the SW part of Room 7, but further NE deep medieval pits had left little but interrupted footings. A few further points were added to the plan when the

---

2. The Site codes are C IX A, C, D; C X C, D, E; and C XV R.
3. In the premises of W.H. Smith and Son, 19 St. George's Street.

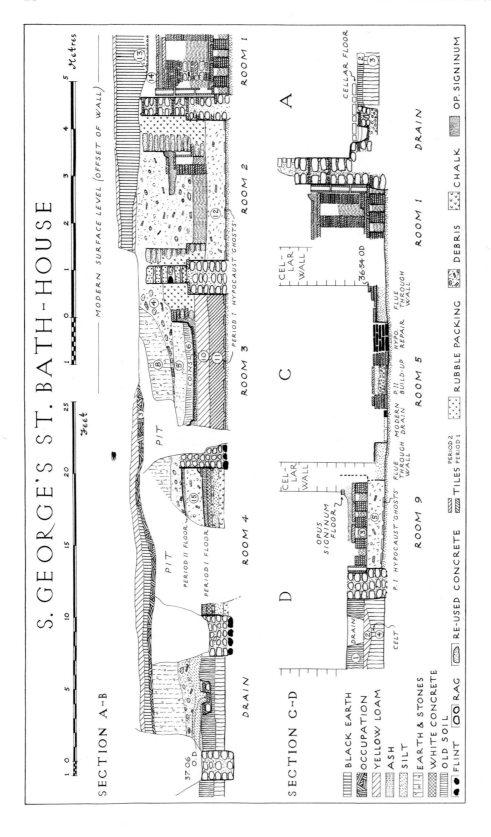

Fig. 3.   St. George's Street Bath-House: Sections A-B, C-D

post-war Woolworth's building was erected on this site.[4] A number of Saxon and medieval pits had been cut through Rooms 4, 7 and 8; their contents are described below (pp. 195–8).

The SE wall of Room 1 could be felt in the position indicated on the plan by means of a ranging-rod pushed into the hypocaust below the modern pavement; in 1982 the position of the wall and of the SW side of the bath-house were confirmed in the work described below in Appendix IX.

PERIOD 1

Dating evidence for the erection of the original building was not plentiful because of the removal of much of the deposits below the floors by Roman excavation for hypocaust chambers, and of many of those elsewhere by medieval pits and later cellars. Below the floor of Cellar A, outside the building on the west side (Fig. 3, Section C-D), were two layers and a gully earlier than the building. Layer 3 produced three Iron Age sherds; Layer 2 yielded the following samian: form 33 East Gaulish, Antonine; 37 Central Gaulish, c. 150–180. The gully contained a sherd of Dr. 31R, Central Gaulish, c. 150–180, part of a mortarium dated 140–200 and jar-sherds of a similar date (Fig. 76, Nos. 1–4). Pottery of slightly later date possibly of the early third century (Fig. 76, Nos. 5–11) was found in a similar pre-building layer in Cellar D (Fig. 3, Section C-D, layer 1) together with sherds of Antonine samian (Dr. 31, 33, 38, 43, all Central Gaulish).[5] The concrete floor-foundations of Room 4 contained the rim of a straight-sided dish of a type resembling Gillam No. 317 which runs down to the early third century. The building can thus hardly have been erected before c. 200–225 and may be slightly later since all these layers have been truncated.

Elsewhere a piece of Dr. 37 (style of Secundus, c. 150–180) lay below the construction-level of the SE external wall of the building.

The arrangement of the rooms in Period 1, as far as it could be established, is discussed below (p. 35). Rooms 1–3, 5–7 and 9 were heated. Room 4 was a cold plunge-bath and was entered from 8. It had a very strongly-constructed floor with two layers of hard concrete below the *opus signinum* floor. The concrete of one of them contained a piece of hard wall-plaster with a light green painted surface as well as the dish-rim already mentioned. All the hypocausts except that of Room 1 were subsequently taken out during the second-period reconstruction, and were identified only by the patches of mortar marking the sites of *pilae* on the original basement floors. A drain (Pl. I) ran round the outside of the building on two sides, that on the NW being rather smaller than the other; the fall appeared to be towards the north. The outlet for a lead pipe, now represented by a hole through the wall lined with opposed *imbrices*, led

4. Thanks are due to Dr. F. Jenkins, for keeping the site under observation.
5. In Cellar D layer 4 produced nothing but part of a polished flint axe and some potboilers; Layer 2 a large Belgic-type jar, perhaps of post-conquest date; Layer 1 contained material down to the early third century as described above.

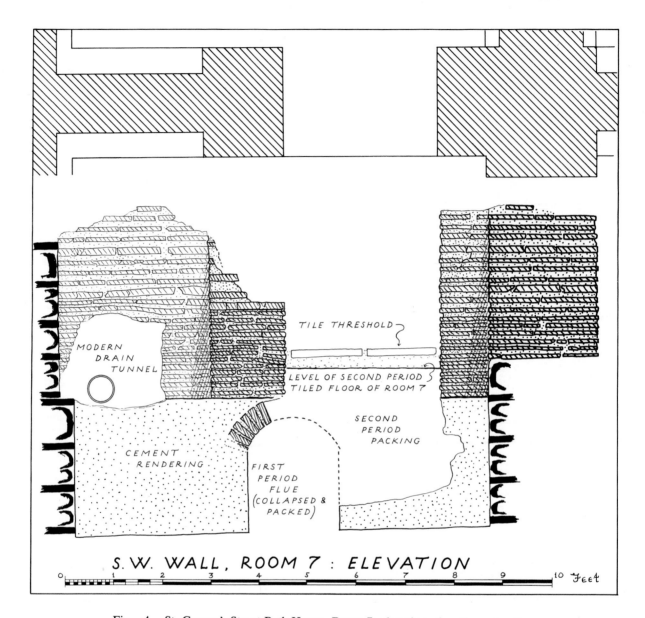

TILE THRESHOLD

MODERN
DRAIN
TUNNEL

LEVEL OF SECOND PERIOD
TILED FLOOR OF ROOM 7

SECOND
PERIOD
PACKING

CEMENT
RENDERING

FIRST
PERIOD
FLUE
(COLLAPSED &
PACKED)

S. W. WALL, ROOM 7 : ELEVATION

0   1   2   3   4   5   6   7   8   9   10 Feet

Fig. 4. St. George's Street Bath-House, Room 7: elevation of south-west wall

out of Room 2, showing that a hot basin (p. 37) had occupied this room in Period 1; a similar pipe led from Room 1. The walls were built of coursed Kentish Rag blocks with tile bonding courses of *tegulae*: the NW external wall was 2 ft. 6 in. (0.76 m.) wide and rested on a wider platform incorporating the inner edge of the drain.

PERIOD 2

At a date satisfactorily fixed by coins as *c.* 355—60 (see p. 35) the building was extensively renovated, and the walls between Rooms 2 and 3, 6 and 7, and 3 and 7 were rebuilt in whole or in part.

Room 1. This was the only room from which the original hypocaust had not been removed: the *pilae* were 13 in. high and over them were bridging-tiles (22 × 22 in.) supporting the upper tiled floor (Pl. VII). Evidently this was still judged sound, and on it was built the second-period hypocaust with *pilae* 38 in. high (Pls. VI and VII). The original wall-flues, coming up from the lower hypocaust, were re-used by smashing the second course to admit hot air at the new level. Opposed *tegulae* had been used instead of box flue-tiles near the corner of the room (Pl. V), perhaps in a repair. The box flues were held in place by T-shaped iron clamps. Over the floor was a layer of rubble (14) which produced sherds of two late fourth-century jars (Fig. 77, No. 16), one of which was apparently hand-finished. Above 14 was a thin gravel floor (13) on which lay a late Saxon cooking-pot (Fig. 78, No. 21) of ninth- or tenth-century date. Above this was black soil containing material ranging from late Saxon to the fourteenth century.

Room 2. Here the original hypocaust had been removed and the level made up with rubble. On this a hypocausted apse was constructed (Pl. IV), largely of big lumps of *opus signinum* (6 × 18 × 18 in.) from some earlier structure. Part of the upper floor with its moulding remained.

Room 3. After the removal of the original hypocaust, a filling of mud and clay was inserted containing a red colour-coated Oxfordshire mortarium of Young's Type C 97 and other third-to fourth-century sherds. Above this a small semi-octagonal cold plunge-bath was inserted constructed of tiles and *opus signinum* (Pls. II, III). This had been done as follows: a rectangular area had been floored with tiles (18 × 12 in.) and the rubble filling held back by a 'false revetment' running parallel with the SW wall; only when this had been done was the oblique side of the bath itself constructed. Sticking upright between the tiles of the floor lay the following coins:

Urbs Roma (330–337)	1	Constantius II or Constans	3
Constantinopolis (330–337)	4	(?) barbarous *Fel. Temp. Reparatio*	2
House of Constantine I (335–342)	1	Illegible	6

Immediately below the tiles of the floor *in situ* lay further coins:

Constantine I (minted 330–337)	2	*Minim*	1
Urbs Roma (330–337)	1	Illegible	4
Constans (341–345)	1		

These had obviously been spilled by the workmen installing the bath, and indicate clearly that the reconstruction took place not later than *c.* 355–360.

The floor of the bath was uniformly covered by a layer *c.* ½ in. thick of charcoal sealing a barbarous 3AE coin of Constantius II (354–358). Above this was dark sticky earth (6) in which was a lump of tufa and a coin of Gratian. This suggested that the building may have been burnt down and left empty for a while. Above this was a light earth filling (5) with much comminuted mortar and plaster fragments, and a few lumps of rubble especially towards the bottom:[6] only above this came (4), collapsed wall-material. Above this again Layer 8 contained a Saxon cooking-pot (Fig. 78, No. 20).

Room 4. The first-period cold bath was filled with rubble which yielded five coins (Claudius II (two), Tetricus II, Carausius and *Constantinopolis*) the rubble was then sealed by a new floor of *opus signinum*, forming a *frigidarium*.

Room 5. The depth of Cellar C left little of Period 2. The spaces between the *pilae* of the first-period hypocaust (Pl. XII) had been packed with rubble which overlay about 2 in. of charcoal sludge; above the rubble, tiles had been laid on *opus signinum* level with the tops of the *pilae*, as a basis for the new hypocaust; but of the latter nothing survived. A barbarous coin of Constantius II (355–358) was recovered from the packing of one of the flues.

Room 6. This was not explored except that portion of it within Cellar C, where conditions were identical with those in Room 5.

Room 7. The original flue between Rooms 6 and 7 had collapsed (Pl. X), necessitating considerable rebuilding of the wall; the rebuilt wall itself was well preserved, and contained a doorway (Figs. 4, 5A, Pl. IX). Part of the thresholds of two other doorways leading to Rooms 3 and 8, less well preserved, was found.[7] Mortar patches on the basement floor showed the position of first-period *pilae* which had been removed (Fig. 5B, Pl. XI): layers of make-up (Fig. 5B (12) and (11)) 3 ft. thick were then inserted (with a good deal of broken tufa blocks among the material) and a tiled floor built just below the level of the door-threshold. Between the floor and the door was a small socket for a timber frame (Figs. 5A, 5B); this probably supported a curtain to confine the heat and steam to the warm suite beyond; there was nothing comparable by the adjoining door to Room 3. In the mortar between the tiles was found a coin of Constans (minted 341–345). A large medieval pit (4) had disturbed the northern two-thirds of this room and a modern drain dug from the surface through Room 8 had sunk sharply along the SE wall of Room 7 and had tunnelled through the Roman wall near the south corner (Pl. XI), leading out through the hypocaust of Room 5 to the modern sewer beneath St. George's Street. Nevertheless in the south corner of Room 7 traces of a ¼-round moulding were found demarcating a curved area patched with cobbles (Fig. 5A). This had been much disturbed by the tunnel; but it probably marked the position of a *labrum* or cold-water basin rather than that of a *pissoir*, since the concrete basis for the floor ran through underneath and there was no proper soak-away. Below the cobbles occurred the following coins:

6.   Also present here was a portion of the lower stone of a quern grooved obliquely on its upper and lower surfaces, *c.* 2 in. thick, of Drybrook Sandstone.
7.   The SE wall of the room still stood 6 ft. 4 in. (1.93 m.) above the basement of the hypocaust.

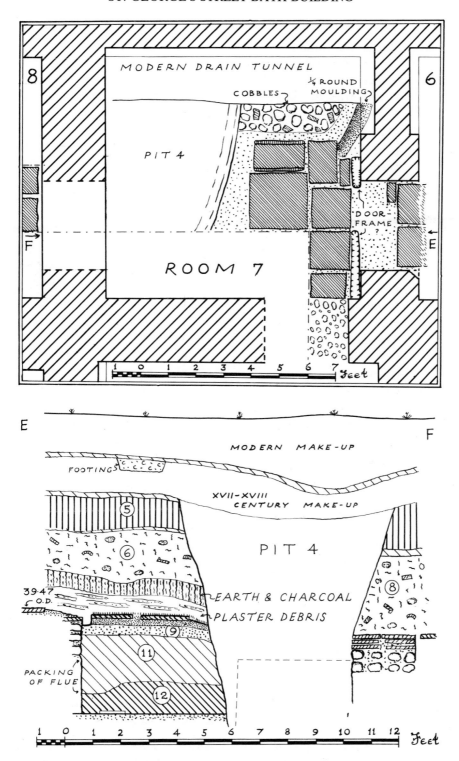

Fig.   5.   St. George's Street Bath-House, Room 7: A. Plan; B. Section E-F. Scale 1 : 40

Tetricus II	1
Barbarous radiate	1
House of Constantine I	3
Theodora	1
Constantine II Caesar	1
Constantius II or Constans (341–345)	2
Constans	4
Barbarous *Fel. Temp. Reparatio*	1
Illegible	1

On the surviving portions of the tiled floor were found 261 coins, as follows:[8]

Urbs Roma	4
Constantinopolis	3
Helena	1
Theodora	2
Constantine II	2
Constantius II	7
Constans	12
Constans or Constantius II	19
House of Constantine I	10 + 1 doubtful
Magnentius	1 + 1 doubtful
Valens	1 barbarous
Arcadius *c.* 390	1 (*Salus Reipublicae*)
Barbarous *Fel. Temp. Reparatio*	59 + 3 doubtful
Illegible	30
Fragments (illegible)	11
Minimi	33
Minimissimi[9]	60
	____
	261

Evidently before *c.* two-thirds of its area was disturbed by Pit 4 this room contained many more than this total. Perhaps it was the *apodyterium*, but this is unlikely because of its position. More likely it was a room where gambling took place, for these coins were scattered

---

8. These coins have been described by B.H. St. J. O'Neil in *Num. Chron.*[4], viii (1948), 226–9. See below, p. 39.
9. Some, both of *minimi* and *minimissimi*, show traces of the legionary-spearing-fallen-horseman type; none shows any other type.

all over the surviving portion of the floor: they had not been concealed. They might, however, conceivably have formed part of a hoard concealed e.g. in the roof, which fell and scattered when the building caught fire.

On the tiled floor lay about 1 in. of charcoal and ash in and under which were the coins; above this was tumbled wall-debris.

Room 8. This was almost completely wrecked by medieval pits. It appears to have been a *frigidarium* in both periods: traces of a ¼-round moulding 4 in. wide belonging to Period 1 were found against the wall; in Period 2 a tiled floor had been constructed 2½ in. higher up.

Room 9. Here again the original hypocaust had been removed, leaving only the 'ghosts' of its *pilae* (Fig. 3, Section C-D, Cellar D; Pls. XIII, XIV). Rubble 14 in. deep was then put in, on top of which the new hypocaust was built. This still had its upper floor in position: there was 7 in. of white concrete above the bridging-tiles (16 × 16 × 3 in.) and 3 in. of *opus signinum* above that; but most of this had been subsequently worn away during re-use of this floor in the recent cellar.

Rooms 10–12. Little remained of these rooms because of pits and cellars. Room 11 had a gravel floor in Period 2: it contained 14 radiate coins of *c.* 270 with one of Carausius and one of the House of Constantine I and overlay a radiate. In Room 12 were traces of a tiled floor in an *opus signinum* bedding, very much decayed.

Date of Period 2. A total of 23 coins, of which 20 were of the House of Constantine, were found in or below the floors of Rooms 3, 4, 5 and 7, and the series ends with one legitimate issue of the *Fel. Temp. Reparatio* type of Constantius II issued between 354 and 358 and four barbarous copies of the same type. These copies are now known to have been made immediately on the issue of the original, and copying had ceased by 358.[10] The absence of the latest issue of Constantius II (*Spes Reipublicae*) and of coins of Valentinian I and Valens closely fixes the second-period reconstruction at *c.* 360.

ARRANGEMENT OF THE BUILDING

Period 1

The building is a free-standing bath-block. The entrance was on the SE, from the street some 34 ft. (10.4 m.) away, and led into the unheated rooms on that side. The two pilasters in Room 11 suggest that the doorway was opposite, in its SE wall. The original floor of this room had been removed, for the gravel floor encountered here contained coins dating it to Period 2.

10. J.P.C. Kent, *Limes Studien*, Basle (1959), 65. (Report of the 3rd International Congress of Frontier Studies); and Kent in P. Corder, *Great Casterton*, iii, 28–9.

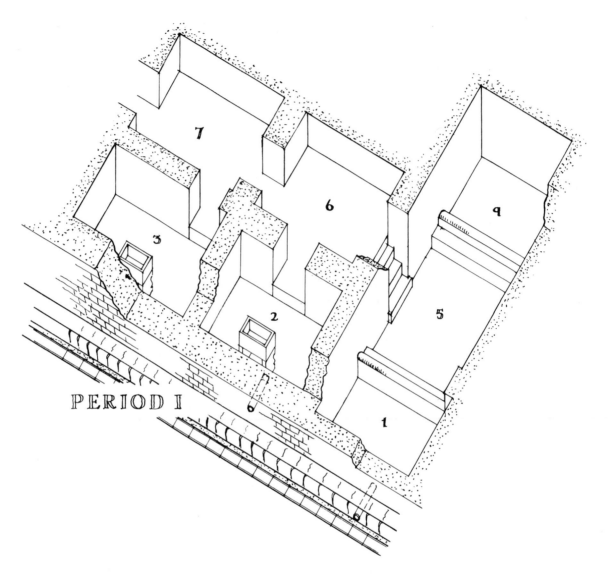

Fig. 6. St. George's Street Bath-House: reconstruction drawing of the Period I Bath-House to show suggested floor-levels (*Drawn by J.C. Frere*)

Rooms 12 and 8 were next entered, Room 12 being presumably the undressing-room (*apodyterium*). Room 8 had a tile-covered offset 1 ft. 4 in. (0.4 m.) wide to its SE wall, level with the second-period floor, which had risen 2½ in. (6.35 cm.) above the original floor-level. This low bench perhaps marks the position for alcoves or cupboards for the bathers' clothing; but Room 8 was certainly also the *frigidarium*, and the main heated rooms (5–7) ran from it to the SW down the centre of the building. As in so many baths, two *tepidaria* (6 and 7) were provided. The furnace must have been outside Room 5, as suggested by its wide central flue (see now p. 326). From these rooms there opened others containing plunge-baths or basins and

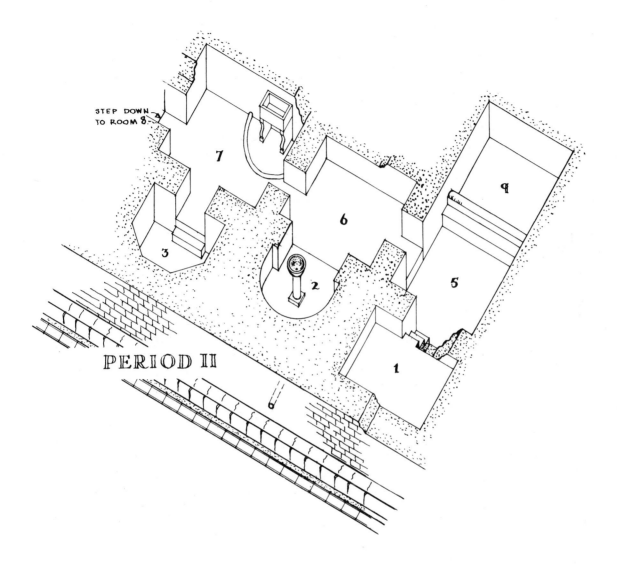

Fig. 7. St. George's Street Bath-House: reconstruction drawing of the Period II Bath-House to show suggested floor-levels (*Drawn by J.C. Frere*)

these formed a third range to the NW (1–4). Room 4 was the cold plunge and must have been entered from Room 8; Rooms 3 and 2, entered from the *tepidaria*, seem each to have held a basin (*labrum*), for their hypocausts were tall (as indicated by the wall-offsets, Fig. 3, Section A-B), and Room 2 had a pipe through the wall, to the drain outside, which started 12 in. (30 cm.) above the offset inside and descended to a point 11 in. above the platform outside. Since this drain started at least 6 in. above the floor, Room 2 could never have been a plunge bath. The wall of Room 3 did not survive high enough for its drain-hole to survive: if it had none, it could have been used for annointing with oil (*unctorium*). Room 5, the *caldarium*, or hottest room, was flanked by two subsidiaries, 9 and 1. The pipe-hole draining Room 1 survived, and as it started inside at the level of the first-period floor (unlike that in Room 2), we can assign a plunge-bath to Room 1. With this agrees its low hypocaust. Room 9 had no traces of a pipe, and no drain was found;[11] but its low hypocaust, of exactly the same height (to judge by the offsets) as that in Room 1, makes it fairly certain that it too was a plunge; for rooms to which *labra* can be assigned do not have this feature. The drain must have run from the southern corner of the room, and skirted round the stoke-hole area.

Thus in Period 1 there were four unheated rooms, one cold bath and seven heated rooms. The floor of Room 8 was 6 in. above that of 11, and the floor of Room 7 (to judge by its offset) was 1 ft. 6 in. (46 cm.) above that of Room 8. Those of Rooms 2 and 3 were 1 ft. (30 cm.) below the floor of Room 7, while in Rooms 1, 5 and 9 the floors were 3 ft. 3 in. below it (Fig. 6).

Period 2

The entrance arrangements remained the same. The floor of Room 8 was raised and the cold bath in Room 4 was filled in and abolished; a tiled threshold connected the two rooms at the new level. Room 7 became the *frigidarium* with a basin near its SE wall and with a cold plunge in Room 3. Room 6 remained the *tepidarium* with a basin in Room 2, where the new floor was at a level at which the drain through the wall could still be used. Room 1 had a new hypocaust too high to carry a plunge; moreover the drain through the wall was now inaccessible; the room now became a *laconicum*. Room 9, however, was given a new low hypocaust similar to the original one and this suggests that the hot plunge-bath remained in this room (Fig. 7).

The general effect of the restoration of the building was thus in the direction of economy: the number of heated rooms was reduced by the substitution of one set of *tepidarium* with *labrum* for the original double set. As a result there were now six unheated rooms, one cold bath and five heated rooms. The proportion of rooms not devoted to bathing has increased, and perhaps it is not without significance that, in one of them in which part of the floor survived, so many *minimi* and *minimissimi* were found; perhaps gambling took place. In this period the floor-level in Room 8 was 9 in. above that in Room 11, and in Room 7 was 6 in. above that in 8. The floor in Room 2, was 9 in. and that of Room 1 was 1 ft. 3 in. above the floor in Room 7, while Room 9 was 9 in. below it (Fig. 7).

An interesting feature of the hypocaust system in both periods was the evident attempt to control the heating, not only in the normal way by distance from the furnace, but also by adjusting the levels of the floors. Thus in Period 1 the *caldarium*, Room 5, had a hypocaust only 13 in. (33 cm.) high, the same as those under the hot plunge-baths each side, but the *tepidarium* in Room 7 (and doubtless also that in Room 6 where the evidence did not survive) had floors raised as much as 3 ft. 3 in. (1 m.) higher, with steps down onto lower hypocausts in Rooms 2 and 3 which, as we have suggested, contained *labra*. In Period 2 the height of the hypocaust in the *caldarium* is unknown, but it may well have been at the level of that under

11. The 'drain' cut through Layer 1 in Cellar D (fig. 3, Section C-D) is modern.

the adjoining hot bath in Room 9 as in the previous period. If so, the hypocaust under Room 1 was 2 ft. (61 cm.) higher, and would require 2–3 steps for entry, while the floor of the *tepidarium* (Room 6) was 9 in. (23 cm.) higher than that in the *caldarium*, and Room 2 with its basin was 9 in. higher again.

It is clear that the hottest air passing through the hypocaust system would tend to rise and thus be trapped in the higher basements. During periods of stoking the effect of this would be mitigated by the rapid passage of the gases through the system and up the wall flues; but it has been shown[12] that once the system was warm stoking could be much reduced; and in these quiescent periods the hot air would not travel fast and would linger in the higher hypocausts. The effect of this in Period 1 would be to increase the heat in the *tepidarium* at the expense of the *caldarium*, and in Period 2 to maintain a greater heat in the *laconicum* (Room 1). This is an aspect of Roman heat-engineering which does not appear to have received much attention.

If latrines existed they will have been placed either in part of Room 12 or perhaps outside it to the NE. Here an irregular piece of masonry was planned by F. Jenkins during the construction of Woolworth's, and towards it the small drain external to the building on the NE leads. There were no 'wet' rooms on this side (12, 8, 4) in either period; probably, therefore, the drain serves a latrine and was flushed by the overflow from a supply-tank for which this masonry formed the support. A fragment of wall was found running parallel with the NE side of the building and 6 ft. 6 in. (1. 98 m.) from it; at first sight this looks like the external wall of a neighbouring building, but subsequent excavations further NE (Area R, p. 69) revealed no trace of further masonry. Perhaps, then, this wall is the external wall of quite a large latrine added to this side of the building and served centrally by the drain. This area was much disturbed and no further traces were observed.

The context of the building

Such a free-standing bath-building with rooms only c. 8 ft. by 9 ft. is too small for a Public Baths owned by the *civitas*: yet it is too elaborate for a private suite, nor is it directly connected with any private house. We have no evidence that private corporations owned such premises, and it is likely that it is a private commercial venture.

The coins in Room 7

There has been some controversy about the coins[13] found on the floor of Room 7. As against 64 legitimate coins of Emperors of the House of Constantine before 361 there are 62 barbarous copies thereof of normal size, 34 similar barbarous copies but of smaller size (*minims*), 60 *minimissimi*, and 41 illegible. There is no doubt today that the barbarous copies are contem-

12. *Saalburg Jahrbuch*, xxxvi (1979), 12 ff.
13. O'Neil., *Num. Chron.*[6], viii (1948), 226–9; Sutherland, *ibid.* ix (1949), 242–4.

porary with the originals, even the copies of smaller size.[14] Later emperors are represented only by one barbarous copy of Valens and one coin of Arcadius. It must be remembered, however, (a) that 43 coins were illegible; none, however, were of a size suggesting the House of Valentinian;[15] and (b) that only *c.* one-third of the floor-area remained undisturbed: we have to assume that the coins recovered represent a fair sample of the much larger total once present, but this assumption is numismatically reasonable.

There is no support for the supposition that Room 7 had a wooden floor.[16] The tiled floor was perfectly adequate and normal: moreover it had on it a moulding of plaster outlining what was perhaps a wash-place. No sockets for floor-joists occurred in the walls, and the first-period offsets, which would have served the purpose admirably, had been carefully buried in the make-up 8 in. below the tiled floor. On the other hand there was a layer *c.* 1 in. thick of charcoal and ash over the floor: since this cannot for reasons just given have been the remains of a wooden floor it is perhaps best interpreted as an indication that the building was damaged by fire, as already suggested by similar evidence in Room 3, where a barbarous *Fel. Temp. Reparatio* coin of identical date was found in the ash. That the fire took place soon after 360 is thus not unlikely, for the coins found in the filling of the external drain also suggested this date,[17] while the ruined rubble filling Room 3 above the ash contained a coin of Gratian. The walls, however, were still standing till sometime after the loss of this coin, and it is quite possible that the two later coins in the group (Valens and Arcadius) are subsequent casual losses which sank into the ash. This theory of an early end to Period 2 seems more acceptable than one which, on the evidence of the coins, involves a period of disuse from *c.* 360 to 390, followed by re-use. For, as Dr. Sutherland pointed out,[18] the absence of the common *aes* coinage of the House of Valentinian I is itself evidence of desertion: but desertion of a fully-functioning building in a city is almost inconceivable.

Our conclusion is that the second period bath-building was burnt soon after its reconstruction and that its ruins gradually fell into decay. It follows that the *minimi* and *minimissimi* are contemporary with the coins of the House of Constantine with which they are associated.[19]

The same conclusion would follow on the other theory, that this collection represents a hoard fallen from the upper part of the room during the fire. Even then the two later coins could not be part of the hoard, which remains closed at *c.* 360; all that would follow would be that the date of the fire would be postponed till after the loss of these coins, *c.* 390–95. But this runs against the weight of the evidence, e.g. from the drain, quoted above; and on the whole it is preferable to hold that Period 2 was of very short duration.

14. See references cited in note 10.
15. These have been re-examined by Dr. J.P.C. Kent. Almost all are almost certainly *minims* of *Fel. Temp. Reparatio* type, and none is of the correct fabric for issues of Valentinian or Valens or later emperors.
16. O'Neil, *op. cit.* (note 13), 228.
17. They were as follows:

Gallienus, one	House of Constantine I (335–342), one
(?)Radiate head, two	Constans (341–345), one
Constantine I, one	Illegible, two

18. *Num. Chron.*[6], ix (1949), 243.
19. This conclusion is supported by the discovery of similar evidence at Bream Down, Somerset; see G.C. Boon, *Num. Chron.*, 1961, p. 179.

II. THE APSED BUILDING

One of the most important discoveries in the St. George's Street area was of a large building with an apsidal east end. This lay on the south-west side of the street, just south-east of Canterbury Lane (Fig. 1, Site 3, and Figs. 8–11) and was excavated in 1949. The site codes were C XV S and T. It was built in the middle of the third century on the site of a previous timber building and remained in occupation until late in the fourth century. The north-west wall of what was probably its northern wing was found in 1947 (C X G) immediately to the east of a Roman north-east to south-west street on the other side of the modern road. Much of the building lay beneath St. George's Street and could not be excavated; but several stretches of wall belonging to the west wing were observed in service-trenches dug along the north-east side of St. George's Street (Fig. 8) in 1951, 1952 and 1975.[20]

THE 1949 EXCAVATIONS

PERIOD I: THE PREVIOUS TIMBER BUILDING

Little activity took place in the area of Cellars S and T before the end of the second century. The old humus (Fig. 11, Section G-H (44)) yielded two sherds of late first-century pottery and was cut by two pits, Nos. 4 and 5, which contained pottery of the period 110–130 and 120–150, respectively (Fig. 81, Nos 59A–72). Not until the period 190–220 was the site occupied by a

20. A continuation of the wall found in C X G was seen in a G.P.O. telephone-cable manhole in November 1952 (Fig. 8, Wall a) and again during trenching for telephone cable-ducts in August 1975, when another wall (b) parallel to it and c. 24 ft. (7.3 m.) to the east was also observed at a depth of 3 ft. below the modern surface. Both walls were 2 ft. wide and built of flint and yellow mortar. A stretch of east—west wall (c) at right-angles to Walls a and b was observed in the same area in 1951 and 1952. It was seen by John Boyle in 1951 in a manhole on the south-eastern side of the Canterbury Lane-St. George's Street junction and located again between September and November 1952 in a trench dug across the south-west end of Canterbury Lane, when it was traced for a distance of c. 18 ft. (5.5 m.). The top of the wall lay c. 2 ft. 6 in. below the surface and it was c. 1 ft. 6 in. wide built on foundations a foot wider. Traces of a concrete floor were observed running under St. George's Street. (Information from Dr. Frank Jenkins. See *Canterbury Archaeology*, 1975–6 (Canterbury City Museums Publication)).

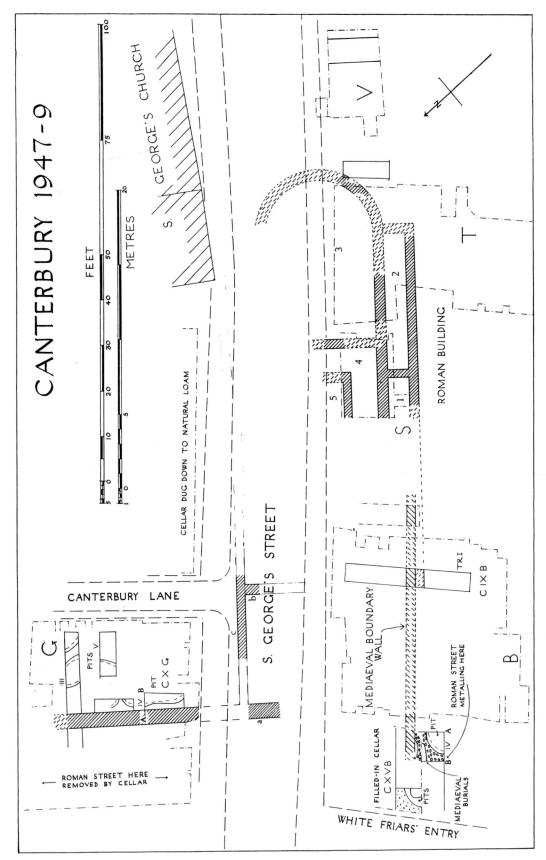

Fig. 8. Apsed Building: general plan of apsed building showing positions of C IX B Trench I and C XV B

timber building. A dish (Fig. 82, No. 87) of a type not made before *c.* 190 was found in a loam floor below Room 4 (Section E-F, S I (4), a layer which is the same as 35 in Section G-H), and a third-century mortarium (Fig. 82, No. 88) was found in a corresponding floor below Room 5. In the cellar area nothing more survived, but behind the cellar wall (Section J-K) two further loam floors (27, 24) were laid down over successive occupation-deposits. Layer 24 was divided from a third floor (23) in which two post-holes were cut, by a deposit of charcoal and ash (layer 23 is not visible on Section J-K). Above 23 was a layer of loam (22) which was either another floor or else a repair designed to counter subsidence. A similar succession of floors (33, 31) and occupation-deposits (32 and 11) were found below Room 1 (Section G-H). More early floors lay to the south of the later masonry building (Section G-H (44, 39); Section L-M (46, 39)). No walls were found unless the irregular gully at the north end of Trench T I (Section N-O (7)) was a trench for a timber-framed wall, and so no plan of the Period I building was obtained.

Date of the Period I Timber Building

S II Pit 4 which underlay the building yielded a sherd of Dr. 37 of Trajanic date and much coarse pottery of the period 110–130 (Fig. 81, Nos. 59B–72); but a date of *c.* 190–220 is indicated by two vessels in primary floors (Fig. 82, Nos. 87, 88). The overlying floors and occupation-levels yielded only second-century samian (Fig. 137, No. 5) and coarse wares which included only vessels of late second- to early third-century date; it seems unlikely, therefore, that the life of the building can have been extended significantly later than *c.* 240. Accordingly it is suggested that the building was erected *c.* 200 and was demolished before 250.

PERIOD II: THE APSED BUILDING

The building (Figs. 8, 9) was very disturbed by modern cellars, but a number of walls 2 ft. 6 in. wide and built of flint and mortar were recovered. It was built *c.* A.D. 250 and fell into ruin in the late fourth century.

Rooms 1 and 2

A corridor 4 ft. 6 in. wide, ran along the south-west side of the building; this was divided between Rooms 1 and 2 by a wall through which there was presumably a doorway. The concrete floor of Room 2 lay *c.* 1 ft. higher than that in Room 1. The west wall of the latter was not found, but Room 2 measured *c.* 30 ft. by 4 ft. 6 in. (9.1 by 1.37 m.). The south wall,[21]

---

21. A rubble-filled trench which probably marked a continuation of this wall to the west had been found in 1949 (Fig. 8, C IX B Trench I) (p. 51).

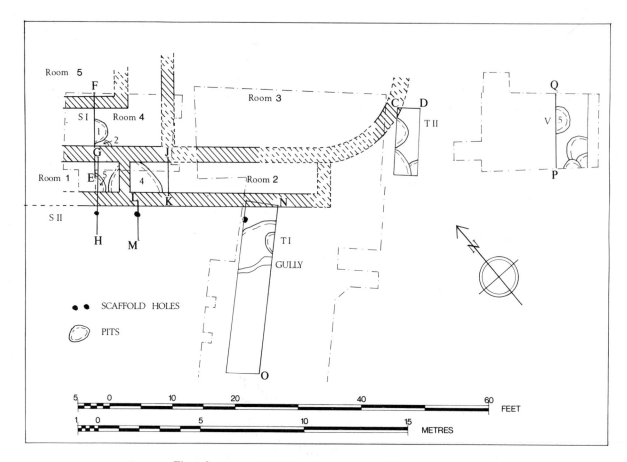

Fig. 9. Apsed Building: detailed plan of Rooms 1–5

which survived in places to a height of *c*. 3 ft. 6 in. and had a double tile-course at the top (Fig. 10, Section G-H; Pl. XV) had foundations which were trench-built through the floors of Period I below. In Section G-H they are trench-built from the level of the disintegrated concrete floor 10, and in Section J-K from below the concrete floor 21; in Section L-M they are sunk from the level of layer 41.

Three holes possibly for scaffolding-poles were found near the south-west face of the wall (Fig. 9 and Fig. 11, Sections G–H, L–M; the hole in Trench T I was 1 ft. 8 in. deep, *c* 12 in. in diameter and dug into yellow loam). Similar holes, assumed to be for scaffolding, had been noted in Canterbury in 1948 outside Room 4 of the St. Margaret Street Baths.[22] Their occurrence is not common, presumably because, then as now, the bottom of the scaffolding usually rested on the surface of the ground.

22.   To be published in a later volume of *The Archaeology of Canterbury* series, 'Excavations in the Marlowe Car Park and associated Areas' (forthcoming).

The corridor did not appear to have been decorated; the walls were roughly rendered from 6 in. above the top of the wall-trench, but flints protruded in places and there was no sign of any wall-plaster.[23]

Room 2 yielded a succession of loam floors and occupation-layers above the original concrete floor (21); in Room 1, however, the original floor (Section G–H (10)) was covered only by a thick occupation deposit (9) of reddish brown soil containing fragments of mortar together with pieces of bone and mussel shells, above which was a layer of black soil (8) yielding carbon flecks and oyster shells.

Rooms 3–5

Room 3 probably measured *c.* 35 ft. by 24 ft. (10.6 by 7.3 m.) and had an apsidal east end. Most of this lay under St. George's Street but the outside face of the apse was found in C XV T Trench II (Fig. 9 and Fig. 11, Section C–D); it was trench-built through a layer of grey earth with charcoal flecks (11) which overlay a yellow loam layer (12) above the natural subsoil. The interior of the room was not examined because of the depth to which the cellar had been cut.

Only a small part of Room 4 could be excavated. It was 6 ft (1.83 m.) wide and L-shaped; perhaps it was part of a portico surrounding a small central courtyard (Room 5).

Room 5 lay almost entirely below St. George's Street and very little information was obtained about it. By tunnelling beneath the street to the north of Trench S I a loam floor 2 in. thick was found, which overlay remains of Period I and yielded a sherd of samian Dr. 37 in the style of Austrus (A.D. 125–145) (Fig. 137, No. 2).

The building must have extended some distance to the north and north-west of Rooms 1 and 5 if the wall found in C X G and the walls found in the service trenches (p. 41) were part of it. There seemed to be at least two rooms (Fig. 8) in the wing bordering the north—south street.[24] C X G Trenches III, IV and V must have lain within the northern room, but the area had been very disturbed by the cellar builders and no floor-levels remained. The only features to survive were pits. One of these (Fig. 11, Section A–B) had a filling of earth and charcoal (4) and yielded seven samian sherds terminating with three of Trajanic or Hadrianic date (Dr. 18/31, 27, 33) and a large group of mid second-century coarse wares (parts of sixty-two vessels) (Fig. 81, Nos. 73–86). It had later been consolidated with rubble (3 and 2) probably when the building was erected. Another pit (G V Pit 1) yielded a large group of vessels of the period *c.* A.D. 100–130 (Fig. 80, Nos. 42–58). Little information was obtained about the southern room except that it measured *c.* 24 ft. by 36 ft. (7.3 by 10.9 m.), and may have had a concrete floor.[25]

The two small trenches and trial-hole dug in cellars on the site of the White Lion Inn in 1947 (Fig. 1, Site 10 and Fig. 8) should have uncovered more of the building; but all produced

---

23. From a medieval layer (S II 26) above Room 1 and underlying Pit 3 (Section G-H) was recovered a large slab of purplish-brown layered stone with polished surface. It was 0.8 in. (21 mm.) thick and is identified as travertine, possibly from a continental source though possibly from e.g. Yorkshire. The slab to judge from its state of wear was probably a flooring slab, but whether it was derived from the Roman building is unknown.
24. Cobbles probably from the edge of the street were found in C X G, Trench III.
25. See note 20.

natural loam immediately below the modern concrete of the cellar floor which had clearly destroyed all Roman and medieval levels.[26]

It is unlikely that the building extended any further south-west than Rooms 1 and 2. Trench T I was too disturbed by medieval pits for certainty that no floors survived;[27] but the three scaffold-pole holes (Fig. 9) are a firm indication that the south wall of Rooms 1 and 2 was external.

No floors were uncovered to east of the apse. Outside the wall in T II (Section C–D) a layer of black occupation-earth (10) overlay the deposits into which the wall-foundations had been cut; layer 10 yielded much late Roman pottery but had remained open into Saxon times since it yielded a sherd of cooking-pot of that period. Trench C XV V, which was cut in the cellar north-east of Cellar T, produced only a series of occupation-layers and pits (Figs. 9, 10).

DATE OF THE APSED BUILDING

A *terminus post quem* for this building is provided by a sherd of Antonine samian Dr. 79/80 and part of a possibly third-century mortarium (Fig. 82, No. 89) from Pit 2 in Trench S I (Section E–F) which predated the north-east wall of Room 1; but a clearer indication of date is

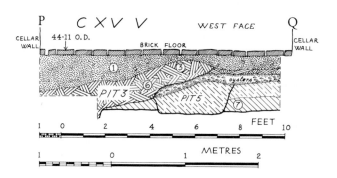

Fig.   10.   Apsed Building: Section P-Q. Scale 1 : 50

26.   It is possible, but unlikely, that the building extended as far north-east as the old Rectory of St. George's Church (destroyed in 1942) in which case the following, brought to notice by W. Urry and D. Harrington may be relevant. The *Kentish Gazette* for Wednesday, 1 February, 1769 stated: 'A new Herculaneum has been discovered in the ruins of Mr. Gregory's house [a Mr. Gregory was the vicar of St. George's Church at this time and the building referred to possibly St. George's Rectory] which was destroyed by the late fire; in the walls of a large arch in the cellar a great cavity was accidentally discovered out of which some ancient pieces of plate etc. were taken'. It should be noted that St. George's and St. Mary Magdalene's Church in Burgate Street were united in 1681 and it is possible that it is the St. Mary's Vicarage that is referred to here.
27.   The Roman gully (Fig. 11, Section N-O (7)) found at the north end and the cobbled surface (10) found at the south end of this trench (Fig. 9) are unlikely to be connected with this building, since they lie too deep.

given by the sequence of Period I floors which themselves did not begin before *c*. A.D. 200. Thus the erection of the masonry building can be dated to *c*. 240–250, and it continued in occupation well into the fourth century. Colour-coated vessels and coarse pottery of fourth-century date (Fig. 82, Nos. 90–104) occur in the later floors and contemporary layers outside, while the destruction-levels yielded vessels of the late fourth century, after *c*. 360 (Fig. 82, Nos. 105–108) and layer 3, a deposit of brown earth over the ruins (Section G—H), yielded a coin of the House of Theodosius.

FUNCTION OF THE APSED BUILDING

As already seen, very little of the building could be excavated and a large part of its plan is unknown. It measured at least 110 ft. (33.5 m.) east–west by 88 ft. (26.8 m.) or more north–south, and was presumably a large town house fronting one of the main streets of the city. Apses became less uncommon as domestic embellishments in the later second century, and the apsidal room here, which lay well back from the street was probably one of the main rooms in the house,[28] possibly the dining room. Whether this room was lavishly decorated and whether it was heated is unknown. The south corridor did not appear to have any embellishments, but this need not be relevant to the adornments of the rest of the house.

It is probably misleading to attempt further analysis of the building on the limited information which we possess. But if this is attempted, there seems to be a resemblance between its eastern wing and the church at Boppard;[29] both measured *c*. 120 ft. east–west, with an eastern apse and narrow south range of rooms. These are similarities and no more; the early date of the Canterbury building and the fact that it went out of use apparently during the fourth century must rule out any suggestion that it may have been a church. Its position towards the edge of the town might be suitable for a religious building of some other cult, but the lack of votive offerings makes this unlikely. It seems best to regard it simply as a large town-house.

DEPOSITS LATER THAN THE APSED BUILDING

The destruction-layers of the apsed building were sealed by deposits of late Roman and early medieval dark earth (e.g. late Roman: S II 3, 29; early medieval: S II 1, 5, 6: see Sections G-H, J-K, L-M). These were cut by pits probably of the thirteenth century (e.g. S II Pit 3).

Within the cellars the latest levels had been removed; but a small stretch of loam floor was found in S II (Section J-K below (1) and another floor-surface in Trench T I (Section N-O (2)). The latter was of seventeenth- or eighteenth-century date and ran up to a wall of flint and

---

28. At Silchester and elsewhere the principal rooms are often situated as far as possible from the street-entrance.
29. For a plan of Boppard and other churches see *Britannia*, ii (1971), 226.

yellow mortar, on top of which the brick wall of the cellar had later been built. A post-hole and timber slot were cut into this floor which sealed medieval pits 3 and 6 which were probably of thirteenth-century date.[30]

In Trench T II, which was dug from the surface, more stratification survived. Three successive cobbled surfaces (Fig. 11, Section C-D (9, 7, and 5)) were found; surface 9 lay to the east of the apse wall and yielded several sherds of eleventh-century pottery (Fig. 82, Nos. 110–112). Surfaces 7 and 5 overlay the wall; 5 produced sherds from three cooking-pots of mid to late eleventh-century date (Fig. 82, No 113). These metalled layers may have belonged to a medieval building,[31] but are more likely part of a cobbled lane.[32] Each surface was covered by a thick layer of occupation-material (Section C-D (8, 6 and 4)). Above layer 4 were two floors (1) and (3). Layer 3 produced sherds of two eleventh-century cooking-pots and layer 1 two twelfth-century sherds. No associated walls were found.

30. In *c*. 1200, according to Cathedral Rental D 124, the area opposite St. George's Church was vacant ground belonging to Odbold, cf. W. Urry, *Canterbury under the Angevin Kings* (London, 1967), 269.
31. There is no evidence in the Cathedral Rentals for buildings here in the twelfth or thirteenth century. W. Urry, *op. cit.* (note 30).
32. William Urry has pointed out that the metalling may represent a lane mentioned in a case heard before the justices at Canterbury in 1214: 'Magister Willelmus de sancto Georgio queritur de obstruccione cuiusdam venelle que est ante hostium ecclesie sue de sancto Georgio que semper in adventu iusticiariorum aperta est et post discessum eorundem clauditur, ad nocumentum ecclesie sue. Et ideo preceptum est quod venella illa aperta sit sicut de iure esse debet et solet'. H.G. Richardson and G.O Sayles, (eds.) *Select Cases of Procedure Without Writ under Henry III*, Seldon Society, vol. 60 (1941), 68. The cobbles discussed here would have met St. George's Street almost exactly opposite the south door of St. George's Church. Although the existing door is of the fourteenth or fifteenth century it is likely that an earlier door lay on the same site.

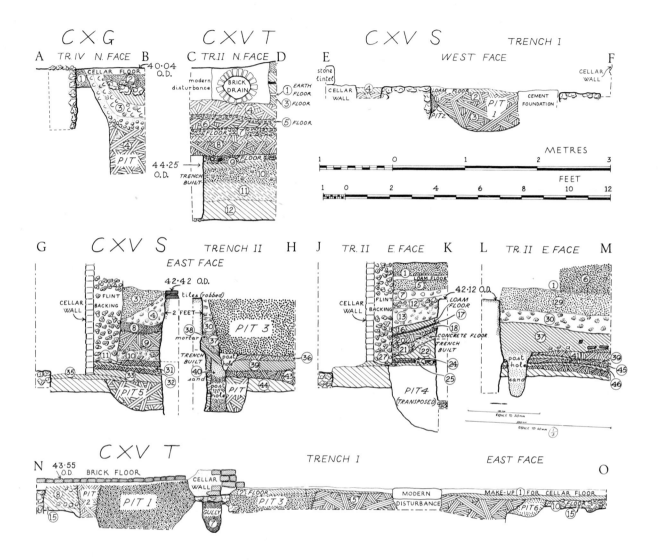

Fig. 11. Apsed Building: Sections A-B, C-D, E-F, G-H, J-K, L-M, N-O. Scale 1 : 50

III. MINOR EXCAVATIONS ALONG ST. GEORGE'S STREET

Between 1946 and 1951 a number of small trenches were dug, mainly in cellars along either side of St. George's Street, east of Rose Lane and west of Canterbury Lane (Fig. 1).

(a) C IX SITE B (Fig. 8)

In April 1947 two small trenches were dug on the south-west side of St. George's Street on the site of the Kentish Observer's offices. In Trench I (Fig. 8) apart from a robbed wall nothing Roman was found; and medieval layers, which dated from the fourteenth century, lay directly above the natural subsoil, indicating that there had been a cellar at that period. The robber trench yielded early nineteenth-century glass bottle fragments; but it aligned with the south wall of the Roman apsed house further east (p. 43) and was taken to represent its continuation. Just north-east of the robber trench the base of a medieval east—west flint wall, 2 ft. wide, was located. This is taken to be a boundary wall belonging to the Austin Friary.[33]

In Trench II (which lay *c.* 60 ft. (18.3 m.) south of the area shown in Fig. 8), a disturbed human skeleton probably from the Friary cemetery was found sealed by seventeenth- and eighteenth-century levels. Four more skeletons from the cemetery were found on Site C XV B (p. 53) and others in a drainage-trench dug in 1953–4.[34]

33. The White, or Austin, Friars were settled in this part of Canterbury by 1325 and remained there until the Dissolution. Mechanical excavators working in the play-ground of Simon Langton School in 1939 uncovered a number of foundations presumed to be part of the Friary (*Arch. Cant.*, li (1939), 210); drainage-trenching to the south of St. George's Street in 1953–54 uncovered the ground plan of a large building which may have been the monastery church. To the north of it were a number of graves (*Arch. Cant.*, lxviii (1954), 204–5). More Friary walls were found in 1960 during excavations on the Simon Langton site (forthcoming report).
34. See note 33.

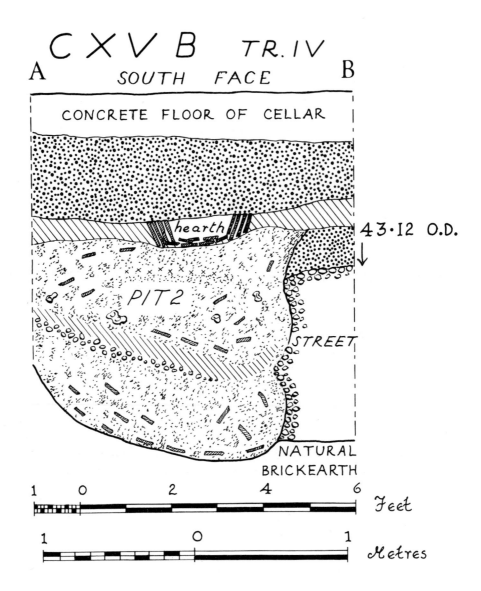

Fig. 12. South of St. George's Street; C XV B Trench IV: Section A-B. Scale 1 : 24

(b) C XV SITE B (Figs. 8, 12)

C XV B was a cellar on the south side of St. George's Street to the east of White Friars Entry (Fig. 8). Three Trenches, II, III and IV, were opened but only Trench IV was productive.

Roman street-metalling was found in Trench IV (Figs. 8 and 12). This was c. 3 ft. 8 in. (1.12 m.) thick and was part of the north-east to south-west street of which c. 40 ft. (12.2 m.) was uncovered in C XV R c. 110 ft. (33.5 m.) to the north-east (p. 70). All the other features were medieval and the street itself was cut by a large medieval pit (Pit 2) which yielded a number of cooking-pot sherds, the latest being thirteenth-century. Above this was a loam floor (2) with tiled hearth (Fig. 12); the floor yielded a thirteenth-century sherd. Four inhumations from the cemetery of the Austin Friary[35] were uncovered together with a fragmentary child burial. They were all orientated east—west and lay south of the east–west wall which had been previously found on Site C IX B Trench I, and which probably formed the north boundary-wall of the Friary Precincts. Inhumation 2, beneath which was Inhumation 4, and Inhumation 3 lay immediately adjacent to the wall with Inhumation 1 a little to the south of 3.[36]

A medieval tile hearth and floor yielding Group III pottery dated to the first half of the twelfth century were also found.

(c) C X SITE J (Figs. 1, 13)

In the summer of 1947 a small area was excavated in a cellar on the south-west side of St. George's Street, just west of White Friars Entry (Fig. 1). Only the lowest levels remained.

The earliest features were a sleeper-beam trench and gravel floor belonging to a Roman building (Fig. 13). The trench was filled with black earth and yielded several third-century colour-coated sherds and a grey-ware dish (Fig. 83, Nos. 114–117); the gravel floor, which was 3 in. thick, lay to the north of this and was covered by a thin occupation-layer (6) which yielded part of a second-century jar (Fig. 83, No. 118) of the period A.D. 160–220.

A large storage-jar (Fig. 83, No. 119) full of black soil, oysters, tile and pottery fragments (Fig. 83, Nos. 120–121) was found in a hollow (5A) to the south of the sleeper-trench. The jar pre-dated the building but it had been cut in half by a later black-filled pit (Pit 1) some of whose contents filled the remaining half of the storage-jar. Several small stake-holes (Fig. 13) were found cut through the hut floor and the filling of the sleeper-trench, but their exact function could not be determined.

Part of the upper stone of a donkey-mill (Fig. 72, No. 1) was found in this trench and this presumably came from a baker's shop nearby. Donkey-mills are rare in Roman Britain, but examples are known from London and Silchester.

35. See p. 51 and note 33.
36. Dr. D.F. Roberts, of the University of Newcastle-upon-Tyne, examined the skeletons and provided Appendix IV below.

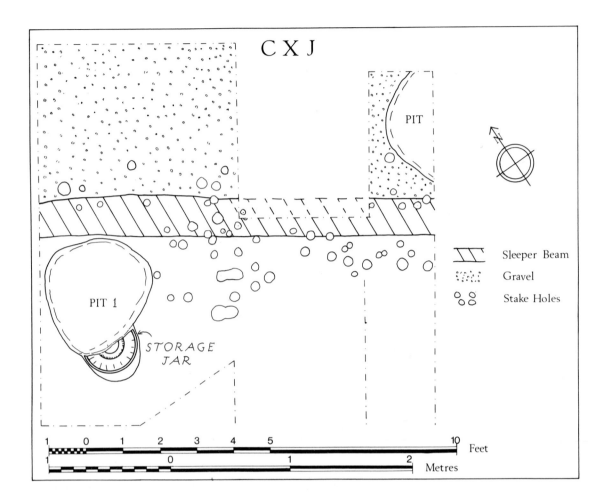

Fig.   13.   South of St. George's Street; C X J: plan. Scale 1 : 30

(d) SITES C XI O AND C XI P (Fig. 14)

Two trenches C XI O and C XI P were dug in December 1947 in cellars on either side of a narrow alley which gave access to the back premises of the Kentish Observer (Fig. 1). Some Roman and post-Roman pits were found.

C XI O

Six pits were excavated in this trench (Fig. 14). Pits 1, 5 and 6 were Roman. Pit 6, the earliest, was undated. Pit 1, whose filling was hard to distinguish from Pit 6, yielded Antonine samian (Dr. 31) and sherds from two late-Antonine or third-century dishes (Fig. 83, Nos.

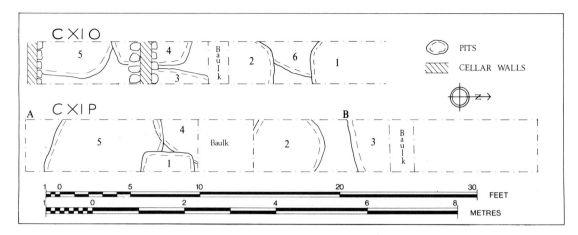

Fig. 14. South of St. George's Street; C XI O and C XI P: plans. Scale 1 : 80

122–123). It was filled with black sticky charcoally material which contained oysters and Roman flue- and roof-tile fragments. Pit 5 produced a coin of Constans; at the base of the pit was *c.* 9 in. of solid sticky black soil, overlaid by 9 in. of lighter clayey soil mixed with lenses of yellow loam. Above this was a deposit of dark sticky soil, *c.* 1 ft. 6 in. thick, which contained fragments of plaster and Roman brick.

Pits 2, 3 and 4 yielded late Saxon pottery (Fig. 83, Nos. 124–126). The brick walls of the cellar rested on flint footings, but it was uncertain whether the two were of different dates.

C XI P

Five more pits were excavated in this cellar (Figs. 14, 15). Of these Pits 2, 3 and 4 were Roman. Pit 2 had a filling of dark sticky earth which in the top half of the pit was mixed with large building-flints, pieces of Roman tile, lumps of iron slag and a few fragments of Kentish Ragstone. It yielded Antonine samian (Dr. 37 and Dr. 31) and part of a flanged bowl of late third- or fourth-century date (Fig. 83, No. 127).

Pit 3 yielded a coin of Valentinian I, the rims of a fourth-century jar (Fig. 83, No. 128) and colour-coated dish. Pit 4 had a filling similar to that of Pit 2 but without the building material. Pit 5, which yielded several sherds of a Saxon spouted pitcher (No. 129), possibly of the second half of the eighth century, was very large, but not fully excavated because of wet conditions. The floor of the pit was of rammed gravel *c.* 6 in. thick, above which was dark sticky earth (4). On top of this was a yellow loamy deposit. The presence of a laid floor might suggest that this pit was a Saxon cellar; but it was sunk in natural brickearth which could hardly have stood for long without revetment, of which there was no sign. Pit 1, in which medieval pottery of Groups II and III dated to between 1050 and 1150 (Fig. 83, Nos. 130–132) was found,[37] was filled with reddish-brown soft vegetable material.

37. For these Groups, see Introduction, p. 24.

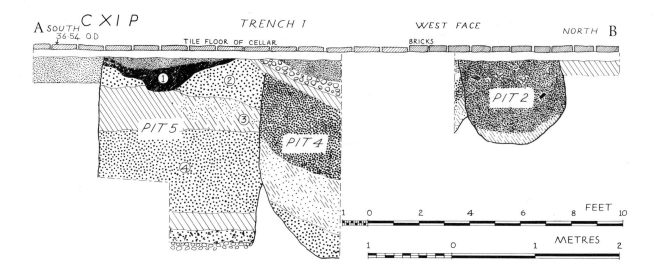

Fig. 15. South of St. George's Street; C XI P: Section A-B

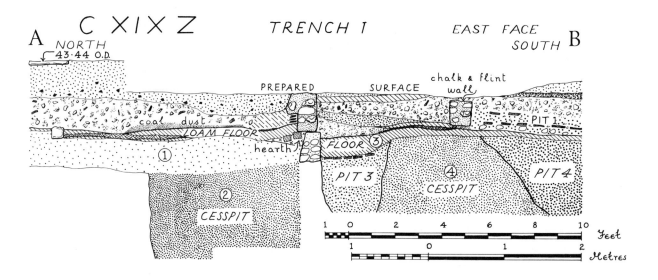

Fig. 16. South of St. George's Street; C XIX Z Trench I: Section A-B. Scale 1 : 48

(e) C XIX SITE Z (Fig. 16)

In April 1951 excavations were carried out south-west of St. George's Street just east of Marks and Spencer's store (Fig. 1) It was hoped to find traces of a south-east to north-west Roman street thought to pass at this point, but the area was very disturbed by thirteenth- and fourteenth-century pits, and no Roman levels survived. Three small trenches were dug from the surface.

Trench 1

Several deep intersecting cess-pits, two of which ((2) and (4)) are visible on Fig. 16, occupied most of the bottom of the trench, but the divisions between them were indistinct. They were filled with fine dark earth and yielded much pottery ranging from the eleventh to the fourteenth centuries (Fig. 85, Nos. 133–137), including two whole but crushed cooking-pots. Other pits were later cut, and of these Pits 3 and 4 are visible on Fig. 16. Both produced fourteenth-century pottery (Fig. 85, Nos. 139–142).

In the later fourteenth century a house with several phases of occupation was built above these pits. A three-phase east—west wall crossed the centre of the trench, and contemporary with this was a succession of floors. The Phase 1 floor in the north room was a grey-green earthy layer (1) in which a number of sherds of late fourteenth-century date were found (Fig. 85, Nos. 144–146). Cut into this floor against the wall was a hearth of pitched tiles which projected in a curve *c.* 1 ft. westwards into the trench. The south room had a loam floor (3) in this phase and in it was part of a fourteenth-century jug (Fig. 85, No. 143). This layer was thicker over Pit 3 without having greatly subsided, and its base was a horizontal layer of tiles; probably laid to combat subsidence. It would appear that the presence of Pit 3 was known. Later the wall was rebuilt in chalk and yellow mortar on almost the same line as before; the north room now had a new floor, this time of loam, on the surface of which was a layer of coal dust probably from an oven. The south room also had a new loam floor.

The wall was then rebuilt on its original line for the second time and a new chalk-and-flint wall was built *c.* 5 ft. 8 in. to the south. The floor in the northern room had been destroyed, but in between the walls a loam floor was found overlying a layer of rubble. The latter was presumably a Phase 2 destruction-deposit. To the south of the new wall the Phase 3 floor had been destroyed by Pit 1 in which a sherd of an early seventeenth-century maiolica plate was found. In Pit 2 there was a seventeenth-century jar-sherd (Fig. 129, No. 831).

In Trench II, which lay *c.* 20 ft. to the south of Trench I, the Roman levels had again been destroyed. At the north end of the trench was a yellow loam floor (2) which possibly belonged to the medieval house found in Trench I. It overlay a layer of black earth (3) which sealed a black-filled pit (Pit 5) and yielded a sherd of a Group III cooking-pot dated to the first half of the twelfth century. Pit 5 contained nothing except a few Roman brick fragments and some iron slag. Another loam floor-surface was seen at the south end of the trench between two medieval pits. This floor was 1 ft. thick with a spread of daub and charcoal (5) on its surface which yielded an eleventh-century cooking-pot (Fig. 85, No. 138); the floor itself overlay a pit of probable eleventh-century date which was filled with black soil. Four late seventeenth- or eighteenth-century pits were cut into the medieval levels and of these Pits 2 and 4 yielded a number of sherds of Dutch maiolica plates, delftware, and stoneware jug sherds besides local ware (Fig. 129, Nos. 832–853).

A similar sequence of a medieval loam floor overlying black sticky medieval soil and cut by seventeenth-century pits was found in Trench III, which was cut between Trenches I and II. Pit 1 in Z III contained maiolica, stoneware and local sherds (Fig. 130, Nos. 854–857; Fig. 136, Nos. 6–7).

(f) C XIV SITE Q (Figs. 17, 18)

C XIV Q Trench I was dug in April 1949 at the south-east end of Iron Bar Lane *c.* 40 ft. (12.2 m.) back from its junction with St. George's Street (Fig. 1). There was no cellar here and deep stratification extending from Roman to modern times survived; but it was only in the medieval and later periods that there were buildings on the site. A second trench was dug in a cellar just below St. George's Street; the only feature here was a Roman pit which was cut into the natural clay below the retaining-wall of the street.

Trench I (Figs. 17 and 18)

Several Roman layers were encountered at the bottom of the trench, but no structures. The lowest level at the north end of the trench (Fig. 18, Sections A-B and C-D (38)) comprised light fine grey earth which dipped down into a pit (39). No dating evidence was recovered from 38 or 39. Above 38 was a layer of sticky grey-black earth (35) which yielded fourth-century sherds together with a possibly intrusive Saxon one. This level dipped down into the filling of a pit (42) which was seen to be cut through the natural subsoil at the extreme south end of the trench. Layer 35 was overlaid by sticky black occupation-deposits (28 and 27) which either represent a gradual accumulation from surrounding occupation or perhaps a deliberate dump. Little dating evidence was recovered from these levels but layer 27 produced sherds of two medieval cooking-pots, one probably of the twelfth century (Fig. 86, No. 147).

In the fourteenth century the first buildings were erected here, and there was intensive occupation throughout that century represented by a number of floor-surfaces earlier, contemporary with and later than three flint-and-mortar walls. The buildings lay on either side of a narrow alley, the primary metalling of which (Fig. 18, Section C-D (32)) seems to coincide with the construction of the first buildings in the area.

No walls were found which were contemporary with Phase 1 of the northern building although the existence of the alley-way makes it clear that it ended on about the same line (Wall B) as the later building. Its primary floor comprised a layer of pebbles and gravel (Fig. 18, Sections A-B and C-D (26)), 4 in. thick, a *terminus post quem* for which is provided by one sherd of a fourteenth-century cooking-pot (Fig. 86, No. 148) and one of a late thirteenth-century jug. On top of this was a black occupation-layer (25) which was overlaid by a secondary floor of yellow mortar (24); above was another occupation-deposit (14) in which a

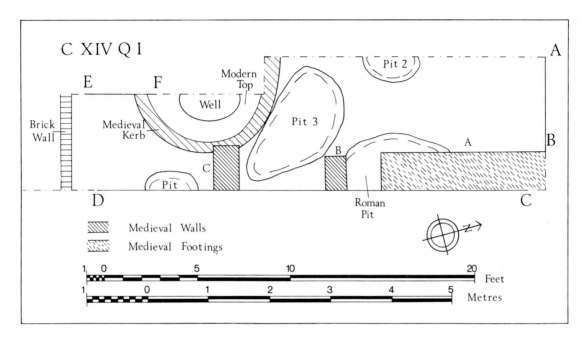

Fig. 17. North of St. George's Street; C XIV Q Trench I: plan. Scale 1 : 60

number of bones and some residual thirteenth-century pottery were found. This was covered by a layer of pebbly earth (13).

Rebuilding now took place, and an east—west wall B was trench-built through layers 13 and 14. But soon after the roof was in position, but before any floors laid, there was a fire and a very black and sooty deposit (10), which contained a number of slates presumably deriving from the collapsed roof (Fig. 74, No. 3), covered 13 and (where this was absent) 14. Layer 10 sealed a pit which yielded a fifteenth-century sherd with apple-green glaze; this provides a *terminus post quem* for the fire. After the fire work on Wall B was resumed and a north—south wall, A, was constructed along the east side of the north part of the trench. Work on this wall may have started before the fire since burnt layer 10 seems to abut it and cover the south end of the footings-trench (Section C-D); further north, however, the wall was clearly trench-built through 10 (Section A-B). The footings extended *c.* 7 ft. 6 in. along the trench but they were capped with flints rendered with mortar only for the first 5 ft. Wall B lay about 2 ft. south of the end of the north—south footings; presumably the gap between the walls was for a narrow door. A gravel floor (9), which yielded a sherd of an early fourteenth-century cooking-pot and part of the shoulder of a jug of similar date (Fig. 86, No. 149), was contemporary with these walls (Sections A-B, C-D). On its surface was a thin occupation-layer (9a) yielding sherds of two more fourteenth-century jugs (Fig. 86, No. 150). The context here shows either that their conventional date is too early, or that the type was long-lived.

Wall A later went out of use and was sealed by a chalk floor (5). Possibly Wall B stood longer than Wall A to border floor 5 on the south, but it too was demolished before long and its remains were covered by a deposit of burnt wall-clay (1). This fact and the narrowness of the foundations suggest that Wall B was carried up in half timber.

The burnt wall-clay also covered the alley, which up to this time seems to have been maintained, although not properly metalled. The original metalling (32) was covered by stony earth (20) above which were a number of slates and pieces of burnt debris presumably from the fire. These were covered by another deposit of stony earth (8).

A succession of floors similar to those already discussed and belonging to two main periods of building lay to the south of the alley.

Period 1

Overlying the medieval black layer (28) (Sections C-D and E-F) was the primary floor of the earliest building. It consisted of pebbly yellow gravel, in which several late thirteenth-century jug-sherds were found, and it had a cobbled surface; a new surface (17) was laid down after the accumulation of a thin occupation-layer. Further occupation-material (16) covered the upper gravel surface and this in turn was overlaid by a new gravel floor (15). Two mortar floors separated by an occupation-layer (12), which in places was covered with slates, overlay 15; the upper surface was covered by a substantial occupation-layer (11) which yielded two late thirteenth- or early fourteenth-century sherds. No walls contemporary with these floors survived but substantial gravel footings (30) which lay beneath the later Wall C very likely belonged to this phase of occupation.

Period 2

Above layer 11 a make-up layer (6) was spread, and overlying this was a chalk floor (5). This seemed to be contemporary with Wall C although the floor had been destroyed by a pit (Pit 1) close to the wall. Wall C was trench-built from the top of the burnt layer above (20) and thus built after the fire. It was later demolished, probably slightly before Wall B — for it was covered by an earth and charcoal deposit (2) above which was burnt wall-clay (1) from Wall B.

A medieval well lay to the west of Wall C; its relationship to the stratification is visible in Section E-F. The well post-dated the Period 1 building, the floors of which were cut by its construction-pit. It was probably in use with the stone-walled Period 2 building although stratigraphically it was earlier in origin; Wall C was built up to the well, cutting away its top, which was capped with large stones (of which only one, 13 in. wide and 6 in. thick, survived) and the well's construction-pit was sealed by chalk floor 5A and its make-up layer (6).

The presence of a wall immediately adjacent to the well was puzzling. It is possible that the well could be approached from two sides, from the alley to the north and the building to the south; but this would be unusual.

The well, which was reconstructed in more recent times, was not excavated.

The only other features of note in this trench were three pits. Pit 1, which post-dated the destruction of the Period 2 building, yielded only residual late thirteenth-century sherds and some roof-slates (Fig. 74, Nos 1–2). Pit 2, which was sealed by layer 10, was more interesting since it had a wooden floor and wooden lining (Pl. XVI). It was 25 in. deep, c. 37 in. in

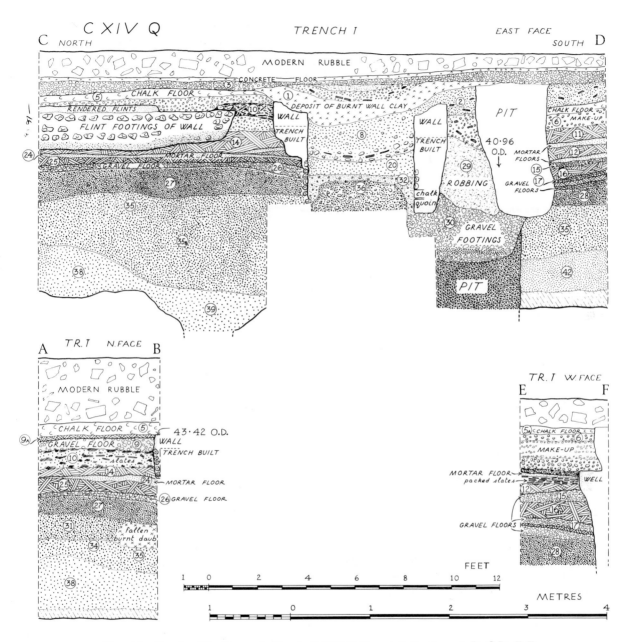

Fig. 18. North of St. George's Street; C XIV Q Trench I: Sections A-B, C-D, E-F

diameter at the top, narrowing slightly towards the bottom. Sherds from two late thirteenth-century jugs, and a third in fifteenth-century ware with apple-green glaze, were found in the filling. Pit 3, which seemed to be cut from above the level of (10), lay between Walls B and C. It pre-dated the well but produced no dating evidence.

Sealing Pit 1 and chalk floor (5) was a layer of gravel, covered by a concrete floor. On the surface of this was a thick deposit of modern rubble.

(g) SITES C X K AND C XIV P (Figs. 19 and 20)

Sites C X K and C XIV P were dug in September 1947 and April 1949 respectively, on the north-east side of St. George's Street, just north-west of its junction with Iron Bar Lane (Fig. 1). Both sites were much disturbed and little information was gained.

SITE K

Site K was in a cellar; two trenches were dug but Trench II was quickly abandoned. In Trench I (Fig. 19) part of a Roman floor was found immediately beneath the concrete floor of the cellar. It consisted of a thin gravel layer containing tile-fragments and bones. The only other Roman feature was Pit 2, which was filled with brown earth, and yielded a sherd of Flavian samian (Dr. 18) stamped **OF VITAL**[, four other Flavian samian sherds (Dr. 18 (three) and Dr. 15/18 — an unusual form), a sherd of mortarium dated A.D. 80–150 (Fig. 86, No. 151) and other coarse-ware vessels (Fig. 86, Nos. 152–153) which extend the date to c. A.D. 80–140. A fourth-century coin from the pit is doubtless intrusive. Pit 2 was cut on the south side by the insertion of a recent vaulted structure which crossed the trench, and on the north by a medieval foundation. On the north side of the latter lay Pit 1 with a filling of black earth which produced sherds of three Saxon cooking-pots (Fig. 86, Nos. 154–156) and a Group III rim-sherd of the first half of the twelfth century. The only other features encountered were the bases of three medieval cellar walls of rather flimsy construction; the most northerly, just mentioned, was in line with the back wall of this part of the modern cellar, of which the length west of the entrance was of medieval build. The west wall of the medieval cellar did not join the northern one and must have turned west in the area destroyed by the vault, probably to form an entrance to the original cellar.

SITE P

Site P (Fig. 20) was a trench dug from the surface and was almost entirely occupied by pits. In the small area where stratification did survive, a layer of grey earth (9), which seemed at one point to dip into a pit, overlay the natural subsoil. The pit was not excavated. Layer 9 was covered by some large flints (not visible on the section), the purpose of which was obscure, and above them was a deposit of black soil (8) which yielded a coin of Valerian (253–259). Layer 8 was difficult to distinguish from similar medieval black-soil deposits (7 and 6) above it which yielded several sherds of Group IV cooking-pots dated to the second half of the

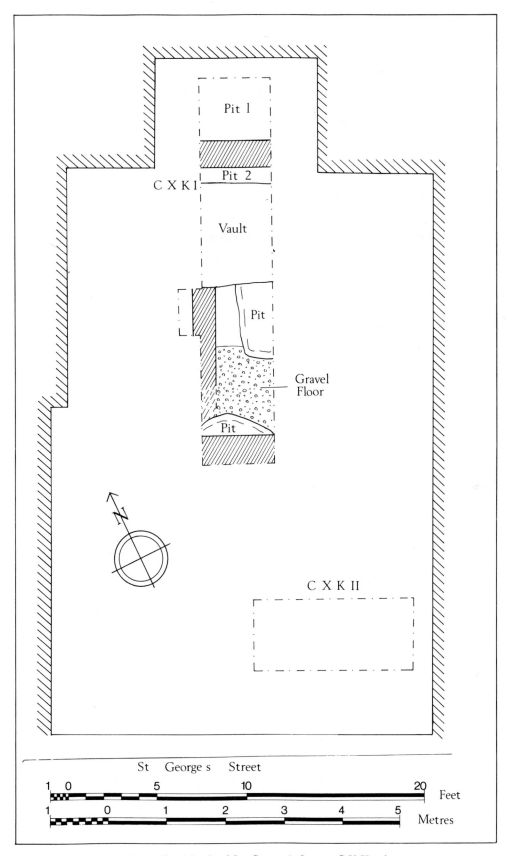

Fig. 19. North of St. George's Street; C X K: plan

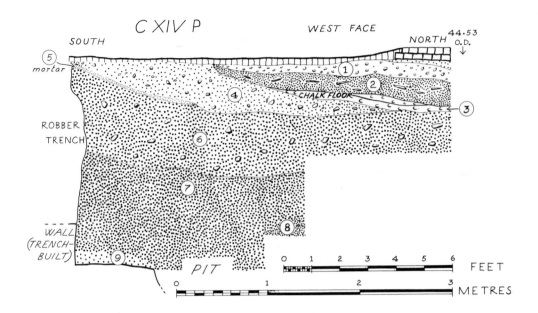

Fig. 20. North of St. George's Street; C XIV P: section. Scale 1 : 40

thirteenth century. An east–west medieval wall which was badly robbed, but had very deep foundations, lay at the south end of the trench; and associated with it were two successive floors of mortar (5) and chalk (3). No dating evidence was recovered from the floors.

In 1166, according to Urry (*op. cit.*, note 30), the ground for 40 ft. to the west of Iron Bar Lane belonged to the sons of Alured de Welles (Rental B 109). In 1200 the Speech House lay in this area (Rental Z Fol. 196) and apparently the name Speech House was still attached to buildings at the western corner of Iron Bar Lane in the sixteenth century.

(h) C XI SITE N (Figs. 21, 22)

The site coded C XI N was dug in January 1948 in a cellar on the north side of St. George's Street between the National Provincial and Barclays Banks[38] (Fig. 1).

Trench I was dug in the lower, west part of the cellar and was unproductive. The only

38. A substantial Roman foundation was found by workmen outside the National Provincial bank in 1954 (Fig. 1(a)). It was 11 ft. 6 in. (3.5 m.) long and 3 ft. (0.9 m.) wide, built of flint and mortar capped by flat Roman tiles. The top lay 6 ft. 6 in. (2 m.) below the present level of the street. (Information from Dr. F. Jenkins.) For this and other walls see further Appendix VIII (C).

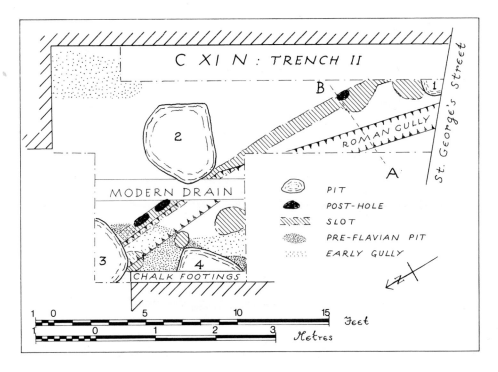

Fig. 21. North of St. George's Street; C XI N Trench II: plan. Scale 1 : 60

Roman features were three pits. Pit 1 was filled with black earth and oyster shells and yielded a sherd of samian (Dr. 18/31) probably of Hadrianic-Antonine date, and sherds from two probably early third-century dishes (Fig. 86, Nos. 157–158). Pit 2 was filled with clean brown loam with patches of earth; this yielded an amphora-stamp (Fig. 136, No. 1).

All the other levels excavated in Trench I were of the seventeenth and eighteenth centuries and were connected with a cellar of which an east—west wall crossed the trench. This was built of chalk and faced with flint and mortar. To its south was a contemporary chalk floor, covered with rubble and cinders. The floor lay on a bedding of chalk, mortar and brick-rubble 6 in. thick in which seventeenth- and eighteenth-century pottery and glass, including the seal of a Pyrmont water-bottle were found. Beneath this, overlying the natural subsoil, was a trodden earthy level which was probably created by the diggers of the cellar cavity. Several post-holes were dug into this and sealed by the rubble make-up. No floor was found in the area to the north of the wall; this was assumed to lie outside the original cellar.

Trench II (Figs. 21 and 22) was dug in the shallower, eastern part of the cellar where more was preserved. The earliest feature was a shallow mid first-century disturbance through which a pit (Fig. 21) had been dug into the natural subsoil and filled with light grey loam with charcoal flecks. The pit yielded pre-Flavian samian (Dr. 27, 29 and 18), a Flavian mortarium and several sherds of coarse pottery (Fig. 86, Nos. 159–163) of the period c. A.D. 50–80. The pit was adjoined on its south side by a shallower area of disturbance which may have been a

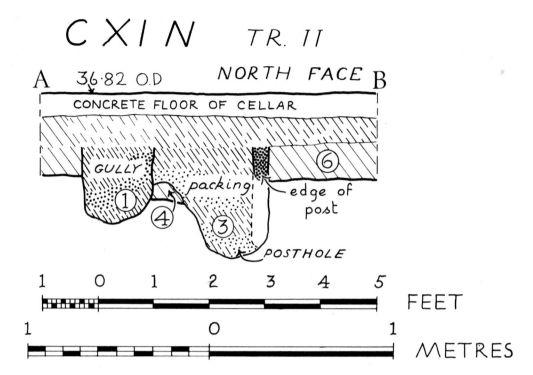

Fig. 22. North of St. George's Street; C XI N Trench II: Section A-B. Scale 1 : 20

drainage gully leading into the pit, but this was uncertain. Parts of two successive Roman timber buildings were found, but the cellar was too small for coherent plans to be recovered. A Period 1 wall was represented by several post-holes and a slot dug into the natural brickearth. Actual post-positions were visible in places; some stood in the centre of the slot, others were close to one edge. The slot (3) was filled with light loam and this yielded a sherd of Flavian samian (Dr. 33). The rim of a late first- or early second-century jar (Fig. 86. No. 164) was found in the packing of one of the post-holes.

In Period 2 the slot was replaced by a square-cut gully, possibly for a sleeper beam. This yielded only a sherd of pre-Flavian samian (Dr. 18R) and a jar (Fig. 86, No. 165) of Flavian date. It was c. 1 ft. 3 in. wide and cut into a layer of charcoal-flecked bright yellow loam (Fig. 22 (6)); at the north end of the trench it was found to have changed direction and here it cut through and overlay the earlier slot, post-holes and mid first-century pit. Layer 6, which sealed the natural where it was undisturbed may have been a Period 1 floor, but this was uncertain; no Period 2 floors were found.

The only other significant feature found in this trench was a deep Saxon pit (Pit 2). This was filled with dark greenish-brown sandy earth with patches of yellow loam and contained many oyster shells and bones[39] together with sherds of three small hand-made Saxon vessels of the

---

39. The bones were examined by Miss Ann Brocklebank whose report is printed in Appendix V.

late sixth or seventh century (Fig. 86, Nos. 167–169). A pierced rim made of soft granular fabric, perhaps of the eighth or ninth century was also found (Fig. 86, No. 166).

Medieval levels had been destroyed by the cellar-builders, but William Urry's examination of the documentary evidence has shown that in *c.* 1166 the land was owned by Cecilia, daughter of Gerald and in *c.* 1200 by the heirs of Alfred de Welles.[40]

40. W. Urry, *Canterbury under the Angevin Kings* (London, 1967), Rental B 109, Rental D 105.

CANTERBURY LANE

KERB

M3

G

IV. AREA R AND MINOR EXCAVATIONS WEST OF CANTERBURY LANE

(a) AREA R (Fig. 23)

The site coded C XV R lay north-east of the St. George's Street cellars, between Iron Bar Lane and Canterbury Lane where a comparatively large area was cleared mechanically in 1949[41] (Fig. 1, Site 4 and Fig. 23).

A 40-ft. (12.2 m.) length of north-east to south-west Roman street[42] joined by a street running to the south-east at right angles was uncovered. Perhaps in the fifth century the streets fell into disuse and a two-period timber hut was built over their intersection. In medieval times numerous pits and wells were dug in the area.

41.   The site was supervised by Mr. J.S. Wacher.
42.   More of this street was located further south in sites C X G (p. 45), C XV B (p. 53) and C XXXI-XXXII S in the Simon Langton School Yard (forthcoming publication).
(a)   Gravel which probably belonged to it was noted by Dr. F. Jenkins on the White Friars site in 1952, but was only c. 9 in. thick. Part of a street at right-angles was also uncovered at this time. (Information from Dr. F Jenkins. Cf. *Arch. Cant.*, lxviii (1954), 204–5).
(b)   To the north-east of site C XV R the line of the street was picked up in a number of drainage-trenches dug in the 1950s.
(i)   The trench dug in September 1951 from Iron Bar Lane to the east end of St. Thomas' Church (Fig. 1, Site 11) located the north-western side of the street. It was badly disturbed by pits but was otherwise similar to the remains in C XV R. It was c. 5 ft. 2 in. (2.55 m.) thick in the centre. A street-ditch c. 5 ft. (1.5 m.) wide and filled with green silt and gravelly pebbles lay to the north-west of the street and beyond this was a series of beaten clay floors belonging to a Roman building. They had been badly disturbed by rubbish pits but seemed to extend for a distance of c. 100 ft. (30 m.) to the western end of the drainage-trench and into its north–south extension. On the primary floor was an irregular hexagonal hearth with chalk walls and tiled floor. A little pottery was found beneath and in the floors; it suggested an early third-century date for the construction of the building. (Information from Mr. J.S. Wacher. A plan of the drain-trench will be deposited in Canterbury Museum).
(ii)   More of the street was observed at various points in a drainage-trench dug from St. George's Street to St. Thomas' Church. The trench ran along the line of the Roman street, but the latter was very badly cut about by pits, one of which (Fig. 23, Pit A) yielded suggestive contents. This lay just north of C XV R Trench III and was a large pit containing debris from a wattle-and-daub building, much thirteenth-century pottery and sherds from at least twenty crucibles. According to Dr. Urry some moneyers had a house in this area in the thirteenth century and it is possible that the pit represents their dump: cf. W. Urry, *Canterbury under the Angevin Kings* (London, 1967), Charter LXVIII .

North-east to South-west Street

This was initially laid down in the mid first century and was subsequently resurfaced about nine times (Pl. XVII) to a thickness of *c.* 4 ft. 6 in. (1.37 m.). It changed direction slightly during the Roman period and assumed a more north-easterly course (see Fig. 25, Section E-F). This may have occurred when the city defences were erected, the street being brought into line with them.

Surface 1 (Fig. 25, Sections C-D, III 29 and E-F, V 17), which was made up of very tightly-packed hard medium-sized iron-concreted gravel, yielded a sherd of Claudian samian Dr. 29 (Fig. 137, No. 1), several *terra nigra* sherds and part of a first-century butt beaker (Fig. 88, No. 170). It was clearly laid down soon after the conquest and like other early streets in Canterbury directly overlay a thickish layer of grey loam (Sections C-D, III 16 and E-F, V 18). The grey loam, beneath which was natural brickearth, yielded a number of Belgic sherds but no Roman material. Almost certainly the layer represents pre-Roman cultivation. It contained many small pieces of chalk which had presumably been spread to marl the soil. This reminds us of Pliny's statements (*N.H.*, xvii, 42) that marling was invented in Gaul and Britain; and (xvii, 45) that chalk (*creta*) was dug in Britain for this purpose from pits up to 100 ft. deep, and that one application was effective for up to 80 years. Although chalk rock forms the solid geology of this part of Kent, beneath Canterbury it lies at a considerable depth below later quaternary deposits; fresh chalk would have to be transported from the hills outside.

The west edge of the street had been largely destroyed in Trench III by a medieval pit, but a layer of greenish gritty silt (15) found to the west of the pit was probably wash from it. A mortarium-rim (Fig. 87, No. 171A) of *c.* A.D. 70–110, a sherd of samian possibly of the second century and a coarse-ware dish (Fig. 87, No. 171B) of the period *c.* A.D. 110–160 were found in III 15, and a sherd of Flavian samian Dr. 18 came from a similar layer (V 23) together with a second-century rough-cast beaker (Fig. 87, No. 172A).

Surface 2 (Sections C-D, III 28 = 14 and E-F, V 22) consisted of very dirty iron-concreted gravel with some larger flints. The surface was generally good, but there were traces of two ruts *c.* 4 ft. 5 in. (1.4 m.) apart, with a cambered rise of *c.* 4 in. between them. In Trench III the metalling overlay a thin layer of dirt; in Trench V it overlay the layer of greenish silt (23) already mentioned. A sherd of samian, probably Dr. 45, of Antonine date, was found in V 22 and this indicates that the first re-surfacing did not take place until after the middle of the second century. A thin layer of dirt accumulated over the gravel before further re-surfacing.

Surface 3 (Sections C-D, III 27 = 13 and E-F, V 20) yielded a scrap of second-century samian and of a second-century reeded-rim bowl, and was made up of gravel similar to that comprising Surface 2, but more loosely packed.

Subsequent re-metalling was on a slightly different alignment, the street taking a more north-easterly course (cf. Figs. 23 and 25, Section E-F, which shows a deposit of black earth (V 19) covering the western 4 ft. of street-surface 3 (V 20)).

There was not much variation in the later surfaces and they do not warrant detailed description. A thin layer of dirt usually accumulated before re-surfacing took place and the respective thicknesses both of dirt and metalling can be seen on the sections. Surface 4 (Sections C-D, III 12 and E-F, V 13) was very worn and uneven with frequent patchings. Surface 5 (C-D, III 25 = 11 and E-F, V 11) had later been patched with a band of gravel, 4 in. thick (Sections C-D, III 24 = 10 and E-F, V 10). Surfaces 6 (C-D, III 23 and E-F, V 9), 7 (III 21 and V 8) and 8 (III

19 and V 6) were unnoteworthy except for a coin of Tetricus II found in the metalling of Surface 8. Surface 9 (C-D, III 17 and E-F, V 5), which produced a coin of Victorinus, was the latest and had a pronounced camber. All the metalling was tightly packed. It took two active workmen three weeks to cut Section C-D, a trench 8 ft. wide.

South-east to North-west Street

Only small areas of this street[43] could be examined in Area R because of extensive disturbance by medieval pits, but it was clear that it had been constructed later than the north-east to south-west street — a conclusion confirmed by the section cut in the cellar just to the east (Site H, Section L-M, see below, p. 77). The buried plough-soil (Fig. 26, Section J-K, IV B (17)) had remained unsealed sufficiently long to incorporate a sherd of Flavian samian (Dr. 27), and was overlaid by two successive occupation-layers (16, 15), which contained coarse pottery of the first half of the second century (Fig. 87, Nos. 172B, 172C); only at this stage was the first metalling laid. In site H (p. 219) pottery of similar date again occurred in a similar context.

Thus the east—west street could not have been laid out before the Hadrianic period, and its real date of construction may have been after the middle of the century to judge by finds in the earliest metalling examined. This layer (Fig. 26, Sections G-H and J-K (13)) yielded one coin of Vespasian or Domitian, a sherd of Trajanic-Hadrianic samian (Dr. 27) and one sherd of Dr. 33 probably of Antonine date together with a dish in BB2 ware of Gillam Type 310 (dated c. A.D. 150–210); layer 12, a spread of occupation-earth which sealed the earliest street, produced late-Antonine samian Dr. 38 and a BB2 dish of *Verulamium* Type 715 of the second half of the second century. However, in all probability there was a metalled surface below layer 13 which was not found in the small area excavated; for layer 14, beneath 13, had all the characteristics of road-silt. It yielded a dish (Fig. 87, No. 172D) dated c. A.D. 125–160. Thus a date of perhaps 130–140 is likely. This estimate of date is confirmed by the section cut in Cellar H nearby (p. 76). The street was re-surfaced on a least four occasions ((11), (10), (9) and (8)), but no useful dating evidence was obtained.

Roman Building North-west of the North-east to South-west Street

Part of a building which had been erected at the beginning or during the first half of the second century was found in Trench R I (Fig. 23). The northern part of the trench had been badly disturbed by pits, and the central area by a post-medieval cellar; but to the south-west of this the remains of two Roman clay walls survived. The east–west wall can be seen on Fig. 25 (Section A-B); it was built over an occupation level (34), beneath which lay loamy layers (39 and 38). No dating evidence was recovered from these deposits. The wall which was made of clay was c. 1 ft. wide and faced each side with a very thin layer of wall-plaster; that on the north side was painted red and on the south white. At intervals of c. 1 ft. was a series of post-holes within the fabric of the wall, slightly staggered alternately to left and right of the

43.   This street had previously been located in 1947 on Site C X H (See p. 76).

central axis. A sherd of Antonine samian Dr. 31 was found in one of them. Only the east face of the north—south wall survived and this too was painted white.

To the south of the east—west wall a deposit of greenish grit (33) had accumulated against it, over layer 34, and yielded a sherd of Hadrianic samian, Dr. 18/31. Both this and the wall, by now demolished, were sealed by layer 29, a spread of clean loam partly, no doubt, deriving from the demolition. Layer 29 contained a piece of Antonine samian (Dr. 31) and a third-century straight-sided dish-sherd. On the north side of the wall the original floor-level on layer 34 was marked by a thin occupation layer containing ash, charcoal, shells and bones (35); it yielded Flavian samian (Dr. 30, 46) and a coarse-ware dish, No. 172E, similar to No. 200 and datable to c. A.D. 110–140. A phase of reconstruction is probably indicated by layer 32 which sealed it, for lime and plaster fragments were mixed with the dirty loam, and what was probably a new floor of clean loam (31) was laid over it. This yielded an early third-century dish of the type shown in Fig. 83, No. 121. Layer 30, of rather dirty loam, equates stratigraphically with layer 29 outside and marks the demolition of the structure.

This was the first occasion in Canterbury when such a clay wall was recognised. Later more examples were found, e.g. in Canterbury Lane (Site C XXIII C, p. 84 below). Their recognition explained the rapid build-up of brickearth layers in parts of the city which had previously been hard to account for.[44] Such buildings would require frequent renewal, and their demolition would create successive deposits of loamy material. The structures themselves are extremely hard to detect in the surrounding matrix of similar material unless, as here, wall-plaster *in situ* betrays them. In this context of frequent renewal, where much of the clay or loam used for new walls was probably simply scraped up from the demolition-layers of their predecessors, the occurrence of residual material must be high.[45] The Flavian sherds in layer 35 were probably residual, but the building does seem to have been demolished soon after the beginning of the third century, for the evidence quoted above is supported by sherds no later than Antonine sealing a pit (see below, Pit 12) which was dug from a higher level than the demolished wall. It will probably be safe to suggest a span of c. 110–220 for the building's existence.

Above the demolished wall, layers 29 and 30 were sealed by a trodden surface of fine gritty black dirt which no doubt represents the floor of the succeeding structure, of which no walls were encountered. Above it was laid a thick deposit of loam (28) possibly representing a second demolition, but also serving as a new floor — for on its surface lay a hearth (28a) made of flat tiles and flints. A thin spread of ash, charcoal and burnt clay overlay the hearth and spread southwards from it. At this level the north-east to south-west wall-trench for a timber-framed partition 1 ft. wide was found crossing the eastern extension of Trench R I, 2 ft. from its eastern end. This wall was cut into layer 28 and was sealed by 27; the trench contained the broken but complete vessel Fig. 88, No. 173, datable to the period c. A.D. 160–200; it must have been old when discarded, for the context cannot be earlier than the middle of the third century.

---

44.   E.g. *Arch. Cant.*, lx (1947), 69, where a build-up to combat 'marshy conditions' was invoked to explain similar deposits in Burgate Street. Somewhat similar problems are discussed in S.S. Frere, *Verulamium Excavations*, i (1972), 9–10.

45.   This was demonstrated at Verulamium: see note 44.

Layer 28 and the hearth were covered by another loamy floor (27), overlaid in turn by a layer of burnt loam and charcoal (26). The few sherds found were all residual. Above 26 in the south-east corner of the trench was a gravel patch (22), *c.* 2 in. thick. This was the latest Roman layer to survive. Subsequent levels at the south end of the trench were of medieval date.

At the north end of the trench very little Roman stratification survived; a large pit, 12, filled with light brown loam, was partly excavated. It had been dug from a level well above the floor of the clay-walled structure and was probably associated with its successor. The pit was sealed with a gravelly make-up (37) carrying a chalk floor which must belong to one of the succeeding phases represented perhaps by layer 28 further south. Layer 37 yielded Antonine samian Dr. 37, 33 and 31.

Late Roman Building on the Street-surface (Fig. 24)

Late in the Roman period, probably in the fifth century, this part of the street went out of use and a two-phase timber-building of irregular oblong plan was built near the intersection. The main part of the building measured *c.* 25 ft. by 12 ft. (7.6 by 3.7 m.) externally and there were indications of two internal partitions; at least one room measuring *c.* 14 ft. by 7 ft. (4.3 by 2.1 m.) lay to the east of this. Two successive floors and a number of slots with post-holes cut into them were found. It was difficult to make a coherent plan of the two phases of the hut because of medieval pit-disturbance, but the two floors were quite distinct. Floor 1 (Fig. 26, Sections G-H and J-K, 7) was made of flint cobbling which contained fragments of broken tile, black dirt, lime and mortar and yielded a radiate coin of the late third century. In places the floor directly overlay the latest street; elsewhere it overlay a silty layer (5). It was covered by a thin layer of dirt (6), on top of which was a secondary floor (4). This was made of closely-packed flints and pieces of broken Roman tile mixed with black dirt and mortar. Little pottery was recovered from the floors, but a coin of Arcadius was found in one of the timber slots.

The building clearly dates to a period after the breakdown of civic discipline, but does not appear to be of Jutish or Anglo-Saxon date. It is probably to be assigned to around the middle of the fifth century on general grounds, and recalls the similar feature found over a Roman street at Winchester.[46] The latter was a rectangular building 15 ft. wide by at least 22 ft. long (4.57 by 6.7 m.), had a cobbled floor and post-hole construction, and was shown by M. Biddle to date between *c.* 400 and *c.* 650. In later studies, however, he has shown that in all probability urban life ended in Winchester during the fifth century, perhaps even as early as the middle of it, and was not resumed on any scale before the latter half of the seventh.[47] In the interim there was a tenuous occupation probably associated with a royal household. The Winchester building, then, is not likely to be later than about the middle of the fifth century unless it was associated with a royal palace; and the finds do not support the latter possibility. It provides an interesting analogy with the building under discussion.

46. *Antiq. Journ.*, xliv (1964), 206; xlvi (1966), 320; xlviii (1968), 270; l (1970), 311–14.
47. M. Biddle in *Vor- und Frühformen der europäischen Stadt im Mittelalter* (Groningen, 1974), 229–61, esp. pp. 234–41; *Scientific American*, vol. 230, No. 5 (May, 1974), 32–43.

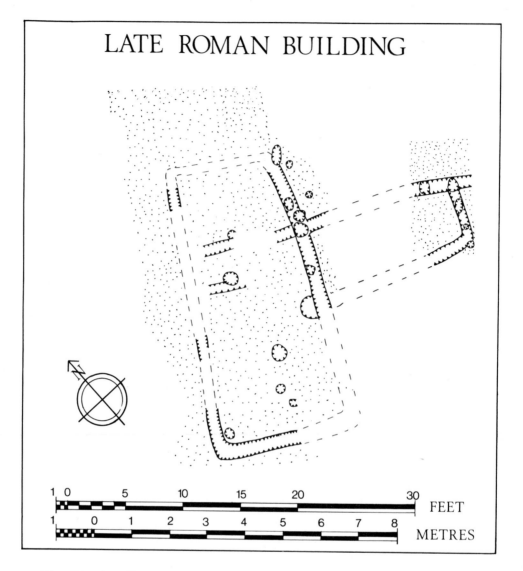

LATE ROMAN BUILDING

Fig. 24. Area R: detailed plan of late Roman timber-framed building. Scale 1 : 96

MEDIEVAL

The Roman streets had been extensively damaged by the fifty or so medieval rubbish- and cess-pits found in the area. Most were unnoteworthy, but some yielded interesting medieval pottery. R I Pit 9 (Fig. 88, Nos. 174–5), R III Pit 2 (No. 176) and R III 4 (No. 177) all produced pottery of the second half of the thirteenth century. Pottery from R IV Pit 2 (Nos. 178–9) and R V Ext. 2 (2) (No. 180) can be dated to the late thirteenth or early fourteenth century. The remaining vessels illustrated (Nos. 181–3 from R IV Pit 1; No. 184 from R III Pit 5; No. 185 from R IV Pit 11; Nos. 186–8 from R III Pit 6; and Nos. 189–92 from R V Pit 1)

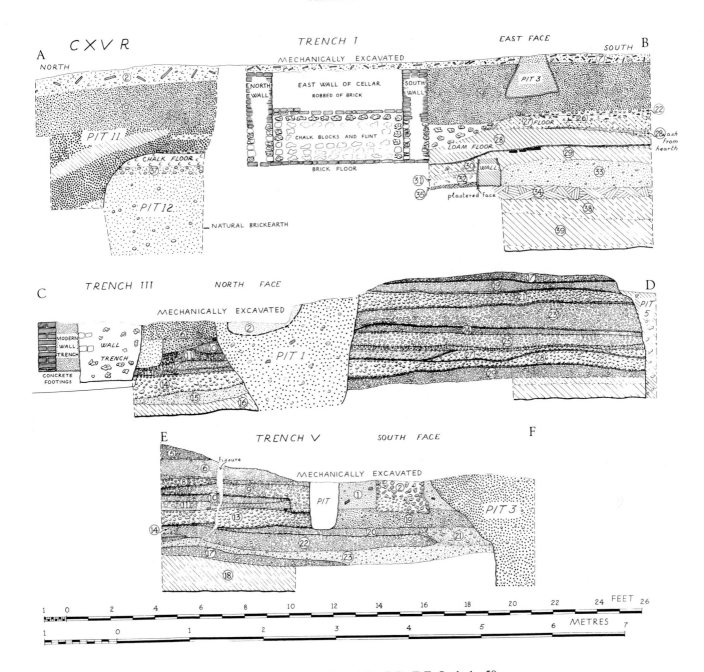

Fig. 25. Area R: Sections A-B, C-D, E-F. Scale 1 : 50

are of fourteenth-century date. Medieval gravel footings for a chalk wall were found in C XV
R Trench III, but no floor-levels survived[48]

A sixteenth-century cellar occupied the central part of Trench I (Fig. 25, Section A-B); this
had a brick floor, on the surface of which the walls had been raised (Pl. XVIII); over this floor
lay a thin deposit of purplish wood ash overlaid by a layer of loose brown earth, *c.* 6 in. thick.
This contained much decayed vegetation, bones and mussels. Above it was a thick filling of
sandy brick-rubble and tile. The cellar walls, which had been partially robbed, were built of
brick except for the bottom seven courses, which were of chalk and flint blocks. The cellar had
a doorway on its north side, outside which was the slot for a timber threshold. A useful group
of post-medieval pottery was obtained from the cellar's filling (Figs. 91–2, Nos. 219–240), and
others from other contexts in the area (Nos. 241–244) (p. 221).

(b) C X Site H and C X Site M (Fig. 23)

In the summer of 1947 excavations were carried out in two cellars on the west side of
Canterbury Lane.

C X H

In C X H part of the south-east to north-west street, already discussed on p. 71, was
examined; its south side was bordered by a timber building. The street covered the whole of
the northern sector of the trench (Fig. 27, Section L-M) and had been relaid three times in the
part remaining below the cellar floor.

Surface 1 overlay a deposit of dark soil (13), except near its south side where a layer of
yellow sand (13a) intervened. Layer 13 overlay a thick brown bed of loamy cultivation-soil
(14). The latter yielded several sherds of late first-century samian Dr. 37 and 18 and coarse
ware of the period *c.* A.D. 100–130 (Fig. 90, Nos. 193–4) in addition to sherds of butt-beakers
of the pre-conquest or Claudian periods. Layer 13 also yielded Flavian samian which included
a Dr. 37 of the period A.D. 85–105 and a group of coarse wares of the period *c.* A.D. 100–140,
indicating that the street was not laid before *c.* 130–140 (see p. 71). A sherd of Antonine
samian Dr. 45 was found in the layer of black earth (11) which accumulated over the metalling.
Street 2 (layer 10), which was probably laid down at the end of the second or beginning of the

48.   Part of another medieval building with three phases of occupation was found *c.* 120 ft. (36.6 m.) to the
      north-west of this, at the west end of the drainage trench dug from Iron Bar Lane to the east end of St.
      Thomas' church in 1951 (see Footnote 42 (b)). The north-east corner of the Phase 1 building lay within the
      trench; the walls were built of stone blocks on loose flint-and-mortar footings. In Phase 2 the building was
      extended to the north, the new wall being built of chalk, flint and dark sandy mortar. The Phase 3 walls lay
      on the Phase 2 alignment but were of chalk. To the east of the building and *c.* 1 ft. 9 in. below the present
      street level was a band of gravel, *c.* 1 ft. 6 in. (0.5 m.) thick, composed of a series of thinner layers. This was
      presumably an earlier version of Iron Bar Lane on an alignment similar to that of the present street.

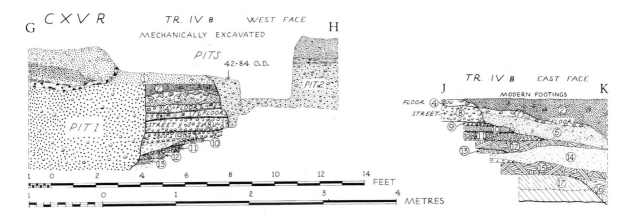

Fig. 26. Area R: Sections G-H, J-K. Scale 1 : 50

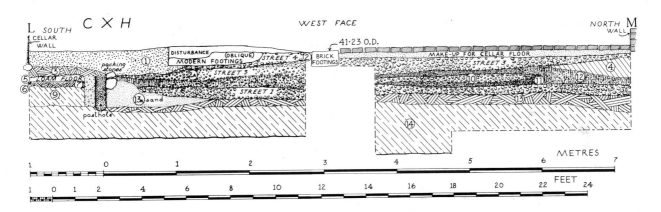

Fig. 27. C X H: Section L-M. Scale 1 : 50

third century did not extend so far to the north as Street 1; it contained pottery of the later second century (Fig. 90, Nos. 202–3). The metalling was covered by a thin layer of dirty soil, above which Street 3 (layer 2a) was laid. This contained sherds of two mortaria (Fig. 90, Nos. 204–205) one of the late second century, the other possibly of the third. At the north end of the trench Street 3 sealed a deposit of yellow clay (4) which may represent a demolished wall; this overlay a thick layer of black earth (12) which had accumulated on top of Street 1 and which yielded four sherds of Antonine samian (Dr. 31 (two), 33, 37) and several contemporary coarse-ware vessels (Fig. 90, Nos. 206–208). In the northern part of the trench the levels above Street 3 had been destroyed by the cellar builders; in the southern part Street 3 was overlaid by a fourth metalled surface. The south side of this was cut by modern footings and all the levels above were destroyed when the cellar was built.

A timber-framed building bordered the south-west edge of the street; it was marked by a foundation-trench, c. 2 ft. wide, filled with fine gravelly sand, which contained in the length exposed four rather irregularly-disposed post-holes supporting the north wall of the structure. The trench had been cut through layer 9 on one side and through a deposit of sand (13) on the other. It is not easy to explain the derivation of the latter, for since it underlies the street it cannot be road-silt. The existing wall was contemporary with a loam floor (5) of the period 190–220; on the section it appears to cut through the latter, but this is only because the posts were not all placed along its north-east edge. There was probably an earlier structure on the site, represented by layer 7, an occupation-deposit containing many oysters, bones and pottery down to A.D. 200, including Fig. 90, Nos. 211–212. This earlier structure ended on the same building-line, and the sand (13) may be associated with it. Layer 9, a grey loamy deposit which underlay the occupation-layer, yielded a sherd of Antonine samian (Dr. 31) and coarse pottery of the period 140–170. Thus the earliest structure here was not erected before about the middle of the second century, and the existing wall and loam floor must be later still. Both the floor and wall were sealed by a dark occupation-layer (3), which was capped by layer 1, a deposit of loose earth and stones, probably road silt. This yielded four sherds of moulded-rim dishes, presumably residual, and was probably of Roman date. There is no sign that the loam floor was renewed, and the building was probably not in use for long.

C X M

Part of a Roman timber building with several phases of occupation was uncovered in C X M (Fig. 23).

The earliest features excavated were two pits; one, in the south-west corner of the trench (Fig. 28, Section N-O, left) was cut into a grey loamy layer (18) which was probably plough-soil unsealed before the late first century. The pit was filled with grey loam, above which was a deposit of clean clay extending beyond the pit to the north.

The second pit (layers 13 and 15) was slightly later in date, being cut into layer 18 and the clean clay above it. Its primary filling was of buff loam mixed with oyster shells, burnt clay, tile and small charcoal flecks (15). This was overlaid by an ashy layer (13) and by a burnt clay deposit (12) which extended beyond the pit to the north, there sealing a layer of dirty clay and oysters beneath which was a gravel spread. Layer 15 yielded a sherd of Trajanic samian (Dr. 33) and sherds of a beaker and dish both likely to date to c. 110–140 (Fig. 90, Nos. 213–214);

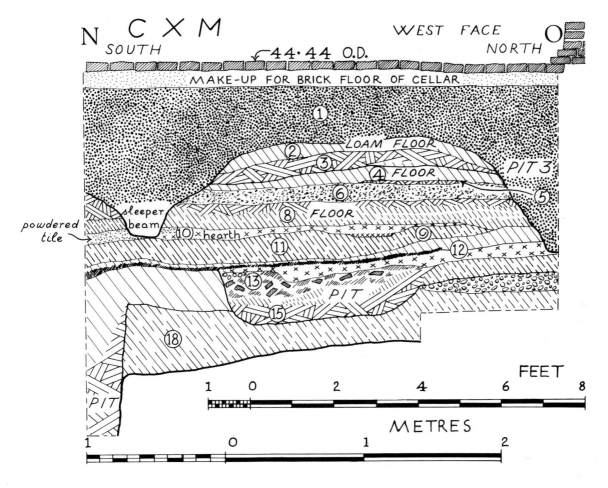

Fig. 28. C X M: Section N-O.

layer 13 contained two sherds of Hadrianic-Antonine samian (Dr. 31) and layer 12 a jar with frilled rim (No. 215). Above this was a thin deposit of charcoal which extended to the south edge of the trench. This was overlaid by a loam layer (11 = 9) which yielded two sherds of Antonine samian (Dr. 33), a mortarium (Fig. 90, No. 216) dated to the mid second century and two BB2 dishes, one of them similar to Gillam Type 222, dated A.D. 150–210 (Fig. 90, Nos. 217–218). Layer 11 was taken to be a floor, for a burnt clay hearth with broken and powdered tiles along its north edge lay on it, and above were three more successive loam floors (Section N–O (8), (4) and (2)). All these floors belonged to a building fronting the north-east side of the street found in C X H.[49] No stone walls were found, and the building was at least partly timber-framed: a south-east to north-west sleeper trench which ran at an angle to the street was contemporary with Floor 8. This floor, which yielded a sherd of samian Dr. 37 (A.D. 150–190) and a number of dish-sherds of types commonly found from c. 200, was covered by a dirty sandy occupation-layer (6); this contained patches of reddish burnt clay and yielded two sherds of Antonine samian (Dr. 31, 33). Layer 6 was in part covered by an earthy occupation-layer (5), above which came a secondary floor (4), in turn overlaid by yellowish earth and charcoal (3). The latter was sealed by a further yellow loam floor (2), associated with which was a red baked-clay hearth. The floor yielded a sherd of third-century straight-sided dish. Here again, as in Trench R I, there seems to have been a fairly rapid succession of structures during the second half of the second century and throughout the third.

At the north end of the trench these floors were cut by Pit 3; elsewhere they were sealed by rich black medieval soil (1), in which twelfth- and thirteenth-century cooking-pot sherds were found.

49. See p. 76. Part of another building fronting the north-east side of the same street was excavated just east of Canterbury Lane (p. 84) and the north-east angle of another (Fig. 1, (b)) was observed by Dr. F. Jenkins in a drainage-trench dug from the north side of St. George's Church in October 1953. The walls had been badly robbed but substantial flint-and-mortar foundations capped by a course of Roman tiles remained. No floor levels survived. (Information from Dr. F. Jenkins).

V. EXCAVATIONS ON THE EAST SIDE OF CANTERBURY LANE

Between 1949 and 1955 an extensive excavation-programme was carried out on the east side of Canterbury Lane (Fig. 1, Sites 8 and 9, and Figs. 27–38). The site codes were C XV N, C XX-XXIV Site C Trenches I-VI, and C XXVIII Site C Trenches XX-XXI.

(a) C XV SITE N, C XX — C XXIV SITE C

Summary

The area was first examined in 1949 when a small trench (C XV N) was dug in the cellar immediately north of Loyn's Bakery to test for the edge of the east–west street found in C X H (p. 76). Two successive late Saxon floors were found overlying remains of a Roman timber building.

Between 1951 and 1953 (seasons C XX-C XXVIII) much further work was undertaken in this area, which was all now labelled Site C. A comparatively shallow cellar (Site C I), lying a little north of that trenched in 1949, was first tested; beneath its floor was found a thick, richly-productive late Saxon layer datable to the period *c.* 850–950 by its association with sherds of Badorf-type ware. This occupation-layer rested on a substantial floor of gravel and cobbles (Pl. XIX) which in turn sealed a thick layer of dark earth containing with rare exceptions only late Roman pottery. This layer, which is similar to one overlying late Roman remains at Winchester,[50] was suggestive of a cultivated soil; it sealed late Roman levels and the remains of earlier Roman buildings.

Trench C III was cut in the small cellar to the south which had already been partially examined in 1949 (C XV, Site N). Subsequently trenches were cut from the surface both in the area between the cellars (Trench C IV) and also eastwards from C I (Trench C II). The area between the cellars had been occupied by a chalk-built house in the late fifteenth century (Building A). But, unusually in Canterbury, the property-boundary had not been maintained; in the eighteenth century Building B was placed on the site of Building A, but with a wall bisecting the latter, and extending northwards into the area of Cellar C. In consequence, when

---

50. *Antiq. Journ.*, xliv (1964), 206.

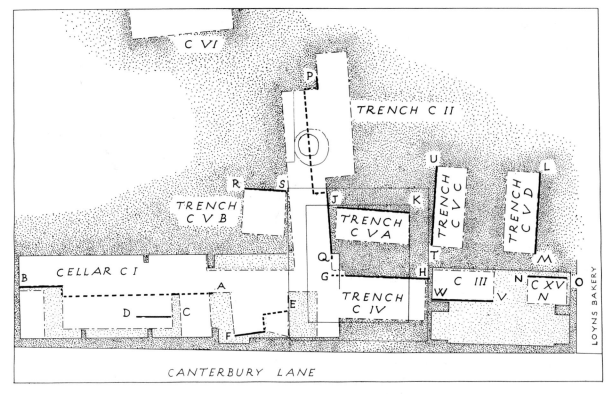

Fig. 29. Canterbury Lane, Plan of C XX–C XXIV Site C Trenches I-VI, showing position of cellars, excavated trenches and published sections. Unexcavated areas stippled.

in the nineteenth century Cellar C I was dug north of Building B it overran the north wall of Building A, leaving only the gravel footings *in situ* (Fig. 32; Fig. 34, Section G-H).

Trench C IV, between the cellars, produced a fine series of stratified layers (Fig. 34) extending from the second to the twentieth century. Trench C II was much more disturbed by pits, lying as it does towards the rear of the medieval premises; but it was remarkable for the fourteenth-century well at its east end (Pl. XX), at the bottom of which were found almost 100 pitchers.

On a subsequent occasion an area adjacent to C II was mechanically excavated to a depth of 5 ft. and Trenches C V A-D were cut by hand from that level. These revealed more of the late Saxon floor and of the Roman buildings. Finally, in 1953 a second area (C VI) was mechanically excavated to a depth of 7 ft. north-east of Trench C II to test the extent of the late Saxon gravel floor. The area was found to be riddled with deep eighteenth-century and earlier pits, but traces of the Saxon floor were found. It overlay 9 in. of late Roman black earth, beneath which was a cobbled floor at 41.36 O.D. — approximately the level of the late Roman cobbled floor in C I (Fig. 33, Section C-D, 22). However, not as much excavation was accomplished in Trench C VI as had been intended, partly because of the delayed arrival of the mechanical excavator and partly because of the need, which had meanwhile arisen, to extend concurrent work on Belgic structures in the Whitehall area. Only three working days remained in which the primary objective of tracing the extent of the Saxon floor could be attempted. This floor (if continuous) appears to cover an area of at least 62 by 66 ft. (18.9 by 20.1 m.).

The earliest archaeological levels were reached only in Trench C XV N and Trenches C III, C V C and C V D. The natural brickearth, whose surface lay at 39.09 ft. O.D., was found to be sealed by a layer of loamy soil (Fig. 36, Section N-O, 12; Fig. 39, Section V-W, 12) containing small chalk lumps and yielding small sherds of Belgic pottery; it was exactly similar to the pre-Roman plough-soil found on the west side of Canterbury Lane in Area R (p. 70). Above this lay successive deposits associated with Roman buildings.

PERIOD I: ROMAN TIMBER-FRAMED BUILDING, PHASE i

The earliest evidence for a structure was the floor of bright yellow gravel found at the bottom of C V A (Fig. 35, Section J-K, 18), lying just above the natural subsoil (here gravel). Trenches C V C and C V D were not dug sufficiently deep to encounter it. The floor lies almost 2 ft. lower, in absolute terms, than the earliest floor found in C XV N and C III; and although the difference is partly due to the previous removal of most of the old plough soil in C V A, the floor there certainly precedes the other. It yielded a sherd of Flavian samian and other pottery of the end of the first century, and was evidently laid down at some date close to 100. Pit XI in C V A, from which came two sherds of pre-Flavian samian (Dr. 18, 27), and some first-century coarse ware (Fig. 93, Nos. 249–250) lay beneath it and had caused this and later floors to dip down from west to east. A burnt loam hearth lay on the floor, and two post-holes (Section J-K, Nos. 5, 6) marked a feature coinciding with the south-east face of the Trench. An occupation-layer (17) had next accumulated, sealing the hearth and post-holes; it yielded three sherds of Flavian samian (Dr. 18, 27, Curle 15) and a few contemporary sherds of coarse ware.

PERIOD I: ROMAN TIMBER-FRAMED BUILDING, PHASE ii

In the middle of the second century some reconstruction occurred. The original room in Trench C V A was now divided by a SE–NW timber partition marked on Section J-K by Post-hole 4; this divided a new loam floor (16A) in the north half of the trench from a new gravel one (16B) in the south. Post-hole 4 was 12 in. (0.3 m.) in diameter, with a dark filling which contained no packing stones. No other post-holes of the partition were recovered because they had been cut away by Pit R 12; but three other small post-holes were seen in the loam floor itself. No. 1 was 10 in. in diameter, 6 in. deep and packed with flints leaving space for a 6-in. post. Nos. 2 and 3 were each 4 in. in diameter and 6 in. deep. A pit (Section J-K, Pit XII) was cut into 16B; this was filled with light grey loam but yielded no finds. A gravel floor, probably belonging to the same south room of Phase ii, was also found in Trenches C V C and C V D (Sections T-U, 10; L-M, 10). A grey occupation-deposit (Section J-K, 15A) covered the floors of both rooms; it contained oyster shells, charcoal and gravel, together with a group of pottery extending to the late second century or a trifle beyond (Fig. 93, Nos. 251–259), and on its surface lay a large piece of crushed amphora. Over 15A extended a thin deposit of burnt ash.

In this phase the building had been enlarged to extend into the area of Trenches C III and C XV N, where nothing hitherto existed. In C XV N (Fig. 36) the old plough-soil was covered by a floor of yellow loam and gravel (11). It extended north into Trench C III (Section V-W, 11) but stopped c. 2 ft. from the north end of that trench; no indications of a timber wall were found in the short length of this edge which was exposed, so probably it had been carried on posts over 4 ft. apart. Although no dating evidence was recovered either in or below the floor, the occupation-layer over it was Antonine. This layer (10) yielded one sherd (Dr. 18/31) of Hadrianic-Antonine and two (Dr. 31, 33) of Antonine samian together with a group of coarse wares (Fig. 93, Nos. 245–248) which extend at least to the end of the second century.

We may associate this southerly enlargement of the Period I building with the construction of the nearby north-west to south-east street, which has been dated c. A.D. 130–140 (p. 71); the beginning of the occupation in C XV N (10) appears to be contemporary with this or only slightly later.

PERIOD I: ROMAN TIMBER-FRAMED BUILDNG, PHASE iii

In Trench C III a new floor of loam (Section V-W, 9) was laid down over the occupation-layer (10), in which it sealed a scrap of Antonine samian, but the floor did not extend into Trench C XV N where N (9) was of much dirtier earthy loam which appeared to be make-up for a later floor. In Trench C III floor 9 was sealed by a thin occupation-layer, above which once again occurred a spread of carbonized material, seemingly representing the burning of the roof. A similar streak of burnt material was found above 10 in the north-east face of C XV N (not visible on Section N-O); but as no floor was found below it there we must assume that this area now lay outside the building as reconstructed. Although the scatter of burnt debris was not extensive over the site, it occurred consistently as the final feature of Period I in widely separated places, and it is probably safe to conclude that the second-century structure perished in a fire.

PERIOD II: CLAY-WALLED BUILDING

Period II levels were uncovered over a wider area than those of Period I. In Period II, the beginning of which can be placed c. 210–220, a new house was built of which parts of c. seven rooms (Fig. 30) were examined.

The building was for the most part built of clay walls which rested on nothing but footings of the same material. The bases of the walls did not carry plaster in situ although wall-plaster fragments in the collapsed debris showed that they had been plastered and painted higher up. This absence made their recognition very difficult: the destruction-layers consisted of horizontal layers of clay which were virtually indistinguishable from the walls in situ; these could be recognised only where floors or occupation-deposits of different texture ended on a straight horizontal and vertical line. It was only the experience previously gained on Site R

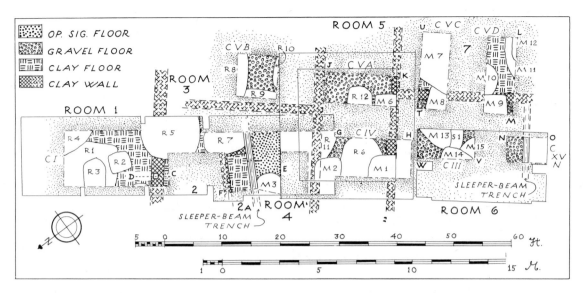

Fig. 30. Canterbury Lane, C XX–C XXIII Site C. Roman, Period II: Plan of clay-walled building. Note: only those trenches are shown which were excavated sufficiently deeply to reach this building. The Roman and medieval pits which cut the building are numbered R 1, M 1, etc.; Scale 1 : 192

(p. 71), where the existence of such a clay wall was initially betrayed by its minimal plaster facing, which enabled understanding and recognition of the present structure. The floors were sometimes of loam, sometimes gravel; only two secondary ones were of cement or *opus signinum*, and beside the latter was one of the only two certain appearances of a normal timber-framed wall (Figs. 30, 33). The other walls were of solid clay with no indications of timber-framing, and they were presumably constructed by tamping clay between shuttering.[51] To this generalisation there was only one apparent exception: in the body of the most northerly clay wall (1/2) a post-hole was found (Figs. 30, 33, Section C-D); but it did not descend to the base of the wall and was probably evidence only of a repair or perhaps of the emplacement of a window-frame or hatch.

It will be apparent from the plan (Fig. 30) that disturbance by later pits was very extensive; insufficient was recovered to give much idea of the building's size or character. The sections recording the vertical stratigraphy are perhaps the more valuable record. Of the clay-walled structure two parallel east—west walls were found, the more southerly of which adjoined a third leading off at right-angles to the south, as well as the angle of another wall and lengths of two more orthodox timber slots. Other walls can be restored from differences in floors on either side.

51. As at Verulamium in Buildings XXI 2 and XXVII 1 (S.S. Frere, *Verulamium Excavations* ii, London 1983). At the first of these, as also at Leicester and at the Farningham and Lullingtone villas, the clay walls rested on platforms of masonry which facilitated their recovery.

Some but not all rooms showed evidence of floor-renewal. Room 1, at the north end, had a floor of loam (Section C-D, 37). Room 2, also floored in loam (Section E-F, 31, 32), was later subdivided. The timber slot which crosses C I and the clay wall to its north enclosing Room 2A are oblique to the main building lines, and are probably later insertions. The original Room 2 must have been bounded at the south end by an east—west wall in the vicinity of Pit R 11, as tentatively indicated on the plan (Fig. 30), dividing its loam floor from the gravel floor of Room 5. Likewise a north—south wall must be restored west of Pit R 9 to divide the loam floor of Room 2 from the gravel floor of Room 3. After the timber partition and clay walls were inserted, Room 2A had an earth floor trodden on the surface of a mixed deposit (Section E-F, 28); and south of the timber partition an *opus signinum* floor (Room 4) was laid over a single layer of pebbles, and became covered with a layer of greenish gritty silt (23) yielding pottery datable to the late third century (Fig. 93, Nos. 260–262).

Room 3 was floored in gravel in Trench C V B (Section R-S, 12) — the lowest level reached in this trench. Room 5 was also floored in gravel (Sections G-H, 20; J-K, 15), but this area can hardly be in the same room as 3. In Trench C V A (Section J-K) a secondary floor of white concrete on gravel (14), very worn and burnt, was laid over an occupation-layer which had accumulated on the original floor (15); but the secondary floor did not survive in Trench C IV (Section G-H) where a thick deposit of fine greenish silt took its place. This silt descended into Pit R 6, and the absence of the secondary floor is probably to be connected with this pit. At a late stage Pit X was dug through the secondary floor (Section J-K) alongside the clay wall; it yielded sherds of third-century pottery dated *c*. A.D. 220–260 (Fig. 93, Nos. 266–269). Both pit and floor were sealed by a substantial layer of charred wood before the clay walls collapsed.

Room 7 had a loam floor (Sections L-M, 7A; T-U, 9), and this too had a covering of charred material. Room 6 had a gravel floor and was bordered on the south by a timber wall-trench (Sections L-M, 8; N-O, 8).

There was a lack of plentiful evidence bearing on the date of erection of the Period II building. It overlay Antonine samian and a coin of Hadrian; and the coarse wares in or under its primary floors did not contain anything certainly later than the late second to early third century (Fig. 93, Nos. 246, 248, 251, 259). A date-bracket of *c*. A.D. 210–220 is accordingly suggested.

Destruction of Period II clay-walled building

At the end of the third century *c*. A.D. 290, there was a serious fire; burning was found above the floor in most of the rooms and in several of them it was possible to see the sequence of destruction. In Room 5 the floor (Section J-K, 14) was badly burnt and covered by a layer of ash, charcoal, charred wood and daub (13), which also sealed Pit 10; this was roof-debris which had evidently collapsed onto the floor while still burning. Above it was a thick deposit of yellow loam (12) containing thin slabs of wall-plaster; the walls had caved in after the collapse of the roof. Both these layers produced late third-century pottery (Figs. 93–4, Nos. 270–278); a pit (Pit 9) cut in this room before the collapse of the clay wall yielded a mortarium sherd probably of the same date (Fig. 94, No. 279). Similarly in Room 7 charred rafters lay above the floor and again yellow loam wall-material (Fig. 35, Section L-M, 7) overlay them. But here the floor was unburnt, indicating that this part of the house had collapsed more gradually after the fire had stopped raging. Fallen clay-wall material was also found in Trench C I (Fig. 33, Sections C-D and E-F, 25), but there was no sign of any burning in this area (Rooms 1, 2A, 2B).

PERIOD III: ROMAN BUILDING

In the fourth century, a new building or buildings were erected on the site, but little of them survived later disturbance. At the north end of C I a layer of fine gravel (Section C-D, 24) carried a surface of rough cobbles; there was no trace of occupation-material on these, however, and they may have been laid as a make-up and support for the loam floor (21) above. No post-holes for a wall were found within the area of the trench. Further north a loam floor contemporary with 21 sealed a coin of Valens. The building, like its predecessor, had been burnt down and its floor was covered by a thick deposit of burnt daub (20) from the walls. This yielded a coin of the House of Theodosius I (379–95). Much of the pottery in the overlying black soil must have been derived from this destruction-level. Part of this or a similar building was found in Trench C V A, where a gravel floor (Section J-K, 10) was found above the destruction-levels of the earlier house. The floor was badly disturbed by pits and little information recovered.

Parts of similar late floors were found (a) in Trench C V C (Section T-U, 6), where it overlay a destruction-layer (7) of the Period II building yielding two sherds of third-century date (Fig. 94, Nos. 280–281) one of them late; and (b) in Trench C III (Section V-W, 5).

PERIOD IV: LATE TO SUB-ROMAN

After the destruction of the Period III building in the early fifth century, the area lay open, and a thick deposit of black soil accumulated (Sections A-B, E-F, 9, 9A; J-K, 7; L-M, 5). This contained a good deal of fine carbon and small pieces of daub brought up from the destruction-level of Period III below it, and is probably best explained as a cultivation-layer. It did not extend into the southern cellar in Trenches C III and C XV N. The layer yielded many sherds of late Roman pottery (Fig. 94, Nos. 282–302) together with a fair amount of residual pottery no doubt derived from pit-digging, and the following coins:

Second century *As*		
Claudius II	268–9	(two)
Tetricus I	270–3	(three)
Tetricus II	270–3	
Carausius	287–93	(two)
Radiates	270–90	(three)
Barbarous radiate	270–90	
Constantius I	293–306	
Constantine I	306–37	(six)
Constantinopolis	330–5	(two)

House of Constantine		(four)
Barbarous *Fel. Temp.*		
Reparatio	348 +	(four)
Magnentius	350–3	
Valentinian I	364–75	(two)
Valens	364–78	
House of Valentinian		
Theodosius I	379–95	
Arcadius	395–408	(three)
House of Theodosius		(fourteen)
minim		

The layer contained no sherds of early Saxon pottery and only a very few sherds of the late Saxon period such as were likely to be intrusive in an unsealed surface (Fig. 95, No. 315). The area contained a number of late Roman pits whose fillings were indistinguishable from layer 9; these pits were presumably dug from time to time in the fifth century when the area was under cultivation. Pit R 2 yielded four coins (Constans, Theodora, Constantius II and House of Constantine) and some late Roman pottery. Pit 4 produced pottery of similar date (Fig. 95, Nos. 303–4), and pottery from other pits is illustrated in Fig. 95, Nos. 305–313.

Late Saxon

Over most of the area excavated the dark sub-Roman earth was sealed by a substantial late Saxon gravel floor (Pl. XIX). It had a good firm surface of cobbles and fragments of Roman tile except at the north end, where it was less regular; here were two surfaces separated by 2 in. of dense black mud. Among the cobbles was part of a grey-ware bottle, imported probably from northern France (Fig. 95, No. 316). This floor was continuous from the north end of C I to the south end of C IV (Fig. 31) which coincided with the south wall of a fifteenth-century chalk-built structure (Section G-H). South of this, in the adjoining cellar, Trench C III was badly disturbed; but towards its north end there was a large late Saxon pit (Fig. 31, S I) and no trace of the floor. In Section V-W, layer 2A was dark soil similar to the pit-filling; perhaps the pit had completely removed the floor, but it is tempting to suggest that the floor ended on the line of what was certainly in later times a property-boundary. This view is reinforced by the fact that in Trench C V D also the floor was missing, and in C V C (Section T-U, 4) it extended only a short distance into the trench.

In Trench C XV N, further south in the same cellar, there was a somewhat different sequence (Section N-O). The black late Roman earth was absent; its place was taken by 6, a light brown powdery earth which was sealed by two successive late Saxon gravel floors (5 and 3), separated by a grey occupation-layer (4). The earlier of the two floors (5) lies at 43.06 ft. O.D., about 6 in. lower than the floor at the south end of Section G-H, where the second gravel floor is missing. It seems probable that the floors in C XV N belong to a different but contemporary late Saxon structure. There was a wall marked by post-holes (Figs. 31, 36) across this trench close to the line of the Roman wall-trench below. The upper floor (3) yielded a bowl sherd in St. Neot's-type ware similar to Fig. 112, No. 515, and the layer of earth, daub and charcoal (2) above this produced a small hand-made pot (Fig. 95, No. 314) as well as a ninth- to tenth-century rim.

The main areas of floor, however, were devoid of post-holes (save for two in Trench C V B), nor were its edges defined. On the west side, Canterbury Lane was apparently not yet in existence, for the floor and the occupation-layer over it were observed beneath the street in a drainage-trench dug in 1953. From beneath the lane the floor extended for at least 46 ft. (14 m.) eastwards, to beyond the medieval well in Trench C II, where it was cut by a later pit, although in the central part of C II an area 12 ft. 6 in. (3.8 m.) long had been removed by later features (Section P-Q). Beyond this point very limited excavations in C VI again revealed part of what appeared to be the same floor, though here much cut by pits of the eighteenth century. Dark soil (4) above the floor yielded a stamped sherd in Ipswich-type ware (Fig. 98, No. 368). Thus the metalling appears to extend over an area at least 62 by 46 ft. (18.9 by 14 m.) and probably 62 by 66 ft. (18.9 by 20.9 m.), an extent too large to lie within even a very large hall.

There were, however, numerous pieces of burnt daub in the occupation-layer, especially towards the north end of C I; and under the cellar wall below the lane, in the area above the Roman timber slot, was another large patch of burnt daub fragments and some sizeable pieces of baked clay containing no wattle sockets. These features suggest the proximity of buildings.

Another find which suggests a roofed area was the discovery in Trench C IV, near the perimeter of Pit M 1, of a double line of bun-shaped loomweights of baked clay which appeared to be lying where they had fallen from a loom (Fig. 31). A careful search of the floor below, however, failed to reveal any indication of post-holes for a loom; but it was observed that under the area occupied by the loomweights, and conforming to their distribution, some large pieces of flint were lying loose over the cobbles, embedded in the occupation-layer 14 (Fig. 34, Section G-H). It was difficult to understand their purpose; possibly they served in some way to support a portable loom. The loomweights themselves were covered and surrounded by a localized layer of burnt cob (Section G-H, 13), which was probably fallen wall-material. Further loomweights were found in the drain-trench below Canterbury Lane.

The floor was everywhere sealed by a thick and extensive layer of occupation-material which yielded much late Saxon pottery (Figs. 97–8, Nos. 323–366) and four sherds of Badorf-type ware[52] imported from the Cologne region during the period c. 850–950 (Figs. 95, 97, Nos. 319–322). The association gives a very useful horizon in the chronology of Saxon wares at Canterbury. For the animal bones from this layer, see Appendix VI.

The occupation-layer also yielded some pieces of Andernach lava quern ½ in. thick, broken clay loomweights (Fig. 69, Nos. 3–4), very many food-bones which included pieces of antler, several well-preserved pieces of dog-dung, numerous oyster and mussel shells and fragments of decayed wood. The latter, encountered in C I, were pieces of twig up to 17 in. (43 cm.) long and between ½ and 1¾ in. (1.2–4.44 cm.) wide, but compressed to a thickness of only ¼ in. (0.63 cm.). Some were branched. They might have served for wattle walling or for a roof. Twenty-three Roman coins were found trampled into the surface of the floor.

Here and there within the layer were small areas of secondary flooring, usually in loam; they

52. The sherds were identified by the late G.C. Dunning; his report (Appendix III below) has been revised with the help of J.G. Hurst.

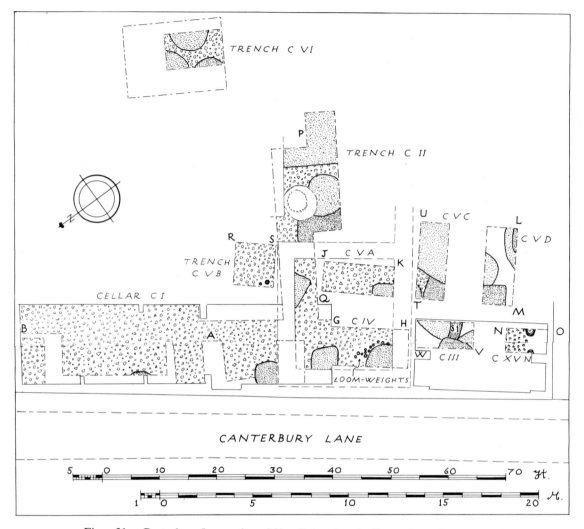

Fig. 31. Canterbury Lane: plan of Site C showing the Saxon floor. Scale 1 : 192

were never continuous or extensive (see e.g. Section P-Q, where the occupation-layer (9, 7 and 5) is separated by localized loam surfaces (8 and 6); compare Section G-H, layers 14, 13, 12 and 11). Towards the south end of Trench C V A (Section J-K, 5), as at the north end of C I, there were two levels of cobbled flooring. A sherd of Badorf-type ware was found in layer 6 which had accumulated between them. In Trench C V B also there were two layers of cobbling though here separated by only ¼ in. of dirt, and in this area was a quantity of iron slag. Later levels in C I yielded two sherds of Pingsdorf ware (Fig. 96).

It is difficult to decide whether the large area of floor represented a yard or a building. Its great extent, the absence of large post-holes, and the huge quantity of filth accumulated over the floor argue for a yard; but indications have been recorded above that there were walls in the vicinity, and the loom at least should have been under cover. It is possible, perhaps, that the rich organic character of the deposit might be partly explained by the decay of successive levels of rush flooring. Yet the area lay far from a street; Canterbury Lane did not yet exist and Burgate Street lies 160 ft. (49 m.) from the north end of C I. Between the two, excavation at Site C XXVIII C (p. 102) revealed part of a late Saxon building. It seems possible that the present area did form a metalled yard with adjacent buildings, lying to the rear of premises on Burgate Street.

MEDIEVAL (Fig. 32)

Many of the trenches were dug in cellars or in part excavated by a mechanical digger, and hence many of the medieval and later levels were destroyed. But in two trenches (C II and C IV) which were dug from the surface a considerable depth of medieval and later stratification survived.

Between the eleventh and fourteenth centuries many pits, producing much pottery, were dug in the area. Pit M 18, which lay behind the contemporary buildings, yielded sherds of several Group II cooking-pots dated c. 1050–1100. Trench C V B Pit 1 and C V C Pit 7 produced early twelfth-century pottery. Pit M 16 (C II Pit 5), which pre-dated the well, yielded sherds of two Group IV cooking-pots and some glazed jug-sherds of the second half of the thirteenth century; C V C Pit 4 and M 7 (C V C Pit 2) produced pottery of a similar date (Fig. 99, Nos. 375–77, and 378–9 respectively) as did M 9 (C V D Pit 3). M 10 (C V D Pit 5) of the same date contained a stone cresset lamp (Fig. 72, No 7). M 11 (C V D Pit 2) contained fourteenth-century pottery and sherds of a London copy of a Rouen jug (Fig. 100, Nos. 383–395).

It was at the south end of the site that the best sequence of medieval structures was found. In Trench C IV (Section G-H) the late Saxon occupation-layer was sealed by a gravel floor (9) on a make-up (14) of dark earth, pebbles and chalk; on the floor lay a black occupation-deposit (8) containing sherds of eleventh- to twelfth-century date. The gravel floor extended to Trenches C II and C V A. In the former (Section P-Q, 4) the overlying occupation yielded residual late Saxon sherds, but the floor itself yielded a twelfth-century cooking-pot sherd. In Trench C V A (Section J-K) the floor (3) yielded sherds of Group II type (second half of the eleventh century) and the occupation (2) above it some sherds of Group III, of early twelfth-century date. In Trench C V B a gravel floor again appeared (Section R-S, 7), but here it was immediately overlaid by a layer of burnt thatch 2–3 in. thick. Both of these layers were sterile; a loam floor (5) was immediately laid over the debris, and this yielded a sherd of Group III type of the first half of the twelfth century. Three post-holes were cut in layer 5 along the east side of the Trench (Fig. 32); they replaced a similar line a few inches to the west in layer 7. Over this secondary floor accumulated a thick occupation-layer (4) which produced several sherds of the same type. Above this, two successive floors (Section R-S, 3 and 2) could be dated to the later twelfth century; floor 2 was cut by a pit (Pit 1) which also yielded twelfth-century pottery.

It was clear that the area of Trench C V B was occupied at this period by a different building from that to the south of it. The fire did not extend to the building examined in C II, C V A and C IV.

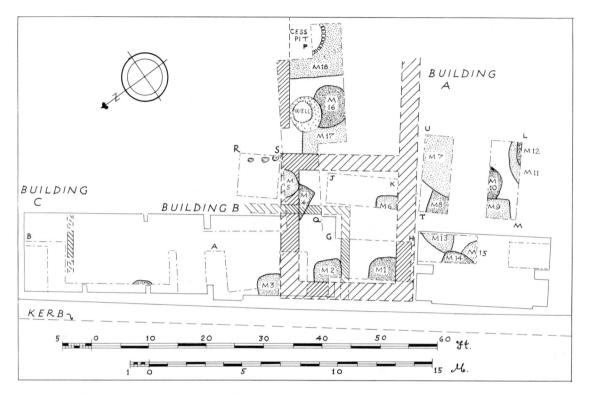

Fig. 32. Canterbury Lane: plan of Site C showing the medieval and post-medieval features. Scale 1 : 192

There, in Section G-H, the original occupation-layer (8) was covered by two successive loam floors (7 and 5) separated by a thin layer of dirt in which was a shell-tempered sherd of thirteenth-century type. In a scoop in 7 was a hearth of burnt loam, 5 ft. 4 in. (1.63 m.) in diameter, lying on loose burnt flints. A slightly different sequence in Trench C V A, 2 m. to the east, showed that here was a different room; the original occupation-layer (Section J-K, 2) was sealed by a floor not of loam but of chalk and gravel. The date of this was probably early fourteenth-century; it yielded sherds of Group IV type of the late thirteenth century and sealed a pit (M 6) which contained similar or slightly later pottery (Fig. 99, Nos. 373–374).

Thus in the Norman period this side of Canterbury Lane was occupied by houses, and the lane was probably established at that time. The buildings must all have been timber-framed, for no traces of masonry were found at these levels.

Probably early in the fourteenth century a well (Pl. XX) was dug at the back of the buildings. It lay in Trench C II (Section P-Q) and was cut through the filling of Pit M 16, which was sealed by the chalk surface at the top of the well and which yielded sherds of two Group IV cooking-pots dated to the second half of the thirteenth century. The well was circular and dug into the natural chalk to a depth of c. 27 ft. (8.23 m.). The bottom 14 ft. was built of large worn chalk blocks; above this level flints were used as well as chalk. The lowest course of chalk rested on an octagonal timber framework,[53] one beam thick; the well bottom lay *c.* 6 in. beneath this.

Sixty-five complete jugs, mostly fourteenth-century handled pitchers, were found in the waterlogged material[54] at the bottom, together with sherds from about forty other jugs (Figs. 101–6, Nos. 396–427); sherds from cooking-pots, dishes and bowls of similar date were also found (Figs. 106–7, Nos. 428–438). These pots were lost or thrown into the well before it was abandoned since above them were a number of large chalk blocks and also pieces of jointed timber planking presumably from the roof and hauling-apparatus, together with a whole pitcher and other sherds (Fig. 107, Nos. 439–442). The pitchers were presumably the pots actually used for drawing up the water, for otherwise it is difficult to explain the presence of so many complete vessels; but if so the well-hook cannot have been efficient. Above the pitchers and the timber (Pls. XXXIV–XXXV) and chalk blocks from the well-head were two deposits (Section P-Q, 12 and 11) of dark sticky soil containing fourteenth-century sherds (Figs. 107–8, Nos. 443–450), on top of which was a thin layer or plug of yellow loam (10); this resembles a floor, but whether it is a floor or a sealing-layer considerable subsidence in the layers beneath is suggested, since it was presumably laid down originally at the surface. Above this were deposits of dark soil and oysters (9), clayey earth (8 and 7), chalk and gravel (6 and 5), and dark earth (4, 3 and 2). Layer 9 yielded one whole jug and a number of large sherds (Fig. 108, Nos. 451–457); but the layers above this contained fewer and smaller pieces of pottery — all however still of fourteenth-century date (Fig. 108, Nos. 458–460). The well thus did not out-last the fourteenth century; but the stratification above it had been removed by a large pit (Pit 1) yielding sixteenth-century pottery (Fig. 109, Nos 461–469).

Other finds from the well included a Caen stone mortar (Fig. 73, No 9), and leather shoe-soles together with a wooden vessel (Pl. XXXV B; Fig. 67).

Late and post-medieval buildings

At the end of the medieval period the first masonry building was erected on the site (Building A, Fig. 32). Parts of two rooms were examined. The front wall adjoined Canterbury Lane which was certainly now if not previously (p. 92) in existence. The walls rested on deep foundation-trenches between 3 and 4 ft. wide and filled with gravel. The front room was a not-quite rectangular structure measuring 17 ft. north–south by 18 ft. 9 in. (5.2 by 5.7 m.). Its south wall, 2 ft. 2 in. (0.66 m.) thick, was built of chalk blocks (Section G-H). The east wall was also of chalk blocks but its east side was flint-faced in the south half of Trench C II though chalk-built in the north half; the west side of this wall had been widened with a flint re-facing 9

53. The excavation of the well was carried out in difficult conditions by Barbara de Seyssel. The late Mr. A.W.G. Lowther examined the timbers; he reported that they were all oak and that some of them had small worm-holes in them of the furniture-beetle type.

54. Puparia from the bottom of the well were submitted to Mr. H. Oldroyd of the Natural History Museum, London. He reported that it was unlikely that flies could survive underwater for any length of time, and suggested that as most of the puparia were empty they had probably been transmitted in one of the pitchers used to draw up the water.

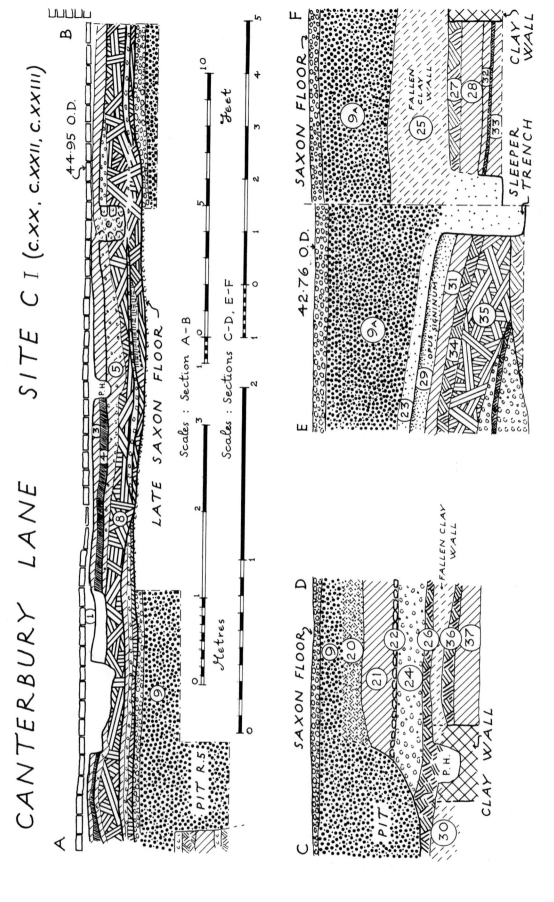

Fig. 33. Canterbury Lane, Site C: sections

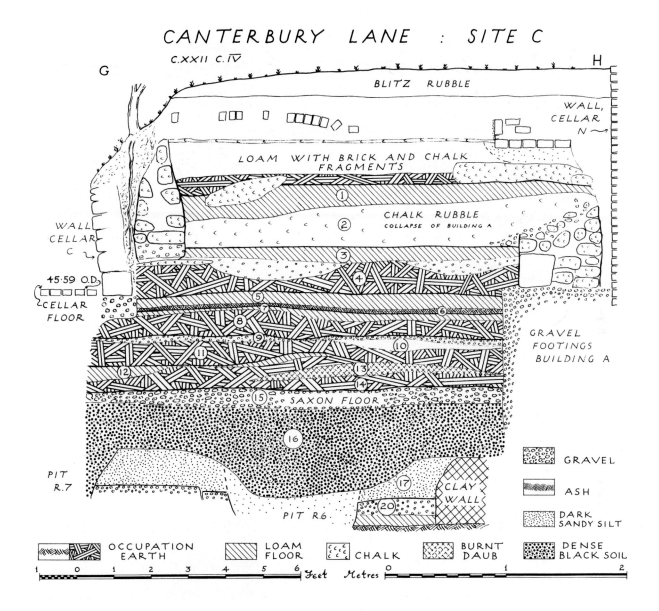

Fig. 34. Canterbury Lane, Site C: section. Scale 1 : 30

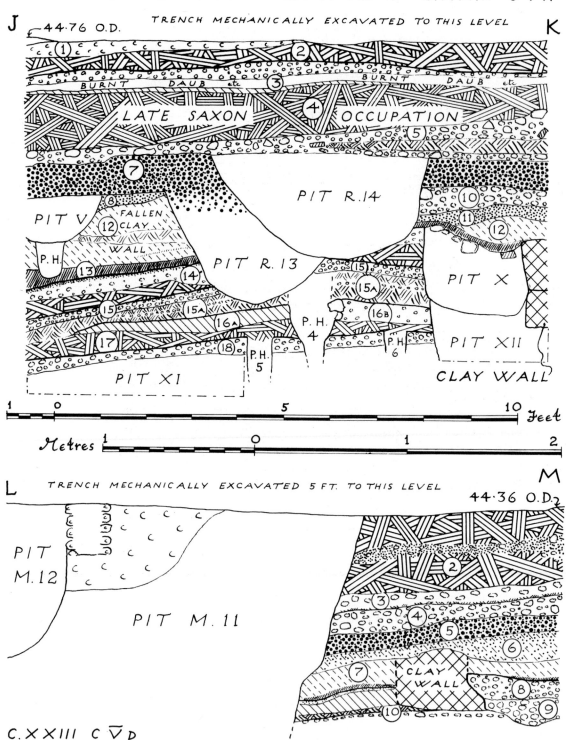

CANTERBURY LANE C.XXIII CⅤA

J 44·76 O.D.

TRENCH MECHANICALLY EXCAVATED TO THIS LEVEL K

① ② ③ ④ ⑤

BURNT DAUB etc. BURNT DAUB etc.

LATE SAXON OCCUPATION

⑦ PIT R.14 ⑩ ⑪ ⑫

⑧ PIT V FALLEN CLAY WALL ⑫ P.H. ⑬ ⑭ PIT R.13 ⑮ PIT X

⑮ ⑮A ⑯A ⑯B P.H. 4 PIT XII

⑰ ⑱ P.H. 5 P.H. 6 CLAY WALL

PIT XI

1 0 5 10 Feet

Metres 1 0 1 2

L TRENCH MECHANICALLY EXCAVATED 5 FT. TO THIS LEVEL M

44·36 O.D.

PIT M.12 ②

PIT M.11 ③ ④ ⑤ ⑥ ⑦ CLAY WALL ⑧ ⑩ ⑨

C.XXIII CⅤD

Fig. 35. Canterbury Lane, Site C: sections. Scale 1 : 24

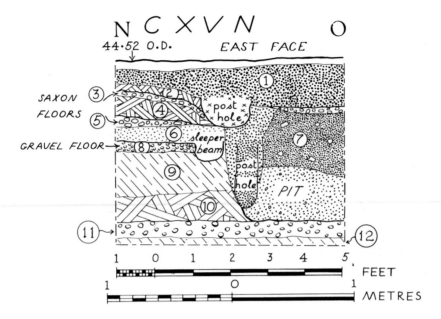

Fig. 36.   Canterbury Lane, Site C: section. Scale 1 : 30

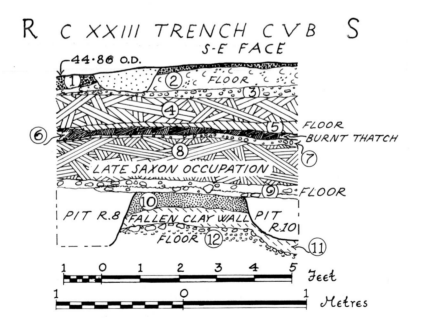

Fig. 37.   Canterbury Lane, Site C: seciton. Scale 1 : 30

VI. EXCAVATIONS ALONG BURGATE STREET AND IN AREA Y

Between 1948 and 1950 four sites were excavated to the south of Burgate Street. Two of these, C X L and C XIV M (Fig. 1, Site 5 and Fig. 44) uncovered parts of Roman timber buildings bordering the north side of the east–west street found in Area Y (Fig. 1, Site 6 and Figs. 44 and 49). C XIV N which lay just east of Iron Bar Lane (Fig. 1) was small and unproductive. Another small site, C XIII T, lay on the north side of Burgate Street (Figs. 1 and 53).

(a) C X SITE L

In 1947 two trenches coded C X L were dug in a cellar on the south side of Burgate Street, west of its junction with Iron Bar Lane[55] (Fig. 44). All the medieval levels had been destroyed, but deep Roman stratification remained and it was clear that the area was occupied throughout the Roman period. Audrey Williams excavated part of a stone-walled building[56] just to the west of C X L in 1945 (Seasons C II-III, Fig. 44) but this building did not extend into the present area.

Trench I extended the whole length of the cellar, but the southern part of it was not fully excavated. At that end of the Trench three pits, 2, 3 and 4 (Fig. 44), had largely destroyed the lower levels. The northern and central parts of the trench were more thoroughly investigated.

The earliest feature was a Belgic pit, perhaps originally a soak-away (Figs. 44, 45, Section A-B (35)) which yielded a Belgic pedestal base (Fig. 114, No. 559); it was cut into the natural brickearth and had a gully leading into it. Both were filled with clean silt with charcoal flecks, and sealed by a thin layer of charcoal and a thick deposit of hard pinkish yellow clay (34); the latter was deposited in the early Roman period and at the time was taken to be make-up to

---

55. A mosaic was found in 1868 *c.* 18 yards (16.5 m.) west of Iron Bar Lane, 8 ft. (2.4 m.) below Burgate Street, and more of the building to which it belonged was uncovered in 1871 together with a second mosaic. *Archaeologia*, xliii (1871), 162, No. 31. *Proc. Soc. Antiq.*, v (1870–73), 128–29. *V.C.H. Kent*, vol. iii, p. 72, No. 19.
56. *Arch. Cant.*, lx (1947), 68 ff.

combat damp conditions preparatory to building.[57] The only pottery found was one sherd of Neronian samian (Dr. 18). Above it were floors and occupation-levels belonging to a succession of buildings which fronted onto the north-east side of the east–west street found in Area Y (p. 168). No stone walls were found and the buildings were assumed to be entirely of timber. Because of the presence of a large pit a baulk was left between the northern and central parts of the trench and there tended to be a slight difference in the stratification of the two areas; they probably represent two different rooms of the same building.

Period 1

The earliest floors (Fig. 45, Section A-B 33, Section C-D 26), which at the north end of the trench (Section A-B) directly overlay layer 34 but further south (Section C-D) overlay grey-green loam (28), are probably to be dated to the late first century. Both were composed of a thin layer of gravel covered by a thin sandy layer, which in 33 yielded a sherd of pre-Flavian samian (Dr. 24/25); above them was a second thin gravel layer. A post-hole was cut into layer 34 from the level of the lower gravel surface. The floors were covered by occupation-deposits of clayey soil and charcoal (Section A-B 32; Section C-D 24); the latter overlay a thin char-coally deposit which had accumulated on the floor. These levels produced several sherds of Flavian samian (Dr. 18, 15/17; and Dr. 18) and a number of sherds of first- and early second-century coarse ware (Fig. 114, Nos. 560–562). Above the occupation-material was another thin layer of ash (31), possibly from destruction by fire although no building-material was found. This yielded sherds of Hadrianic date (Fig. 114, Nos. 563–565).

Period 2

The building was refurbished, perhaps *c.* A.D. 140, and loam floors (Section A-B 30; Section C-D 23) which yielded a second-century jar (Fig 114, No. 566), were laid immediately above the Period 1 burning. A hearth was cut into 23. A secondary floor (29) of smooth pebbles was laid above (30) in the western part of the northern area and above this (but not visible on Section A-B) was a black ashy layer (28) covered by occupation-material (18). Further south (Section C-D) occupation-material (22) lay over 23; it yielded mid second-century sherds and

57.   The surface of natural brickearth in this trench lies at 31.7 O.D. which is over 6 ft. lower than in Canterbury Lane some 260 ft. (80 m.) to the south-east. At the neighbouring site (C II-III) to the west, Audrey Williams recorded it as even lower, at *c.* 30 ft. (*Arch. Cant.*, lx (1947), 69). At the east end of St. George's Street it lay at *c.* 44 ft. O.D. (*Arch. Cant.*, lix (1946), 69), whereas under the Butchery Lane Building natural brickearth occurred at *c.* 33 ft. O.D. under the SW part of the house but at *c.* 25 ft. O.D. under its NE wing. The present-day water-level of the river Stour near the Whitehall site and London Gate is 27 ft. O.D., but Dr. Jenkins has shown that in early Roman times it probably lay at *c.* 22 ft. O.D. (*Arch. Newsletter*, June 1954, 34 f.). It seems possible that a gully or extinct watercourse runs near Burgate Street towards the river, in which case a deposit of make-up would be understandable. However, later excavations (pp. 72 and 84) showed that some early Roman buildings possessed clay walls which were very difficult to disentangle from the fallen clay levels derived from their demolition. A rapid build-up of clay from buildings is possibly therefore partly responsible.

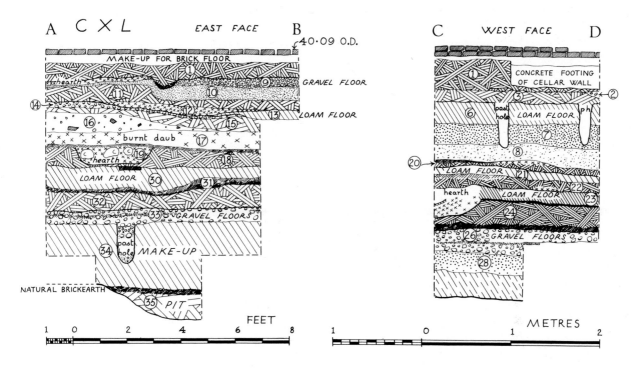

Fig. 45. South of Burgate Street; C X L: Sections A-B, C-D. Scale 1:40

over it was a secondary loam floor (21) covered by another spread of occupation soil (20); the latter yielded Antonine samian and more mid second-century sherds (Fig. 114, Nos. 569–570). Hearths were cut into both layers 18 (cf. Section A-B (19)) and 20. This house was later burnt down; the evidence of destruction was far less ambiguous, certainly in the northern part of the trench, than at the end of Period 1. A thick layer of burnt daub (17) lay above 18 sealing the hearth (19); and above this was a debris-layer (16) which was also found in Trench II (6), which lay to the east of the north end of Trench I. The debris was absent further south although a deposit of charcoal was found above layer 20. The debris layer (16) yielded Antonine samian and a fairly large group of sherds which may extend in date down to c. 220 (Fig. 114, Nos. 571—578).

Period 3

The erection of the Period 3 building followed the fire without any appreciable interval. In Section A-B the debris (16) was covered by a charcoally occupation-layer (15) (= Trench II (5)) which yielded late second- and early third-century pottery (Fig. 114, Nos. 579–586); above this was a thin layer of gravel (14) containing early third-century sherds (Fig. 115, Nos. 587–588); in Section C-D layer 20 was covered by a brown gritty deposit (8 and 7) which represents silt from the adjacent street. It was above layer 7 that the Period 3 floor of loam (6) was laid; a continuation of this extended just into the south corner of the northern area (Section A-B

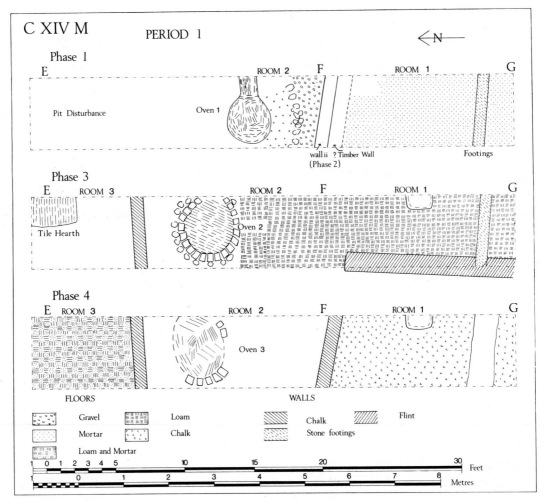

Fig.   46.   South of Burgate Street: C XIV M: plans. Period 1.   A. Phase 1,   B. Phase 3,   C. Phase 4.
Scale 1 : 80

(13)), yielding a late second- to early third-century jar (Fig. 115, No. 589); to the north of it was an area of burnt clay, presumably from a hearth. Several post-holes were cut into 6. Above it was an occupation-layer (3) which was the equivalent of (11) in Section A-B. These layers yielded sherds of third-century date (Fig. 115, Nos. 590–597). Layer 11 was covered by a sandy layer (10) sealed by a gravel floor (9) into which a baked clay hearth had been cut. Above layers 9 and 3 was a thick deposit of occupation-material (1) which yielded eight coins:

Herennius Etruscus	250–251
Victorinus	269–271
Barbarous *Fel. Temp. Rep.* (two)	350 +
Constans (three)	333–350
Gratian	367–383

and much late Roman pottery (Fig. 115, Nos. 598–602). A number of post-holes were cut into this but their function was unknown. Subsequent levels had been destroyed by the cellar builders.

Trench II, to the east of the north end of Trench I, was badly disturbed by pits and not excavated below the destruction-levels of the Period 2 building.

(b) C XIV SITE M

Four small areas were examined in site C XIV M, which lay to the east of C X L (Fig. 44) near the corner of Iron Bar Lane. Trenches I and IB[58] were dug from the surface to the rear of the cellar; here there was much disturbance by medieval pits in the lower levels, but an interesting sequence of medieval and post-medieval structures was examined. Trenches II and III lay within the cellar where the Roman levels were preserved. Part of a timber building fronting the north-east side of the east–west street found in Area Y (p. 168) was excavated.

TRENCHES I AND IB

It was only at the extreme north end of Trench I that any Roman layers survived. Here a small area of pebble floor was uncovered (Fig. 48, Section E-F (28)); this yielded a sherd of late Antonine or early third-century samian (Dr. 31) and overlay a layer of light mixed loam (30) containing a second-century sherd and another layer (29, not showing in the section) which yielded two third-century dishes. A thin layer of charcoal lay above the floor and on top of this was a thin loam deposit, possibly representing a re-flooring. These layers were cut by a large pit (26) which was filled with earth and large chalk blocks and produced three more sherds of late Antonine samian (Dr. 31R, 36 and 37 (Fig. 137, No. 3)) and other vessels of probably mid third-century date (Fig. 116, Nos. 603–606). A layer of yellow loam (25) containing wall-plaster fragments, which was possibly a floor, sealed the pit (into which it had sunk) and extended to the north of it. This yielded a sherd of a mortarium datable c. 240–300 and an 'à l'éponge' sherd of Gaulish origin (Fig. 116, Nos. 607–608). Above (but not extending as far as Section E-F) were first a layer of black ash (24) ¼ in. thick, and then a badly-damaged *opus signinum* floor (23). This was covered by grey ash (22) in which four coins were found (Tetricus I (270–73), Tetricus II (270–73) and two illegible of the third or fourth century) together with a sherd of colour-coated beaker (Fig. 116, No. 609). A thick deposit of compact black earth (19), which contained much building-material (probably debris from the demolition of the building), sealed layer 22. This also yielded four coins (Antoninus Pius (138–61), radiate (270 +), Carausius (287–93) and one illegible of the third or fourth century), together with a Rhenish-ware beaker sherd and a hand-made dish in grey ware probably dating

58.   The baulk dividing Trenches I and IB was later removed.

after 360 (Fig. 116, Nos. 610–611). Thus the building had been demolished by soon after the middle of the fourth century.

All subsequent levels were post-Roman. At the north end of the Trench above 19 were two gravel floor-surfaces (17 and 18) divided by a thin layer of oysters and dirt. Sealing these floors was a stony brown layer (15) which yielded a sherd of early eleventh-century cooking-pot (Fig. 117, No. 637), above which was a hearth with a post-hole to its north. These layers were sealed by a deposit of dark earth and pebbles (14) producing sherds of two cooking-pots dated to the first half of the twelfth century. Cut into layer 14 were two thirteenth-century rubbish-pits (16 and 13). A continuation of 13 and possibly other rubbish-pits with similar black filling destroyed all earlier levels in the southern part of the trench (Section E-F (33); Section F-G (13)). Layer 13 yielded a number of sherds of thirteenth-century pottery.

Sealing the pits was a succession of buildings (Fig. 46) dating from the fourteenth century to modern times. Throughout successive rebuildings three rooms were present in the trench, and are numbered 1-3 from the south towards the north.

Medieval Buildings: Period 1

In Period 1, in which there were several different phases, part of the bulding was probably a bakery: a sequence of three circular bread-ovens, carefully built of tiles pitched in clay, was found in Room 2.

Phase 1 (Fig. 46A)

Parts of two Phase 1 rooms were excavated. The south room (1) had a mortar floor (Fig. 48, Section F-G (12)) which overlay a make-up of loam (16) probably deposited to level off the pit. Further north, Room 2 was floored with gravel (Section E-F (32)); no dividing wall was identified but it was presumably of timber and must have lain just south of the Phase 2 wall visible at the north end of Section F-G (Wall ii). Contemporary with the gravel floor in Room 2 was a large oven (1) (Pl. XXI) of tiles pitched in clay; this was *c.* 3 ft. 6 in. in diameter and of rather rough construction with a flue on the east side. Much of the tile walls of the oven had been destroyed, but the southern extent of the structure was marked by a circle of flints within which was a red burnt area. The gravel floor in this room was covered by an occupation-layer and this was sealed by a reddish burnt deposit (20) representing a hearth which partially covered the by-now ruinous oven. Above it was a thin layer of charcoal (Trench I (12)), which dipped into the later wall-trench of the Phase 2 wall. The floors of Phase 1 in Room 3 had been destroyed by Pits 13 and 16.

Phase 2

Subsequently minor alterations took place. A new wall was built between Rooms 1 and 2 (Section F-G, Wall ii) and Room 1 was given a new floor of gravel (Section F-G, Trench IB (9)), into the north end of which a small tile-lined hearth was cut. The south end of Trench IB was very disturbed by a modern pit and brick wall; east—west stone footings were found which could represent the south wall of Room 1 in Phases 1 and 2; however, floors identical to those in Room 1 were found to the south of the footings and it is more likely that they were inserted from a higher level.

Phase 3 (Fig. 46B)

Room 1 now had a new west wall, but its north wall (Sections E-F, F-G, Wall ii), which had separated it from Room 2, was removed and its site was sealed by an occupation-level (Section F-G (8A)). Above this was a loam floor (Sections E-F (9), F-G (8)) which covered both rooms. In Room 2 this layer sealed an earlier floor of chalky loam (10) yielding a sherd of late thirteenth-century cooking-pot. A second oven (Pls. XXI-XXII) was cut into the north end of 9; this lay very slightly to the north of Oven 1 and was of similar construction. A black layer contemporary with the use of Oven 2 covered layer 9. Further north in Room 3 there was a hearth of pitched tiles set in layer 8 (Section E-F); this layer yielded part of a contemporary quern in Mayen lava (Fig. 72, No 5).

Phase 4 (Fig. 46C)

In Phase 4 Room 3 was reconstructed and a new dividing wall built in chalk between it and Room 2. Room 3 now had a loam and mortar floor laid down over Trench I layer 8, sealing the earlier hearth.

Room 2 was still a bake-house and had a new pitched-tile oven, 3, (Pls. XXIII-XXIV) which lay a little to the north of Oven 2. This was cut into a make-up layer (5) which covered Oven 2 and contained a fourteenth-century pipkin (Fig. 117, No. 638). The northern part of Oven 3 had been destroyed by later rebuilding. The new wall between Rooms 1 and 2 lay on almost the same line as the Phase 2 wall. Room 1 was now floored with chalk (Trench IB, 6) into which a small oblong pit was cut.

Period 2 (Fig. 47)

In the fifteenth century the building ceased to be a bake-house. The chalk walls were demolished and new walls built on similar alignment.

The new south wall of Room 3 lay 1 ft. to the south of its predecessor. It was later rebuilt in brick and all that remained of the original wall were its robbed footings. Room 3 was floored with loam which overlay occupation-layer 6. A fifteenth-century jetton was found in layer 6 and this provides the *terminus post quem* for this period. A fire-place (Pl. XXVI) with brick walls still standing to a height of 1 ft. was cut into the floor against the south wall of Room 3. The new south wall of Room 2 lay very slightly north of its predecessor and was built of tile (Pl. XXV). This room had a thin chalk floor (Trench I, 4) which sealed several hearths on the surface of 5. There was a second fire-place at the north end of the room but the bricks had gone and only mortar, resting on a layer of yellow sand, remained.

Room 1 had a loam floor (Trench IB (5)).

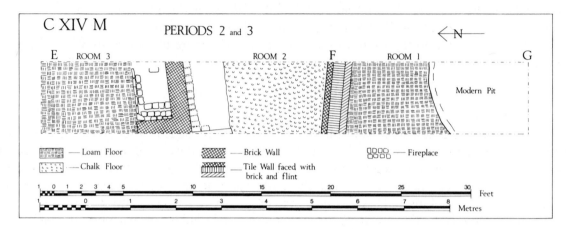

Fig. 47. South of Burgate Street; C XIV M: plan, Periods 2 and 3. Scale 1 : 80

Period 3

The Period 3 building made use of the Period 2 walls although much rebuilding was necessary. The tile wall between Rooms 1 and 2 was refaced on its south side with flints and on its north side with brick and flint (Pl. XXV) from above the level of floor 4 in Room 2. Room 1 was given a new loam floor which lay above a make-up layer (Trench IB (4)); the floor in this room was at a considerably lower level than the floor in Rooms 2 and 3 and presumably there was a step up into Room 2. In Room 2 a thick make-up (3) was deposited over floor 4 and a brick floor was laid down. Its northern edge had later been removed when modifications were made in modern times.

The wall between Rooms 2 and 3 was now (or possibly earlier) totally rebuilt on the Period 2 line in brick with a rubble core. Room 3 now had a loam floor which overlay a thick make-up layer and into which a fire-place had been cut in exactly the same position as in Period 2. No dating evidence was obtained for Period 3.

In modern times the rear part of the premises was demolished; a brick retaining-wall was erected on the floor of Room 2 and the area south of it became a garden.

TRENCHES II AND III

In Trenches II and III, which were not excavated down to the natural subsoil, the Roman levels lay directly under the cellar floor. Two rooms of a Roman house were found, but the west room lay only just within the area examined.

The east room had a succession of floors. Above a layer of loam (Section H-J II (14)) and a deposit of grey sandy occupation-earth (13), which correspond with the pre-building layers in Trench I, lay a thin yellow mortar floor covered by a thin occupation-layer (12) which yielded a sherd of late Antonine samian, Dr. 33, and a coin of Antoninus Pius. This was covered by a deposit of charcoal, above which was a yellow loam floor (11) and a contemporary tile hearth. A stamped amphora sherd dated *c.* 140–180 and a third-century dish (Fig. 116, Nos. 612–613) were found in the floor, which was probably laid in the period *c.* 215–235 and corresponds with the gravel floor (28) in Trench I. The loam floor (11) did not extend to the north end of Trench II, but a probable continuation of it to the west was found in Trench III (Section K-L (9)). Stratigraphically earlier than this floor in Trench III was a hearth overlying a thin band of sand and ash (12) (which yielded a coin of Hadrian) and sealed by ash (10) in which two coins, of Antoninus Pius (138–61) and Lucilla (161–69), were found. Floor 9 overlay these layers and should be contemporary with Floor 11 in Trench II and accordingly laid down *c.* 215–235. Over the floor and hearths in both trenches was a deposit of occupation-material (Sections K-L (6); H-J (10 and 6)) in which three coins were found: one of Vespasian in III 6 and one each of Trajan and Victorinus in II 10. In the area of the Trench II hearth a thin gravel surface was found dividing the occupation-layers 10 and 6. This occupation spans the period *c.* A.D. 235–270.

In the last quarter of the third century another loam floor was laid; this was substantial in Trench II (Section H-J (7)). A thinner loam floor (5), possibly belonging to the same room, was found in the eastern part of Trench III (Section K-L); the east edge of it was cut by two post-holes, one oblong, the other square, which probably belonged to a timber partition. The floor was covered by occupation-material (II (5); III (2 and 4)). No dating evidence was recovered from II (5), but III (4) produced a coin of Claudius II and many sherds of pottery (Fig. 116, Nos. 614–629). Of these only No. 628 is likely to date after 300; the rest are of the third century or else residual pieces, and the deposit can be assumed to have become sealed by *c.* A.D. 310–320. In Trench II it was covered by a chalky floor (4) which contained several small brick *tesserae*. A similar chalky deposit was found above 2 in Trench III but this did not extend to Section K-L. Possibly contemporary with it was the hearth and sleeper-beam trench found at the extreme west end of Trench III (Pl. XXVII), both of which were covered by a layer of charcoal (8) in which seven coins were found (Faustina I (138–40); Claudius II (two) (268–69); Victorinus (269–71); Tetricus II (271–3); radiates (two) (270+)). The stratification suggests that these coins were still in circulation to *c.* 315–330. Layer 8 also yielded a group of pottery of third-century character (Fig. 117, Nos. 630–636). The cellar floor had removed all later levels in Trench III. In Trench II a brown loamy layer (3), into which a post-hole was cut, covered 4, and above this was chalky pebbly material (2), possibly the remains of another floor. The cellar floor covered this.

(c) C XIV SITE N

A trench was dug in a cellar south of Burgate Street, just east of Iron Bar Lane (Fig. 1). The only feature found was a Roman pit; this was filled with dark sticky material (4) above which was a deposit of yellow loam (3). Layer 4 yielded a large sherd of a Dr. 37 (A.D. 140–160) (Fig. 137, No 4), a radiate coin (270+) and a number of sherds of third-century pottery (Fig. 117, Nos. 639–646). Two coins, Tetricus I (270–73) and a barbarous radiate (270+), were found in

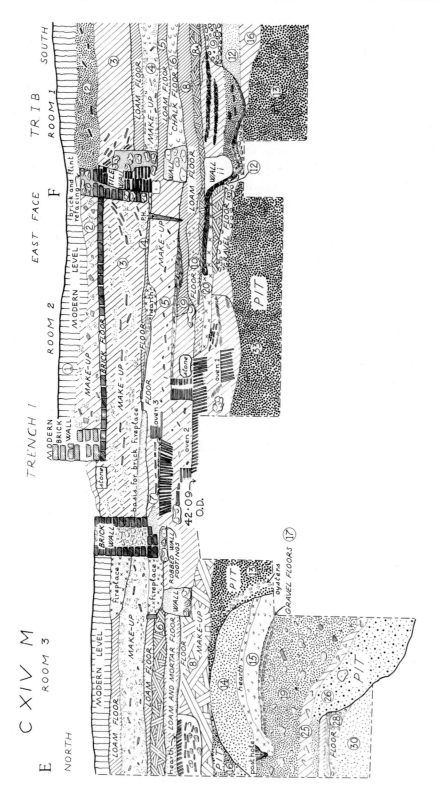

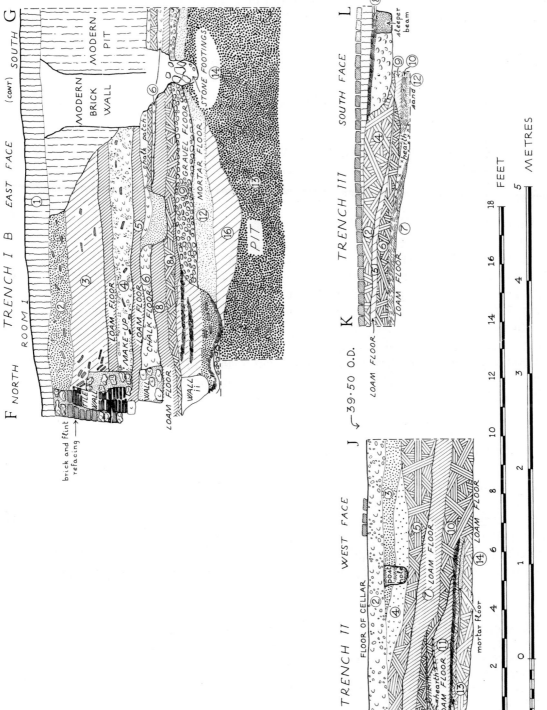

Fig. 48. South of Burgate Street; C XIV M: Sections E-F, F-G, H-J, K-L. Scale 1 : 40

layer 3. A coin of Arcadius (395–408) was found in a deposit of loam mixed with plaster and concrete which lay to the south of this pit. This was probably debris from a nearby Roman building.

(d) AREA Y

Area Y, which was excavated in April and August 1950, lay *c.* 25 m. south of Burgate Street and the same distance west of Iron Bar lane (Fig. 44).

A. ROMAN

An east—west Roman street was found, as expected, running at right-angles to the north–south street uncovered in 1949 (Area R p. 70); it appears to be orientated towards the West Gate.[59] The timber buildings found on sites C X L (p. 110) and C XIV M (p. 113) and the masonry building excavated by Audrey Williams in 1945 (*Arch. Cant.*, lx (1947), 68 ff.) fronted the north side of this street (Fig. 44); remains of similar buildings were uncovered in Area Y fronting its south side (Fig. 49).

A metalled lane was found running south at right-angles to the main Roman street, dividing the *insula*; this was too narrow to be a principal street, but had been maintained for a considerable period.[60]

East—west street

The main street was uncovered in Trenches Y I and Y V (Figs. 44, 49), where the top of the street lay *c.* 6 ft. below the modern surface. The metalling was 4 ft. 6 in. (1.37 m.) thick and overlay a deposit of yellow loam, possibly a floor, beneath which was a layer of Belgic plough-soil containing flecks of charcoal. The north edge of the street did not lie within the area excavated; the south edge was destroyed by pits (Fig. 49, Pits 2, 28 and 29). A feature resembling a sleeper-trench was found running east–west in Y V, cut into the surface of the

---

59.   The first indication of this street had been found by Mr. John Boyle and Dr. F Jenkins at No. 47 Burgate Street (Fig. 44, Site A) in 1946–8 (*Arch. Cant.*, lxiii (1950), 82–91). No one then appreciated that Roman streets could achieve a thickness of almost 1.5 m. of metalling, and on this site the metalling was much mutilated by pits and cellar-digging. The gravel was at first interpreted as part of the podium of a late building (*Arch. Cant.*, lxi (1948), 5 and fig. 4), but its true identification was made clear by discoveries on the present site and in Area R (p. 70).

60.   Similar lanes are known at Amiens and probably existed at Silchester, where they are visible in *Insulae* VII and XI on aerial photographs but have not been excavated. Cf. G. Boon, *Silchester: The Roman Town of Calleva* (2nd ed., 1974), 98.

street; little survived for examination, but it may have been part of a fifth-century structure such as that examined in Area R (p. 73). No dating evidence was recovered from it or from the metalling below.

North—south lane

The lane which ran south at right angles to the east—west street was only 8 ft. (2.44 m.) wide. The metalling, which was badly damaged by pits, was *c*. 2 ft. 6 in. thick (Fig. 51, Section A-B, Fig. 52, Section C-D, Y III 3, 25–17); it had probably been laid down between two houses about the middle of the second century,[61] and went out of use perhaps soon after the middle of the third. It overlay a layer of dirty grey occupation material (Y III 3 (26)), which contained many oysters and produced sherds of Flavian samian (Dr. 29, 18/31, 27) but also two sherds unlikely to be earlier than *c*. 130 (Fig. 118, Nos. 646–647). The original metalling was a layer of dirty gravel (25) (Section C-D), covered by gritty dirt (24) above which was a deposit of hard gravel (23), and dirty gravel (22). This was overlaid by a thin occupation-layer (19), above which were two more gravel surfaces (18) and (17). Layer 24 yielded two sherds of Hadrianic-Antonine samian and coarse ware of similar date (Fig. 118, Nos. 650–652). The lane went out of use probably soon after 250 and was covered by a Roman house extension.

Roman buildings

It was difficult to obtain coherent plans of the buildings because of pit damage and the impossibility of full excavation, but it was clear that throughout the Roman period a succession of timber-framed buildings bordered the east—west street.

Roman building east of the lane

This area had been occupied throughout the Roman period by a succession of timber-framed buildings which were destroyed by fire at the end of the fourth century, perhaps *c*. 390–400.

The lowest levels were only partially excavated; the earliest floor uncovered was of gravel (Section E-F); this was covered by occupation-material (Y III 2 (28)) which yielded a sherd of Flavian samian (Dr. 18) and coarse ware of the mid second century (Fig. 118, Nos. 648–649). Above this was a gravel floor (27A) to the west of which was one of loam (27), but no sign of a partition was detected. Both floors were covered by a thin spread of charcoal above which was a thick layer of loam (24) — probably, in part at least, the product of the demolition of a clay wall. This yielded a sherd of Hadrianic samian (Dr. 18/31) and it probably formed a floor

---

61. In Section C-D (Fig. 52) the top surface of the lane is layer 17. Above this is a floor of *opus signinum* (11) which must imply that at this stage the lane had been built over; accordingly the upper layers of gravel (10, 17) are taken to be later floors rather than metalling. Interpretation is hindered by the presence of several large pits west of the street (Fig. 49). However, supporting this view is the fact that in Section E-F the total thickness of the street-metalling is not more than 20 in., and in Section A-B 28 in.

contemporary with the first phase of a timber slot (Sections C-D and E-F, Y III 3 (21)) which ran north—south along the east edge of the lane. The slot turned east *c.* 4 ft. from the edge of the main east–west street. Sometime later it was recut on the same alignment (Sections C-D and E-F (20)) and a second slot 12 in. wide and 8 in. deep was now cut *c.* 13 ft. 8 in. to the east (Section E-F (51)). The first contemporary floor (Y III 2 (26)) yielded a sherd of Antonine samian (Dr. 38). The second wall-trench did not extend as far north as Section C-D, where a chalk floor crossed its line. Probably therefore there was a doorway at this point, most of which had been removed by Pit 10. From the eastern wall a narrow slot, only 6 in. wide, ran off to the east to a large post-hole (2) beyond which it was destroyed by Pit 7; the post-hole yielded a sherd of a mortarium dated to after A.D. 250 (Fig. 118, No. 653) which presumably arrived there when the building was destroyed in the late fourth century. The western room (Room 1) which measured 12 ft. 4 in. (3.8 m.) east–west was floored with *opus signinum* (Section E-F, Y III 2, (25)) and Rooms 2 and 3 with gravel and loam containing plaster-fragments (26).

Probably soon after 250 the lane went out of use and the building to its east was extended over it. The north—south timber beams had already been replaced slightly to the west of their earlier position; the beam which formed the west wall of Room 1 now actually overlay the metalling of the lane (Section C-D (6)). The east wall of Room 1 was also moved slightly to the west. The situation is obscured in Section E-F by the intervention of Pit 11; but in the rest of the trench a shelf 10 in. wide and covered with charcoal lay just to the west of the earlier slot. Floor Y III 2 (21) ended along its line and it was assumed to be the base of the new timber-framed wall.

The new Room 4 over the lane was floored with *opus signinum* (Section C-D, Y III 3 (11)) and was later re-floored with successive layers of dirty gravel (10, 7) separated by an occupation-layer (9), which yielded a red colour-coated sherd which cannot be earlier than *c.* 260 and in Canterbury is likely to be rather later. Room 1 also had a new floor of rough *opus signinum* (Section E-F, Y III 2 (21)) laid over a level of make-up (23). Rooms 2 and 3 were floored with chalk (Section C-D, Y III 2 (20)).

There were indications that the building had been destroyed by fire. The destruction-layer (Section E-F, Y III 2 (18)) sealing the eastern wall contained charcoal and burnt daub, and in the western wall-trench (Section C-D, Y III 3 (6)) the charred remains of the sleeper-beams survived at the corner of the room; the trench yielded fourth-century pottery (Fig. 118, Nos. 655–657), a coin of Valens (A.D. 364–78) and part of a white pipe-clay figurine of a seated Mother-Goddess (Pl. XXXII A). Layer Y III 2 (18) also yielded a sherd of fourth-century pottery (Fig. 118, No. 654) and an Anglo-Gallic jetton of Edward I, which must be intrusive from the adjacent pits. Two coins of the House of Theodosius I were found in the corresponding destruction-deposit in Trench Y II 1 (10).

Three or four more rooms probably belonging to this building were located further south in Trenches Y II 1–3. The area between Y III and Y II was unexcavated except for a small trench Y IV, which was almost entirely occupied by pits; but as the timber slots found in Y II and Y III lay on the same alignment and only *c.* 6.5 m. away it is very likely that they were part of the same building. These trenches were less thoroughly excavated and the various phases are less clear. Room 5 was floored with *opus signinum* Y II 1 (11) (not extending as far as Section A-B and bordered on the south-east by a small length of wall-trench); this floor overlay a layer of dirty loam containing fragments of painted wall-plaster and charcoal (13) (Section A¹-B) — presumably destruction-debris from an earlier phase not excavated. It yielded a sherd of a jar possibly of fourth-century date. To the north of the *opus signinum* floor was a small area of gravel (12) which may represent the position of the timber-framed north wall of the room. Both the floor and the gravel were covered by a destruction-deposit of black earth containing charcoal and burnt daub (10). It produced third- to fourth-century pottery, some of which was burnt, together with a coin each of Carausius (287–93) and Constantine I (*Urbs Roma* 330–37) and two of the House of Theodosius (379–95). In Trench Y II 2 a small area of Room 6 where not destroyed by pits was floored with loam (Y II 2 (9) in Section A¹-B), above which was much burnt wall-debris (8 and 7). Room 7 had a loam floor above which more demolished plaster and wall-debris occurred (Y II 3 (20) in Section A-A¹), into which a post-hole had been cut. The western wall of Room 7 (not visible on Section A-B because of pits) had two phases. The second possibly belonged to the time when the building was extended over the lane as had happened further north. Here two successive *opus signinum* floors ran over the lane (Y II Part 3, 13 = 21 and 14A); above this was a deposit of debris (II 3 (20A)) and dark earth containing burnt material (II 4 (14A)) which yielded part of a rouletted bowl of Argonne ware, form 37.

Roman building west of the lane

A succession of Roman floors and occupation-levels was found in Trench Y I to the west of the lane, but the area excavated was too small and too disturbed by pits to enable coherent plans to be recovered. The earliest floors were mostly of loam and probably belonged to several phases of timber building bordering the east—west street and similar to the sequence found east of the lane. A complete second-century jar (Fig. 118, No. 658) was found in occupation-material over one of these floors. Later in the Roman period a building with stone footings occupied the area. Two very small stretches of badly-robbed footings, one running north—south, the other east—west were found in Trench Y I (Fig. 49). Two phases of floor seemed to be contemporary with these, but disturbance was such that no dating can be assigned save that they are post-Antonine. At the south-west end of Y I gravel floors overlaid by mortar floors were found both north and south of the east—west footings. The wall must have turned before reaching Trench Y II 4; here a mortar floor (16) (Section A-A¹), probably contemporary with that in Y I, overlay an earlier loam floor (18). Layer 18 yielded a sherd of third-century Castor-ware 'box' lid.

B.   MEDIEVAL AND LATER BUILDINGS

In the medieval period a large number of pits were dug in the area, destroying many of the Roman levels. The pits produced pottery dating mainly to the fourteenth century. Pit 16 yielded sherds of several fourteenth-century jugs and a cresset lamp (Fig. 118, Nos. 659–661), and Pit 17 (Section A-B) yielded jug sherds of similar date (Fig. 118, Nos. 662–664). Pit 18 produced a sherd possibly of the fifteenth century.

Post-dating most of the pits was a succession of stone buildings originally constructed in the mid to late fourteenth century (Fig. 50) and representing a considerable expansion into the rear areas behind the frontage of Burgate Street. It was interesting to note that many of the original medieval walls were rebuilt in the seventeenth and eighteenth centuries and that these rebuilds were often capped by recent footings, thus preserving the medieval property-boundaries right up to the Second World War.

One building erected in the late thirteenth or early fourteenth century seemed to be of timber, but few details were recovered. This had a cobbled floor (Fig. 51, Section A¹-B, Y II 1 (8) and Y II 2 (5)) which overlay a deposit of black medieval debris Y II 1 (9) and Y II 2 (6). A sherd of a Group IV cooking-pot (Fig. 119, No. 671) dated to the second half of the thirteenth century was found in the floor. Several post-holes lined with flint and chalk and a slot containing decayed timber were found, but no coherent plans obtained. The post-holes can be seen beneath the drain in Trench Y II 1 (Fig. 50). The floor was covered by more black dirt (Section A¹-B, Y II 1 (7), Y II 2 (3)) which produced several fourteenth-century jug- and dish-sherds including Fig. 119, No. 670.

Stone Buildings

Very little information was recovered about the earliest masonry building here which only just entered the north end of Trenches Y I and Y III 4. Wall A was 27 in. wide and built of tiles, possibly for bonding the wall-junction. From it a robber-trench ran south-west along the section-face (Section C-D, 52) while in Trench Y I a 3-ft. wall of flints and ragstone set in yellow sandy mortar ran off to the north-east: its junction with Wall A was obscured by robbing and by Pit 5. This wall overlay a pit which yielded a Group III cooking-pot rim and a glazed jug-sherd, so cannot be earlier than the early fourteenth century. North of the wall and west of Wall A was a thin floor of gravel and chalk (Y I 15) sealing dark late Roman earth: over the floor was a layer of occupation-earth (Y I 14) which yielded jug-sherds of the four-teenth century.

A later building sealed the robbed wall and about this more information was recovered.

Building 1

This building, which was initially constructed during the fourteenth century, was rebuilt and added to at various stages up to the twentieth century, and was sufficiently large to extend into Y II to the south.

Period I

Room 1 lay in Trenches Y III 3–4 and measured 17 ft. 7 in. (5.3 m.) from north-west to south-east. The NW wall B¹ (Section C-D) was 1 ft. wide, built of flint, and at the north end of Y III 4 was recessed to receive a tile fire-back in front of which was a large hearth of pitched tiles (Pl. XXIX). The first-period south-east wall C¹ entered the south-west end of Y III 3 where three courses of flint survived (Section E-F), but further north it had been rebuilt in

Period III (Section C-D, Wall C²) and the original wall had been replaced by chalk footings (Pl. XXX). The room probably extended as far as the south-west end of Y IV where a flint wall was found underneath the later Wall K. This flint wall was later than the south-east wall of the room, which it abutted; but this difference was probably only structural. The room was floored with loam (Section C-D, Y III 3 (2A) (2B) and Y IV (14)), cut into which were several tile hearths (Fig. 50) and, in Trench Y IV, two post-holes. Against the north-east baulk of Y III 3 was a large semicircular oven floored with pitched tiles. In the east corner was an oblong mortar base with three patterned glazed tiles (Fig. 69, Nos. 9–11) still *in situ* and imprints of *c.* 19 others in the mortar.

Very little of the area to the north-west of Room 1 was available for examination because of Pit 5. A deposit of gravelly sand (Section C-D, Y III 4 (7)) covered by occupation-material (6) and more pebbly earth (5) ran up to the west side of the wall and probably belonged to a yard outside the building. Similar layers occurred in Trench Y I.

About 6 ft. 6 in. (2 m.) to the north-west of Wall B was a two-period drain built of chalk blocks. The first phase of this drain, in the north part of Y I, overlay the early wall mentioned on p. 124 and was contemporary with Period I of the present building. It was 5½ in. (14 cm.) wide and deep and was floored with tiles lying horizontally; its sides and roof were made of squared chalk blocks 5–7 in. wide and 12 in. long. Incorporated in its structure was a plain unglazed oval-sectioned jug-handle, probably of the fourteenth century.

The first-phase drain was found to extend to the south part of Trench Y I, where it had been replaced by a new drain whose construction-trench destroyed its farther course. The new length of drain took a slightly different alignment but it too was clearly contemporary with Wall J, the west wall of the Period I house, with which it was connected by a flange of mortar. The new drain was 9½ in. (23 cm.) deep and 6½ in. (16.5 cm.) wide and was constructed of squared chalk blocks 5–7 in. wide and 10 in. long laid transversely to the axis of the drain. The roofing-tiles (Fig. 70, No. 18) used for the floor of the drain beyond the turn were still laid parallel with the original axis. Owing to subsidence it was not clear in which direction the drain was running, but almost certainly it ran south to a soakaway beyond the building. Wall J itself showed no sign of rebuilding, and was superseded in Period III; both phases of chalk drain therefore belong to the earliest phases of the building.

The area south-east of Room 1 was outside the original building but was later covered by an extension to it.

Room 2 lay to the south-west of Room 1 and was excavated in Y II 3–4. Its south-east wall C lay on the same line as the south-east wall of Room 1. The south-west corner of the room (and of the building) and a stretch of its west wall (J), 1 ft. wide, were found in Trench Y I; it was thus *c.* 6 ft. wider from north-west to south-east than Room 1, measuring *c.* 23 ft. 6 in. (7.2 m.) and was *c.* 16 ft. (4.8 m.) from north-east to south-west. In Period I this room was divided by a north—south timber partition represented by a slot (Fig. 50) which was cut into Pit 17 (Section A-A¹). This pit produced several sherds of fourteenth-century pottery (see p. 275). Both rooms were originally floored with loam (Y II 3 (7), (11A)) which yielded two late thirteenth- or early fourteenth-century jug-sherds, and then by mortar (6) from which came a glazed floor-tile (Fig. 69, No. 8). The latest floor in the western room, a thick layer of pebbly earth and tile (Section A-A¹, Y II 3 and 4 (3)) yielded sherds of the early sixteenth century (Fig. 120, Nos. 677–679).

Period II

This period involved only the reconstruction of Wall B, the west wall of Room 1, which had sagged outwards in the neighbourhood of the fireplace, causing the collapse of the south end of the tile backing (Pls. XXVIII, XXIX). The wall was partly refaced, partly rebuilt in chalk blocks and Caen stone; it rested on a thin layer of unburnt loam sealing the ash of the hearth. This refacing contained at its base a soft light yellow brick measuring $8\frac{1}{8} \times 3\frac{6}{8} \times 3\frac{1}{8}$ in. ($206 \times 146 \times 79$ mm.).

By the end of Period II, in the early seventeenth century, the building had fallen into disrepair; the floors and hearths of Room 1 were covered by a thick deposit of loam (Y III 3 (1)) (Section C-D) which contained many tiles and patches of ash and charcoal and which probably represents the demolition of the half-timbered walls of the upper part of the structure. No pottery was recovered from this, and the date of demolition is uncertain.

Period III

Rebuilding, however, is likely to have followed fairly closely on the demolition, and the reconstruction which marks Period III can be assigned, as stated, to the early seventeenth century.

In *Room 1* a new south-west wall (K) was built of chalk above the earlier flint wall. The south-east wall (C) was totally rebuilt (Pl. XXX) at the northern end of Y III 3 (Section C-D) where a new wall-trench (38) was cut through the Period I loam floor and destruction-level and a wall of chalk blocks (C²) was inserted. This trench yielded a sherd probably of the sixteenth century. The new wall lay very slightly west of its original line; at the extreme south-west end of Trench Y III 3 the rebuilding was less total and the new wall was built on the remains of Period I: three courses of chalk blocks survived above the remains of the original flint wall.

Wall B² of Period II remained in use as the north-west wall of Room 1, which had a chalk floor in this period. This was found at the south end of Y III (Section E-F (36)) where it overlay a deposit of occupation-material (35); the floor was also found in Y IV (6). It was clearly contemporary with chalk wall K and overlay dirty loam and tile (7) which yielded a salt-glazed stone-ware sherd of the seventeenth century.

Room 2. The timber partition now went out of use and its trench was filled by a deposit of loose dark brown earth (Section A-A¹, Y II 3 (2A)) and sealed by the gravel basis of the new floor (1); a new south-east to north-west wall (G) was constructed across the middle of Y II 3–4. This turned north-east at the west end of Y II 4, there overlying an earlier hearth, and was traced for *c*. 15 ft. 4 in. (4.7 m.); it did not align with Wall B in Room 1, but must represent the rebuilding of the outer wall of the house on a new line. During the last week of the excavation Wall G was traced northwards to examine its relationship with Wall B. The latter was traced for a short distance beyond the end of the former (Fig. 50) before it was robbed away; but the relationship between the two was found to be destroyed by a nineteenth-century cylindrical brick drain which passed between the two. The reconstruction of Walls C and K in Period III has already been described. The new room to the north-east of Wall G was floored with puddled chalk which rested on a rubbly gravel basis (Y II 4 (1); Y II 3 (1)) which produced two stone-ware jug sherds and coarse ware of late sixteenth- and early seventeenth-century date (Fig. 120, Nos 672–676). The area to the south was floored with pebbly earth (Y

II 3 (3); Y II 4 (7)) which yielded a stone-ware jug-base of late fifteenth- to early sixteenth-century date and other sherds (Fig. 120, Nos. 677–679).

Period IV

Sometime probably during the eighteenth century further reconstruction took place and additions were made. In Room 1 (Section C-D) both walls B³ and C³ were rebuilt on the old lines. Wall B³ incorporated a red brick measuring 8⅝ × 4½ × 2¼ in. (22 × 11.5 × 5.7 cm.) together with part of a plain Romanesque capital. South-west of the reduced Room 2 of Period II¹. Wall H (Fig. 50) was built to enclose a new room: all that remained of it was one course of mortared flints and stone above three footing-courses of flint bedded in loam. To the north-west of the wall was a gravelly floor (5) and to the south-east a floor of loam (8). No dating evidence was recovered.

Also assigned to Period IV is an extension added to the south-east side of Room 1. It overlay pits yielding much fourteenth-century pottery but was probably considerably later. The walls of this, like Wall H, were of rather flimsy construction and they lacked proper footings. Most of the area within the angle of the two walls had been destroyed by a later pit (Section E-F), but stratification did survive immediately inside the north-east to south-west wall. Here just beneath the edge of the wall was a gravel deposit (Y III 2 (11)) above which was a layer of puddled chalk (10) overlaid by loam, lime and chalk (9); these were taken to be builders' levelling-layers. Above was a layer of loam (8), possibly a floor, covered by mortary rubble (7) and another thin loam deposit (6). A deposit of broken tiles and loam (2) covered this. Layer 2 yielded sherds of a stoneware jug, but the other levels only residual fourteenth-century pottery. To the north of the east—west wall and possibly contemporary with it were two successive loam floors (Y III 2 (16) and (15): Section C-D) covered by a tile floor (not visible on section) above which was chalk and stone debris (12). Cut into these layers was a circular structure built of chalk blocks. It was not a well, as at first suspected, and was interpreted as a base for a wooden pillar.

Trench Y V was much disturbed, but contained part of a pitched tile hearth which appeared to be backed against the remains of a wall. It overlay a pit (Fig. 49, Pit 29) which yielded a group of fourteenth-century pottery (Fig. 119, Nos. 666-669).

Trench Y III 1 was found to be occupied by a brick-built cistern (Pl. XXXI) overlying a large fourteenth-century pit. The cistern was not quite rectangular, measuring 2 ft. 8 in. wide by *c.* 6 ft. 10 in. internally, and had been partly robbed of its bricks. The brick floor was dished along its long axis, being 4 in. deeper in the middle than at the sides; at some stage the floor had been renewed to the same pattern above 1 ft. of make-up; some fish-bones were recovered from the rubble filling above this as well as two early sixteenth-century stoneware jugs (Fig. 120, No. 680); but there was no sign of silt on the floor. It is perhaps best interpreted as a rain-water cistern.

In the nineteenth century a drainage tunnel was dug across the site in a north-east to south-west direction; it recalls the similar tunnel cut through the St. George's Street Baths (p. 32). The date of this must be subsequent to 1868 when the streets were trenched for the insertion of main drainage by James Pilbrow (*Archaeologia*, xliii (1871), 151–64).

Much of the building remained in occupation until World War II. Walls B⁴ and C⁴ were each rebuilt in brick, and Walls L and M (Fig. 50) were also both of comparatively recent date.

Fig. 51. Area Y Trench II: Sections A-A¹, A¹-B

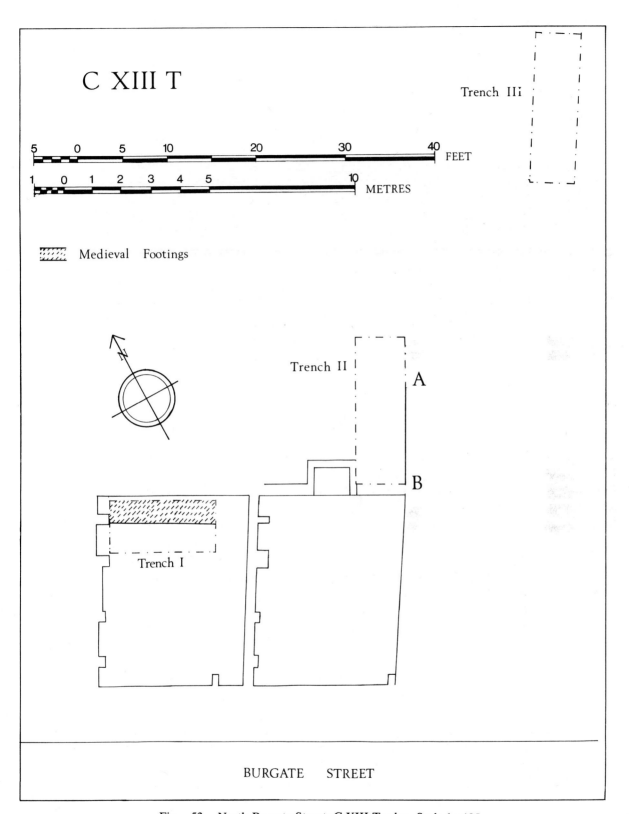

C XIII T

5   0   5   10   20   30   40 FEET

1   0   1   2   3   4   5   10 METRES

Medieval Footings

Trench III

Trench II

A

B

Trench I

N

BURGATE   STREET

Fig.   53.   North Burgate Street; C XIII T: plan. Scale 1 : 125

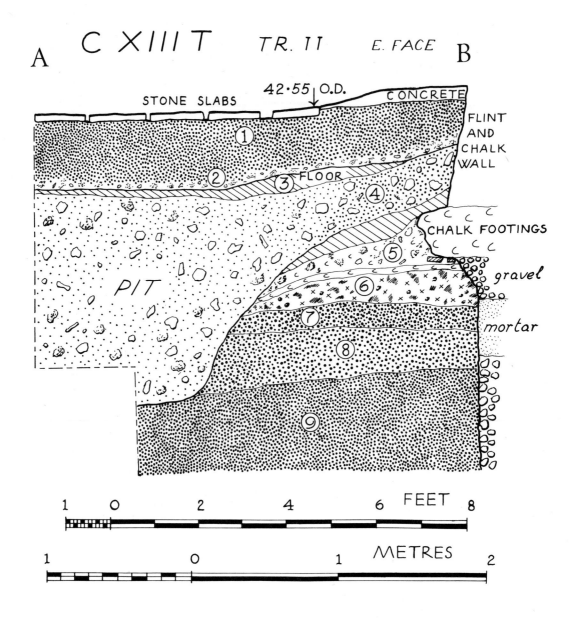

Fig. 54. North of Burgate Street; C XIII T: section. Scale 1 : 25

Trench I was dug in a cellar and here footings of an east—west medieval wall were cut into the Roman garden soil.

Trenches II and III were dug from the surface behind the cellar. The lowest level excavated in Trench II was a layer of late Roman black soil (Fig. 54, Section A-B (9)) yielding several sherds of pottery (Fig. 122, Nos. 705–709) and a coin of Constantine I. This was covered by two more deposits of garden soil (8) and (7); the former produced medieval sherds of the second half of the eleventh century. Above layer (7) was a burnt deposit (6) containing much iron slag and yielding an early twelfth-century sherd and another of late twelfth- to early thirteenth-century date (Fig. 122, No 712); this was overlaid by what may have been a chalk floor, sealed by chalky rubble (5), a layer which yielded much sixteenth- to seventeenth-century pottery. A substantial wall on deep gravel foundations had been built from this level, and the layers above 5 had been destroyed by a large pit apparently filled in the early seventeenth century. Sealing the pit was a loam floor (3), which yielded sherds of the early seventeenth century (Fig. 123, Nos. 713–716). Above the floor was first a layer of demolition-debris and plaster fragments (2), containing part of a pot-quern in Mayen lava (Fig. 72, 6) and pottery down to *c.* 1750, and then 14 in. of old garden soil (1) sealed by paving. Layer 1 yielded a quantity of eighteenth-century stamped or inscribed stoneware mugs (Fig. 123, Nos. 723–730).

Trench III was disturbed by modern pipes and not fully excavated. Several pits were found, one of which produced a sherd of fifth-century Jutish pottery (No. 61) (to be published in *The Archaeology of Canterbury*, vol. v (Marlowe area report).

A disturbed skeleton probably from the lay cemetery of the cathedral was found in Trench IV which lay in a cellar behind Burgate House.

VII. C XV X: BUS STATION SITE

In the summer 1949 six trenches were dug along the south-east side of St. George's Lane just inside the city walls, on the site of the new Bus Station (Fig. 55). The tail of the Roman bank, or wash from it, was found in Trenches II and V and this has been discussed in a previous report.[62] Elsewhere the Roman levels were very disturbed by later pits and little of interest was recorded (Figs. 59–60).

(a) Roman

In Trench I the earliest deposit excavated was a layer of light brown earth (23) (Fig. 56, Section A-B) which produced a coin of Valentinian II (388–92) together with contemporary and residual pottery. Most of this deposit was cut away by Pits 1 and 9.

The Roman levels in Trench III were slightly less disturbed. The earliest layer excavated was a deposit of thick yellow and grey loam (Fig. 57, Section H-J (22)). This produced Antonine samian and pottery of the period 150–200. Overlying 22 was a similar layer (20) which contained several third-century sherds together with a flanged bowl of unusual form which probably dates to the fourth century (Fig. 124, No. 733). The layer was cut by a pit (21) (Sections H-J, J-K) which yielded a third-century sherd. In the second half of the fourth century a building was constructed in this area but no coherent plan could be obtained. It had a pebbly floor (16) into which several post-holes were cut and which was bedded on a make-up (19) of rubbly brown earth containing fragments of brick, burnt clay and charcoal. A sherd of late fourth-century pottery (Fig. 124, No. 734) was found in the floor.

No Roman levels were excavated in Trench IV; in Trench V the only Roman layer behind the tail of the bank was a stony deposit of the fourth century (22). This was cut by a medieval pit (9) which yielded an unusual stamped bowl in Oxfordshire ware (Fig. 124, No. 732). In Trench VI the only Roman features were two pits (Pits 5 and 6).

(b) Post-Roman

A useful series of pottery dating from the early Saxon period to the twelfth century, and from the post-medieval period, was recovered from the many pits in the area and from the deposits sealing them.

---

62. S.S. Frere, Sally Stow and Paul Bennett, *Excavations on the Roman and Medieval Defences of Canterbury, The Archaeology of Canterbury*, ii (1982), 62–4.

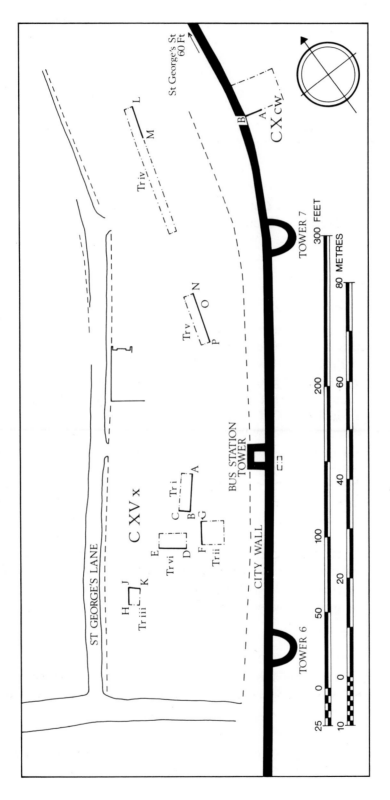

Fig. 55.   Bus Station. General Plan of Trenches

Pit 6 in Trench I (Section A-B) was Saxon, datable to the sixth century, and Pit 9 (which produced no finds) was probably contemporary. Pit 9 was cut into a deposit of grey brown earth (22) which yielded sherds of fifth- or sixth-century hand-made cooking-pots (Fig. 124, Nos. 744–748). Sherds probably of the sixth century (Nos. 749—752) were also recovered from layer 21 which sealed 22 but did not extend as far as the section-face. The pit was sealed by a thick deposit of brown earth (7) which yielded Saxon sherds down to the tenth century as well as early Norman pottery of Group III type.[63] Pit 6 itself, which was filled with black earth and large flints, was the earliest of five intersecting pits at the south end of the trench. It yielded several sherds of fifth- and sixth-century Saxon pottery (Fig. 124, Nos. 735–738).

The medieval pits probably all belonged to the period between the end of the eleventh and the middle of the twelfth century. Pit 4, with a filling of grey earth, was cut through a layer of grey-yellow soil (16) identical with layer 7 and containing material down to the twelfth century. The pit itself produced sherds of Group III type dated c. 1080–1150 (Fig. 125, Nos. 764–765), as well as three late Saxon cooking-pot rims of types dated c. 850–950 in Canterbury Lane. No pottery was recovered from Pit 5, which cut both Pit 4 and Pit 6. Pit 3 cut Pits 4 and 5, but produced only residual pottery of Group II-III type as well as hand-made and late Saxon sherds (Fig. 124, Nos. 742–743, 762). Pit 1 was the largest of the medieval pits in Trench I. It was filled with gravelly earth below which was a layer of black earth with oysters. The pottery in it was of much the same date as that recovered from Pit 4 (Fig. 125, Nos. 766–768).

The only other features of note in Trench I were two patches of loam floor. The earlier (Fig. 56, Section B-C (9)) lay at the south end of the trench and sealed Pit 6. Four small post-holes irregularly positioned were cut into this surface and on top of it was a light brown occupation-deposit (8) containing much charcoal and some oysters together with cooking-pot sherds of the second half of the eleventh century. The later floor (Section A-B (2)) was found in the northern part of the trench sealing Pit 1. This floor and the pits were covered by a thick layer of black earth (1), containing pottery mainly of the seventeenth century (Fig. 127, Nos. 796–814) and representing a cultivated garden; above this layer were the remains of a pre-war building.

In Trench II several Saxon layers were found above the supposed Roman bank (Fig. 57, Section F-G (17) and (18)). Layer 13 was a deposit of clean yellow gravel yielding a hand-made Saxon handle (Fig. 124, No. 739); above this was a gravel layer (12) producing a shell-tempered Saxon sherd perhaps of the ninth to tenth century. To the south of layer 12 and overlying Roman Pit 3 was a thin layer of dark earth with charcoal flecks (16) which yielded two fifth-century Jutish sherds (Fig. 124, Nos. 740–741) as well as grass-tempered sherds of a later date. Layer 16 and part of 12 were covered by gritty earth (15) which produced two Saxon hand-made sherds, one of them in sixth- or seventh-century grass-tempered fabric. Gravelly layers 8, 14 and 9 contained residual Saxon material, but layer 8, the lowest, also

---

63. For some medieval pottery from Canterbury it is convenient to use the classification of the groups discussed in *Arch. Cant.*, lxviii (1954), 128 ff. The dating of these is now considered to be as follows:

Group I	c. 975–1025
Group II	c. 1050–1100
Group III	c. 1080–1150
Group IV	c. 1250–1300

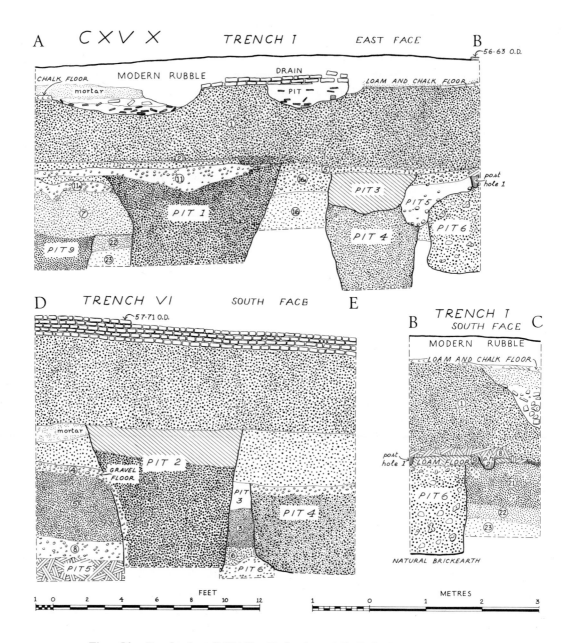

Fig. 56. Bus Station. C XV Site X, Sections A-B, B-C, D-E. Scale 1 : 64

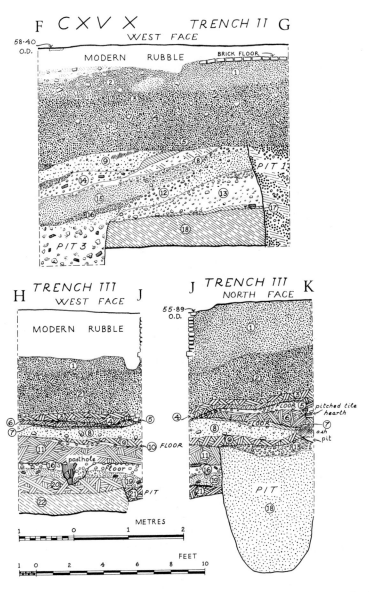

Fig. 57. Bus Station. C XV Site X, Sections F-G, H-J, J-K. Scale 1 : 64

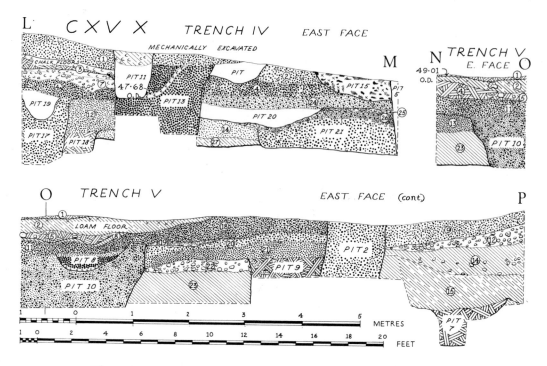

Fig. 58. Bus Station. C XV Site X, Sections L-M, N-O. Scale 1 : 64

yielded a rim of Group III type (*c.* A.D. 1080–1150). Sealing these were thick post-medieval deposits of dry powdery brown earth containing oysters; the pottery is illustrated in Fig. 126, Nos. 780–795.

In Trench III a large pit (Fig. 57, Section J-K (18)) was cut through the Roman levels and was filled with grey-brown earth. It yielded a late Saxon sherd of late ninth- to early tenth-century date together with a residual Roman graffito (Fig. 124, No. 731).

Above the Roman deposits and sealing this pit were three successive thirteenth- and fourteenth-century floors (Sections H-J and J-K). The first of these (10) was of earth and gravel; above 18 the gravel (here labelled (13)) was considerably thicker than elsewhere, presumably to counter subsidence. A layer of occupation-debris (9), into which an ash pit was cut, overlay the floor and yielded a sherd of a thirteenth-century jug. A make-up layer of cobbles and large flint pebbles (8) sealed 9; above them was a second floor (7) of earth and yellow loam which produced sherds of two late thirteenth-century cooking-pots and a crucible (Fig. 125, Nos. 769–70). An occupation-level (6) covered the floor and was sealed by a third floor (5) of gravel, in which were two fourteenth-century sherds (Fig. 125, Nos. 771–2). A pitched tile hearth was cut into this floor and both were covered by occupation-layers 3 and 4; the latter also produced fourteenth-century sherds. Sealing layer 3 was a thick deposit of greenish earth and clay (2) with fourteenth-century sherds, above which was dark brown earth (1) with pottery ranging from the fourteenth to the sixteenth century (Fig. 125, Nos. 722–779). Above this was modern rubble.

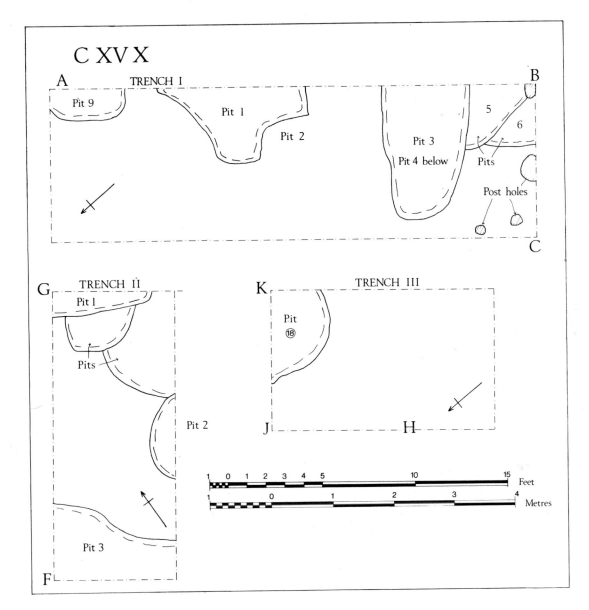

Fig. 59. Bus Station. C XV Site X, Plan of Trenches I-III. For positions, see Fig. 55. Scale 1 : 60

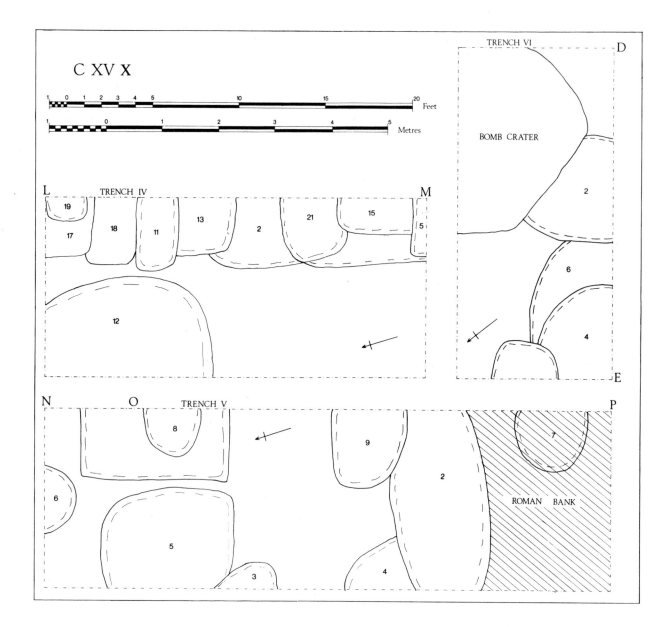

Fig. 60.   Bus Station. C XV Site X, Plan of Trenches IV-VI. For positions, see Fig. 55. Scale 1 : 64

Trench IV, a long north—south trench prepared by a mechanical excavator and excavated by some very unskilled paid labour, was found to be occupied by more than twenty pits dating from the Saxon period through to modern times (Fig. 58, Section L-M). The only useful find was a late Saxon spouted pitcher (Fig. 124, No. 763).

Trench V (Section N-O) was likewise occupied by pits. Two, Pits 10 and 8, were late Saxon (Fig. 124, Nos. 760–761). They were both sealed by a deposit of dark soil (11) which was continuous with layer 18 to the south, and contained late ninth- to early tenth-century sherds (Fig. 124, Nos 754–755) apparently residual, since in a deposit of grey loam (13), below 11, there was a Group II cooking-pot rim dating to the second half of the eleventh century as well as another late Saxon cooking-pot (Fig. 124, No. 758). Above 11 were two successive floors. The first (8) was of dirty yellow loam containing burnt clay and charcoal together with sherds of Group II type. Above was a blackish occupation-deposit (5) sealed by a second loam floor (2) which yielded more eleventh-century sherds. A brown occupation-layer (1), which contained a coin of Henry II (of 1180–89) as well as a hand-made Saxon pot (Fig. 124, No. 753), covered the floor. The only other features in this trench were medieval pits containing eleventh- and twelfth-century pottery with a residual late Saxon cooking-pot in Pit 1 (Fig. 124, No. 759).

In Trench VI (Fig. 56, Section D-E) again the main features were medieval pits with pottery ranging from the eleventh to the thirteenth century. Pit 4 yielded residual Saxon sherds, including one in Ipswich ware (Fig. 124, Nos. 756–757).

PART II : THE FINDS

A. THE COINS

I. COINS FROM THE ST. GEORGE'S STREET BATH-BUILDING[64]

1–6.   Gallienus, six *antoniniani*. *RIC* 177, 208, 253, 256, 308, illegible

C IX A I Pit 8. Third century.

C IX D III (6). Gravel. Mid fourth century.

C IX A III Pit 1. Medieval.

C IX D II (2). Roman building-debris.

C X D Trench A (1). Roman building-debris.

C IX A IV. Drain outlet from Room 2.

7–17.   Claudius II, eleven *antoniniani*. *RIC* 54, 104, 109, as 261 (four), 266, 283, illegible (two)

C IX D I. Room 11: on surface of Period II gravel floor.

C IX D II (4). Modern disturbance.

C X D Trench A (1). Roman building-debris.

C IX A V (15) (two). Room 4: in debris between Period I and II floors.

C IX D I (3). Medieval pit.

C IX D I (6). Room 11: Period II gravel floor make-up.

C IX D III (6) (two). Gravel. Mid fourth century.

C X D Trench A in surface of (2). Dark earth beside Roman wall.

C IX A I (2). Loam outside baths. Late second or early third century.

18–20.   Victorinus, three *antoniniani*. RIC 114, illegible (two)

C IX D I (5). Room 11: in Period II gravel floor.

C IX D I (6). Room 11: Period II gravel floor make-up.

C IX A V Pit 1. Medieval.

---

64.   The coins were identified by C.M. Kraay, R. Reece and B.H. St. J. O'Neil.

21–30.   Tetricus I, ten *antoniniani*. *RIC* 77, 88–91, 90, 100 (two), 102, 111, 130–3, illegible (two)
C IX A V (2). Roman building-debris.
C IX D III. Above hypocaust.
C X C II (11). Room 7: clay filling of hypocaust.
C X D Trench A Pit 1. Medieval.
C IX D II (4). Modern disturbance.
C IX A V Pit 1. Medieval.
C IX D III (6). Gravel. Mid fourth century.
C IX D II (2). Roman building-debris.
C IX A V. Room 2: on Period II hypocausted apse.
C IX D I (5). Room 11: on surface of Period II gravel floor.

31–34.   Tetricus II, four *antoniniani*. *RIC* 234, 254–9, 270–2, 272
C IX A V (8)–(9). Late Roman and medieval earth.
C X C II. Room 7: below cobbles.
C IX A V (15). Room 4: in debris between Period I and II floors.
C IX D I (5). Room II: on surface of Period II gravel floor.

35–36.   Tetricus I or II, two *antoniniani*. Rev. *Spes, Pietas*
C IX D I on (7) sealed by (6). Room 11, beneath Period II gravel floor.
C IX D I (6). Room 11: Period II gravel floor make-up.

37–43.   Carausius, seven *antoniniani*. *RIC* 98, 130, 319, 331, 457, *Pax* (two)
C IX D I (4) (three). Room 11: occupation on Period II gravel floor.
C X D Trench A on surface of (2). Dark earth beside Roman wall.
C IX A V (15). Room 4: in debris between Period I and II floors.
C IX D II (4). Modern disturbance.
C IX D I (6). Room 11: Period II gravel floor make-up.

44–53.   Radiates, ten *antoniniani*. Rev. *Laetitia* (two), *Pax*, illegible (seven)
C IX D II (2). Roman building-debris.
C X D Trench A (1). Roman building-debris.
C IX D I (6) (three). Room 11: Period II gravel floor make-up.
C IX D I (5) (two). Room 11: in Period II gravel floor.
C IX D I. Room 11: on surface of Period II gravel floor.
C IX A IV (1) (two). Drain.

54–61.   Barbarous radiates (eight). All illegible
C X C II. Room 7: below cobbles.
C IX D I (4). Room 11: occupation on Period II gravel floor.
C IX D I (5). Room 11: in Period II gravel floor.
C IX D I (5). Room 11: on surface of Period II gravel floor.
C IX D I (6). (four). Room 11: Period II gravel floor make-up.

62–64. Constantine I (three). Rev. *Gloria exercitus* (three)
C IX A V (two). Room 3: below tiles of cold bath.
C X C II. Room 7: on Period II floor.

65–81. House of Constantine I (seventeen). Rev. *Gloria exercitus* (fourteen), illegible (three)
C X C II (three). Room 7: below cobbles.
C X C II. Room 7: on Period II floor (eleven).
C IX A IV (1). Drain.
C IX A V. Room 3: between tiles of cold bath.
C IX D I (6). Room 11: Period II gravel floor make-up.

82–85. Constantine II (Caesar) (four). Rev. *Gloria exercitus* (four)
C IX A V Pit 1. Medieval.
C X C II. Room 7: below cobbles.
C X C II. Room 7: on Period II floor (two).

86–93. *Urbs Roma* (eight). Mints: Trier, Lyons, illegible (six)
C IX A. Room 3: below cold-bath floor.
C IX A. Room 3: between tiles of cold bath.
C IX A IV (1). Drain (primary).
C X D Trench A Pit 1. Medieval.
C X C II. Room 7: on Period II floor (four).

94–102. *Constantinopolis* (nine). Mints: Trier (two), Lyons, illegible (six)
C IX A V. Room 3: between tiles of cold-bath floor (four).
C IX A V (15). Room 4: in debris between Period I and II floors.
C X C II. Room 7: on Period II floor (three).
C IX D II (2) (hybrid coin). Roman building-debris.

103. Helena. Rev. *Pax Publica*
C X C II. Room 7: on Period II floor.

104–107. Theodora (four). Rev. *Pietas Romana* (four)
C X C II. Room 7: below cobbles.
C X C II. Room 7: on Period II floor (two).
C IX A V. Room 4: over Period II floor.

108–129. Constans (twenty-two). Rev. *Victoriae* (seventeen), *Securitas, Gloria exercitus, Fel. Temp. Rep., Phoenix* (three)
C X C II. Room 7: on Period II floor (twelve).
C X C II. Room 7: below cobbles (four).
C IX A V. Room 3: below cold-bath floor.

C X C II. Room 7: in mortar between tiles of floor.
C IX A IV (1). Drain (primary)
C IX D I (4). Room 11: occupation on Period II gravel floor.
C IX D I (1). Roman building-debris.
C IX A I. Unstratified.

130–140.   Constantius II (eleven). Rev. *Gloria exercitus* (three), *Victoriae* (three), *Fel. Temp. Reparatio* (five).

C IX A. Room 3: on cold-bath floor.
C IX C I. Room 5: blocked hypocaust-flue.
C X C II. Room 7: on Period II floor (seven).
C IX D I (3). Medieval pit.
C IX D I (1). Roman building-debris.

141–175.   Constans or Constantius II (thirty-five). Rev. *Gloria exercitus* (three). *Victoriae* (eight), *Fel. Temp. Reparatio* (twenty-four)

C X C II. Room 7: on Period II floor (nineteen).
C X C II. Room 7: below cobbles (two).
C IX A V. Room 3: between tiles of cold bath (three).
C IX A V Pit 1. Medieval.
C IX D I (1) (four). Roman building-debris.
C X D Trench A (2). Dark earth beside Roman wall.
C IX D I (4) (three). Room 11: occupation on Period II gravel floor.
C IX D II (2) (two). Roman building-debris.

176–242.   Barbarous *Fel. Temp. Reparatio* (fallen horseman) (sixty-seven)

C X C II. Room 7: on Period II floor (fifty-nine, plus three uncertain).
C X C II. Room 7: below cobbles.
C IX A. Room 3: between tiles of cold-bath floor (two).
C X C II (6). On top of mortar layer.
C IX D I (1). Roman building-debris.

243–245.   Magnentius (three). Rev. *Victoriae* (two), illegible

C IX D II (2). Roman building-debris.
C X C II. Room 7: on Period II floor (two).

246.   Valentinian I. Rev. *Gloria Romanorum*

C X C II Pit 3. Medieval.

247.   Valens (barbarous issue)

C X C II. Room 7: on Period II floor.

248. Gratian. Rev. *Gloria Novi Saeculi*
C IX A V (6). Room 3: sticky earth above cold-bath floor.

249. Theodosius I. Rev. illegible
C IX A II Ext. (3). Medieval.

250. Arcadius. Rev. *Salus Reipublicae*
C X C II. Room 7: on Period II floor.

251–297. Illegible (forty-seven)
C IX A V. Room 3: between tiles of cold-bath floor (six).
C IX A V. Room 3: below tiles of cold-bath floor (four).
C X C II. Room 7: below cobbles (one).
C X C II. Room 7: in mortar between tiles of floor (one).
C X C II. Room 7: on Period II floor (twenty-nine).
C IX A IV. In drain (two).
C IX D I (3). Medieval pit (one).
C X C II Pit 1. Medieval (one).
C IX D I (1). Roman building-debris (two).

298–308. Fragments. Illegible (eleven)
C X C II. Room 7: on Period II floor (eleven).

309–343. *Minimi* (thirty-five)
C X C II. Room 7: on Period II floor (thirty-three).
C IX A V. Room 3: below tiles of cold-bath floor (one).
C IX A V Pit 1. Medieval (one).

344–403. *Minimissimi* (sixty)
C X C II. Room 7: on Period II floor (sixty).

Room 3: Hoard of seven coins found beneath Period II cold-bath floor
Constantine II. Rev. *Gloria exercitus.*
Constantine I or II. Rev. *Gloria exercitus.*
Urbs Roma. Mint: Lyons.
Constans (two). Rev. *Victoriae, Fel. Temp. Reparatio.*
Constantius II. Rev. *Victoriae.*
Barbarous *Fel. Temp. Reparatio.*

II. COINS FROM THE APSED BUILDING[65]

1.   Titus (under Vespasian), *dupondius*. *RIC* Vespasian 777b
        C XV S I (3). Pit pre-dating apsed building. Late second or third century.

2.   Trajan, As. Rev. illegible
        C XV V I (7). Loam above natural. A.D. 140–200.

3.   Claudius II, *antoninianus*. *RIC* 14/15
        C XV S II (12). Destruction-layer of apsed building. Fourth century.

4.   Tetricus I, *antoninianus*. *RIC* 140
        C XV S II unstratified, or Pit 7. Late Roman.

5–6.   Tetricus II, two *antoniniani*. *RIC* 272; illegible
        C XV S II (12). Destruction-layer of apsed building. Fourth century.
        C XV S II (6). Medieval.

7–11.   Radiates. Rev. *Spes* (one); illegible (four)
        C XV V (1). ? Saxon.
        C XV S II (1). Medieval.
        C XV S II Pit 7 (two). Late Roman.
        C XV T II Pit 2. Medieval.

12–13. Barbarous radiates (two). Rev. Illegible
        C XV S II (6). Medieval.
        C XV V (1). ? Saxon.

14.   Constantius II. *CHK* i, 94
        C XV T I (5). Saxon.

15.   Gratian. *RIC* ix, p. 66. No. 15
        C XV V I (4). Pit. Fourth century.

16.   House of Theodosius I. *CHK* ii, as 565
        C XV S II (3). Late Roman dark earth.

17–29. Unidentifiable.

---

65. The coins were identified by R. Reece and B.H. St. J. O'Neil.

III. COINS FROM MINOR EXCAVATIONS ALONG ST. GEORGE'S STREET[66]

1.   Valerian, *antoninianus*. *RIC* 70
        C XIV P I (8). Late Roman black soil.

2.   Radiate. Rev. illegible
        C XI P I Pit 3. Fourth century.

3.   Constans. *CHK* i, as 102
        C XI O I Pit 5. Fourth century.

4–5.   House of Constantine (two). *CHK* i, as 48
        C IX B II (2). Pit. Seventeenth or eighteenth century.
        C XIX Z I (2). Medieval.

6.   *Urbs Roma*. Rev. illegible
        C X K I Pit 2. First century (coin intrusive).

7.   *Constantinopolis*. Rev. illegible
        C XI P I (2). Pit. Fourth century.

8.   House of Valentinian I. Rev. illegible
        C XI P I Pit 3. Fourth century.

9.   Philip IV of France (1285–1314), double parisis
        C XIV Q I (11). Occupation-material. Early fourteenth-century.

10.   Cambrai: Bishop Gui de Collemède (1296–1306). *Chautard, 'Type Esterlin'*, pl.
        XVII, 8.
        C XIV Q I (4). Mortary gravel on chalk floor (5). Fourteenth century or later.

11.   French reckoning counter. Fifteenth-century. Probably imitated from the silver
        coins of Charles VI and VII
        C XIX Z II Pit 3. Eighteenth century.

12.   Charles I, copper farthing token. Lord Maltravers' issue *c.* 1635–40
        C XIX Z II Pit 1. Eighteenth century.

---

66. The coins were identified by C.M. Kraay, R. Reece and B.H. St. J. O'Neil.

13.   James I or Charles I, copper farthing token
       C XIX Z II Pit 2. Eighteenth century.

14.   German jetton
       C IX B II (1). Eighteenth-century earth.

15–21.   Unidentifiable.

IV. COINS FROM AREA R[67]

1.   First-century *As* (Vespasian or Domitian). Rev. illegible
      C XV R IV B (13). Primary metalling of east–west street; early to mid second century.

2.   Antoninus Pius, *dupondius*. Rev. illegible
      C XV R I Ext. II Pit 1. Late Roman or medieval.

3.   Faustina I, *As*. *RIC* (Antoninus Pius) 1162a
      C XV R I (7). Medieval.

4.   Gallienus, *antoninianus*. *RIC* 639
      C X M Pit 1. Late third of fourth century.

5–6.   Postumus, two *antoniniani*. *RIC* 318, 1871
        C XV R II (6). Medieval.
        C XV R IV (4). Dark soil above north—south street.

7–8.   Claudius II, two *antoniniani*. *RIC* 54, illegible
        C XV R IV (4) (two). Dark soil above north—south street.

9.   Victorinus, *antoninianus*. *RIC* 78
      C XV R III (17). Surface 9 of north—south street.

10–11.   Tetricus I, two *antoniniani*. *RIC* 128, rev. illegible
          C XV R IV (4). Dark soil above north—south street.
          C X M (1). Medieval.

67.   The coins were identified by C.M. Kraay, R. Reece and B.H. St. J. O'Neil.

12–14.   Tetricus II, three *antoniniani*. *RIC* 247 or 248, 270, 272–4
           C XV R III (1). Medieval.
           C XV R I Ext. II Pit 1. Late Roman or medieval.
           C XV R III (19). Surface 8 of north—south street.

15.   Probus, *antoninianus*. *RIC* 112
           C XV R I Pit 11. Medieval.

16–17.   Carausius, two *antoniniani*. *RIC* 55, 101
           C XV R IV Pit 13. Fourth century.
           C XV R I Pit 7. Medieval.

18.   Allectus, *quinarius*. *RIC* 128
           C XV R IV Pit 2. Medieval.

19–23.   Radiates (five). Rev. illegible (five)
           C XV R I (25). Medieval.
           C XV R II (6). Medieval.
           C XV R IV Pit 1. Medieval.
           C XV R IV Pit 13. Fourth century.
           C XV R IV B (7). Floor of late Roman building.

24–25.   Barbarous radiates (two). Rev. illegible (two)
           C XV R III Pit 1. Medieval.
           C XV R IV Pit 13. Fourth century.

26–27.   Third century (two). Illegible
           C XV R IV B (2). Dark soil above late Roman building.
           C XV R V Ext. 2 Pit 3. Fourth century.

28.   House of Constantine. Rev. illegible
           C XV R I Pit 9. Medieval.

29.   Constantius II. *CHK* ii, as 2039
           C X M (1). Medieval.

30.   Constantius II or Constans. Rev. illegible
           C XV R II (6). Medieval.

31.   Barbarous *Fel. Temp. Reparatio*
           C XV R IV (1). Medieval.

32–33.   House of Valentinian (two). *CHK* ii, as 78, as 80
C XV R IV B (3) (two). Destruction of late Roman building.

34–35.   Theodosius I (two). *CHK* ii, as 163 (two)
C XV R IV (1). Medieval.
C XV R IV B (2). Dark earth above late Roman building.

36–37.   Arcadius (two). Rev. illegible (two)
C XV R IV. Timber slot of mid fifth-century building.
C XV R IV B (2). Dark earth above late Roman building.

38–43.   Third or fourth century (six). Illegible.
C XV R I Pit 7. Medieval.
C XV R II Pit 1. Medieval.
C XV R III (1). Medieval.
C XV R III Pit 1. Medieval.
C XV R IV (4). Dark soil above north–south street.
C XV R IV Pit 1. Medieval.

44   Edward I (1272–1307), penny. Canterbury mint
C XV R IV (2). Fourteenth-century loam.

45   Medieval fragments
C XV R I (25). Medieval.

Unidentifiable (fourteen).

V A. COINS FROM CANTERBURY LANE (C XX — C XXIV SITE C)[68]

1.   Vespasian, *As*. *RIC* 502
C XXII C I (9c). Dark earth below late Roman cobbles.

2.   Titus or Domitian, *As*. Rev. *Spes*
C XXII C I (9c). Dark earth below late Roman cobbles.

3.   Domitian, *sestertius*. Rev. illegible
C XXI CI (10). Fourth-century pit (R 5).

68.   The coins were identified by C.M. Kraay, R. Reece and B.H. St. J. O'Neil.

4. Hadrian, *As*. *RIC* 811
    C XXII C III (7). Loam below Period III building.

5. Faustina I, *sestertius*. *RIC* (Antoninus Pius) 1143
    C XXIII C V A Pit 2. Late Roman (R 14).

6–7. Faustina II, two *Asses*. *RIC* (Marcus Aurelius) 1636, illegible
    C XXIII C V D Pit 5. Medieval.
    C XXI C I (10). Fourth-century pit.

8–9. Second century, two *Asses*. Illegible
    C XXII C I (9). Late Roman black soil.
    C XXII CI (23). Occupation on *opus signinum* floor of Period II building.

10. Septimius Severus, *denarius*. *RIC* 516
    C XXII CI on surface of (22). Late Roman cobbles.

11. Gallienus, *antoninianus*. Rev. illegible
    C XXII C I Pit B. Fourth century (R 4).

12. Postumus, *antoninianus*. *RIC* 389
    C XXIII C V B (9). On Saxon floor.

13–15. Claudius II, three *antoniniani*. *RIC* 44, illegible (two)
    C XX C I (9A). Late Roman black soil.
    C XXII CI Pit B. Fourth century (R 4).
    C XX C I (8). On Saxon floor.

16–18. Claudius II (posthumous), three *antoniniani*. *RIC* 261 (two), illegible
    C XXII C I (9). Late Roman black soil.
    C XXII C I Pit C. Fourth century (R 3).
    C XXII C I (8D). In Saxon floor.

19–32. Tetricus I, fourteen *antoniniani*. *RIC* 87, 100 (two), 130 (three), 140, illegible (seven)
    C XX C I (9A). Late Roman black soil.
    C XX C I (8). In Saxon floor.
    C XXII C IV Pit 1. Medieval.
    C XXII C I Pit C. Fourth century (R 3).
    C XX C I unstratified.
    C XXII C II Pit 6. Late Roman.
    C XXII C I (9). Late Roman black soil.
    C XX C I (7). Medieval.

C XX C I (8) (two). Saxon occupation-material.
C XXII C I (8D) (two). In Saxon floor.
C XX C I (9). Late Roman black soil.
C XXII C I (20). Destruction layer of Period III building.

33–35. Tetricus II, three *antoniniani*. *RIC* 270, 272, barbarous *Pax*
C XX C I. In Saxon floor.
C XV N I (3). Saxon floor.
C XX C I (9A). Late Roman black soil.

36–40. Carausius, five *antoniniani*. *RIC* 121, 149, as 895, 898, illegible
C XX C I (8A). Saxon.
C XXII C I Pit C. Fourth century (R 3).
C XX II C I (9) (two). Late Roman black soil.
C XXII C I (8D). In Saxon floor.

41–50. Radiates (ten). Rev. *pax, Laetitia,* illegible (eight)
C XXII C II (27). Late Roman black soil.
C XXII C II. On Saxon floor.
C XXII C I (21). Period III loam floor.
C XXII C I (8). Saxon occupation-material.
C XXII C I (8D) (two). In Saxon floor.
C XXII C I (9) (two). Late Roman black soil.
C XXII C IV (4). Medieval.
C XV N I (4). Occupation between two Saxon floors.

51–55. Barbarous radiates (five). Rev. illegible
C XXII C I Pit C. Fourth century (R 3).
C XXII C I (9). Late Roman black soil.
C XXII C III (4). Medieval.
C XXIII C V A (6). Occupation between two Saxon floors.
C XV N I (3). Saxon floor.

56. Maximianus Herculius. Rev. *Genio Populi Romani*
C XXI C I (8D). In Saxon floor.

57. Constantius I. Rev. *Genio Populi Romani*
C XXII C I (9). Late Roman black soil.

58–60. Theodora (three). Rev. *Pietas, Pax* (two)
C XXII C I Pit A. Late Roman (R 2).
C XXII C I (8D). In Saxon floor.
C XXII C III Pit 4. Roman.

61–69.   Constantine I (nine). Rev. *Marti Conserv., Soli Invicto, Sarmatia Devicta, Victoriae* (three), *Virtus Exercit.* (two) *Gloria Exercitus*
C XXII C I (8D) (two). In Saxon floor.
C XXII C I (9) (six). Late Roman black soil.
C XXII C I (20). Destruction-layer of Period III building.

70–77.   *Constantinopolis* (eight). *CHK* i, 52, 59, 66, as 52 (four), 746
C XXIII C V D (4). Medieval.
C XXIII C IV (16). Late Roman black soil.
C XXII C I (8D). In Saxon floor.
C XXIII C V B (9) (two). Saxon floor.
C XX C I (9A). Late Roman black soil.
C XXII C I (8D). In Saxon floor.
C XXIII C V B (9). Saxon floor.

78–80.   *Urbs Roma* (three). *CHK* i, as 51
C XXII C I (8D). In Saxon floor.
C XXII C I (20). Destruction-layer of Period III building.
C XXIII C V D Pit 3. Medieval (M 9).

81.   Constans. *CHK* i, as 75
C XXII C I Pit A. Late Roman (R 2).

82.   Constantius II. *CHK* i, 89
C XXII C I Pit A. Late Roman (R 2).

83–93.   House of Constantine (eleven). *CHK* i, as 53 (two), as 87 (six), as 137 (three)
C XXIII C V A (4A). Saxon occupation-material.
C XX C I (9) (four). Late Roman black soil.
C XX C I (two). In Saxon floor.
C XXII C I Pit A. Late Roman (R 2).
C XXII C I Pit B. Fouth century (R 4).
C XXII C I Pit C. Fouth century (R 3).
C XXII C II Pit 6. Late Roman.

94–99.   Barbarous *Fel. Temp. Reparatio.* (fallen horseman type) (six)
C XX C I (8). On floor.
C XXII C I (8D). In Saxon floor.
C XX C I (9). Late Roman black soil.
C XXII C I (9A) (three). Late Roman black soil.

100–101   Magnentius (two). *CHK* ii, 56, as 56

C XXII C IV (18). Late Roman.

C XXII CI (9). Late Roman black soil.

102–104   Valentinian I (three). *RIC* ix, p. 66, 17a, Rev. *Gloria Romanorum, Securitas Reipublicae*

C XXII C I (9). Late Roman black soil.

C XXII C I (9A). Late Roman black soil.

C XXIII C V A (4A). Saxon occupation-material.

105–108   Valens (four). *RIC* ix, p. 64, no. 9b, p. 147, no. 15b, Rev. *Securitas Reipublicae, Gloria Romanorum*

C XXII C I (9). Late Roman black soil.

C XXII C I (8). Saxon occupation-material.

C XX C I. In Saxon floor.

C XX C I (10). Fourth-century pit (R 5), probably pre-dating Period III building.

109.   House of Valentinian. Rev. *Gloria Romanorum*

C XXII C I (9A). Late Roman black soil.

110–111.   Theodosius I (two). *RIC* ix, p. 102, 37b, Rev. *Victoria Auggg*

C XX C I (9). Late Roman black soil.

C XX C I. In Saxon floor.

112–117.   Arcadius (six). Rev. *Victoria Augg* (six)

C XXII C I unstratified.

C XXII C I (9) (two). Late Roman black soil.

C XXII C II (27). Late Roman black soil.

C XXII C II Pit 4. Medieval.

C XV N I (5). Saxon floor.

118–135.   House of Theodosius (eighteen). Rev. *Victoria Auggg* (fifteen), *Salus reipublicae* (three)

C XX C I. In Saxon floor.

C XX C I (8D). In Saxon floor.

C XX C I (9) (six). Late Roman black soil.

C XX C I (9A) (five). Late Roman black soil.

C XXII C I (20). Destruction-layer of Period III building.

C XXII C II (27) (two). Late Roman black soil.

C XXIII C V A (5). Saxon floor.

C XXIII C V A (7). Late Roman black soil.

136–138.   Minims (three). Rev. illegible

C XXII C I (8D). In Saxon floor.

C XXII C I (9). Late Roman black soil.
C XXII C II Pit 6. Fourth century.

139. Edward III (1327–77) worn silver penny
      C XXII C II Ext. Eighteenth-century pit.

140. Charles VI (1380–1422) or VII (1422–61) of France. Base silver gros, possibly
      contemporary forgery
      C XXII C II unstratified.

141. Nuremberg counter. Georg Schultes (1553)
      C XXII C IV. In slot of cellar wall.

142. Nuremberg counter. Hans Krauwinckel (*c.* 1580–1610)
      C XXII C II Pit 1.

143. Flemish or German counter. Sixteenth or seventeenth century.
      C XXII C IV. Slot of cellar wall.

144. Trade token (1658). Hythe, Kent. *Williamson* i, p. 372, No. 356
      C XXII C II unstratified.

145. Charles II (1674) copper farthing
      C XXII C II Pit 1.

146. George II (1727–60) half penny
      C XXIII C V unstratified.

147–211. Illegible (sixty-five).

V B. COINS FROM CANTERBURY LANE (C XXVIII SITES C XX AND C XXI)

1–2. Tetricus I, *antoniniani*. Rev. illegible (two)
      C XXVIII C XX Pit 13 (probably intrusive).
      C XXVIII C XXI (25). Medieval.

3.   Carausius, *antoninianus*. Rev. illegible
      C XXVIII C XX (33a). Saxon black soil.

4–7.   Barbarous radiates (four). Rev. *Fortuna, Invictus,* illegible (two)
C XXVIII C XX (33). Saxon black soil.
C XXVIII C XX Pit 12. Saxon.
C XXVIII C XXI (29). Medieval.
C XXVIII C XXI (25). Medieval.

8–9.   *Urbs Roma.* (two). *CHK* i, as 51, 65
C XXVIII C XX (13). Medieval.
C XXVIII C XXI (16). Medieval.

10.   Constantius II. *CHK* ii, as 25
C XXVIII C XXI Pit 1. Medieval.

11.   Edward I (1272–1307). Penny.
C XXVIII C XX Pit 3B. Late thirteenth to fourteenth century.

12.   Thirteenth-century silver half-penny
C XXVIII C XX (28). Brown soil in bottom of late fifteenth- or sixteenth-century cess-pit.

13.   Fourteenth-century English counter
C XXVIII C XXI (5). Fourteenth-century gravel floor.

14.   Fifteenth-century German counter
C XXVIII C XX (5). Make-up for sixteenth-century building.

15.   Francis I of France (1515–47). Base metal denier tournois *Ciani* 1187
C XXVIII C XX Pit 2. Seventeenth century.

16–17.   Henry III of France (1574–89) (two). Double tournois *Ciani* 1463, 1465
C XXVIII C XX Pit 2 (two). Seventeenth century.

18–25.   Unidentifiable (eight).

VI. COINS FROM AREA Y AND SITES ALONG BURGATE STREET.[69]

69.   The coins were identified by C.M. Kraay, R. Reece and B.H. St. J. O'Neil.

1. Vespasian, *sestertius*. Rev. illegible
   C XIV M III (6) on surface of (7). Occupation-material above late second-century floor.

2. First century, *As* (pierced). Rev. illegible
   C XVII Y V Pit 1. Medieval.

3–4. Trajan, two *sestertii*. Rev. illegible (two)
   C XVI Y I (24). Medieval.
   C XIV M II (10). Occupation-material above late second-century floor.

5. Trajan, *dupondius*. Rev. illegible
   C X L I (12). Hearth contemporary with Period 3 floor (13).

6. Hadrian, *sestertius*. Rev. illegible
   C XIV M III (12). Ash below hearth.

7. Sabina, *sestertius*. *RIC* (Hadrian) 1032
   C XIV M III in Post-hole 2. Cut into floor (5). Late third century.

8. Antoninus Pius, *sestertius*. Rev. illegible
   C XIV M I (19). Roman building-debris.

9–10. Antoninus Pius, two *Asses*. Rev. illegible (two)
   C XIV M II (12). Occupation-material. Second half of second century.
   C XIV M III (10). Ash above hearth. Late second century.

11. Mid second-century *sestertius*. Rev. illegible
    C XIV M II (6). Occupation-material above late second-century floor.

12. Faustina I, *sestertius*. Rev. illegible
    C XIV M III (8). Charcoal deposit. Fourth century.

13–15. Faustina II, three *sestertii*. *RIC* (Antoninus Pius) 1383. Rev. illegible (two)
   C XVI Y I (31A). Medieval.
   C XVI Y I (19). Medieval pit.
   C XVI Y I (24). Medieval.

16. Lucilla, *denarius*. *RIC* (Marcus Aurelius) 786
    C XIV M III (10). Ash above hearth. Late second century.

17.   Commodus, *As*. Rev. illegible
           C XVII Y III Part 3 (3) (= 23). Medieval.

18.   Trajan Decius, *antoninianus*. Rev. *Salus Aug*
           C XVI Y I (19). Medieval pit.

19.   Herennius Etruscus, *antoninianus*. Rev. *Pietas Augg*
           C X L (1). Late Roman occupation-material.

20–22.   Claudius II, three *antoniniani*. *RIC* 34–38. Rev illegible (two)
           C XIV M III (8) (two). Charcoal deposit. Fourth century.
           C XIV M III (4). Occupation-material above late third-century floor.

23–25.   Victorinus, three antoniniani. *RIC* 61. Rev. illegible (two)
           C X L (1). Late Roman occupation-material.
           C XIV M II (10). Occupation-material above late second-century floor.
           C XIV M III (8). Charcoal deposit. Fourth century.

26–27.   Tetricus I, two *antoniniani*. Rev. *Fides*, illegible
           C XVII Y III Part 3 (6). Destruction-layer of Roman building over lane.
           C XIV N (3). Late third-century pit.

28–29.   Tetricus I or II, two *antoniniani*. Rev. *Spes* (two)
           C XVII Y II Part 3 Pit 4 (= Pit 16). Medieval.
           C XVII Y III Part 3 (6). Destruction-layer of Roman building over lane.

30–31.   Tetricus II, two *antoniniani*. *RIC* 70, 254–8
           C XIV M I (22). Ash above third- or fourth-century floor.
           C XIV M III (8). Charcoal deposit. Fourth century.

32.   Aurelian, *antoninianus*. Rev. *Fortuna*
           C XIV N I (1). Medieval.

33–36.   Carausius, four *antoniniani*. *RIC* 141, 895, Rev. illegible (two)
           C XIV M I (19). Roman building-debris.
           C XIV M IB on (9). Medieval floor.
           C XVII Y II Part 1 (10). Destruction-layer of Roman building east of lane.
           C X L II (1). Late Roman black soil.

37.   Allectus, *quinarius*. *RIC* 124
           C XIV M I on (18). Medieval floor.

38–45.   Radiates (eight). Rev. *Pax, Spes,* illegible (six)

C XIV M I (19). Roman building-debris.
C XIV M III (8) (two). Charcoal deposit. Fourth century.
C XIV M III (1). Late Roman occupation-material.
C XIV N (4). Late third-century pit.
C X L II Pit 1 (three). Late Roman.

46–48. Barbarous radiates (three). Rev. illegible (three)
C XIV M I (22). Ash above third- or fourth-century floor.
C X L II (1). Late Roman black soil.
C XIV N (3). Late third-century pit.

49. Constantine II. Rev. *Beata Tranquillitas*
C XVII Y III Part 2 (17). Medieval.

50. Constantine II. *CHK* i, 56
C XVII Y III Part 3 (3). Medieval.

51. House of Constantine. *CHK* i, as 87
C XVII Y III part 4 (18). Black soil over *opus signinum* floor of building over lane.

52–53. *Urbs Roma* (two). *CHK* i, 205, Rev. illegible
C XVII Y III Part 3 Pit 4. Late Roman.
C XVII Y II Part 1 (10). Destruction-layer of Roman building east of lane.

54. *Constantinopolis*. *CHK* i, 185
C XVII Y II Part 3 Pit 3 (= Pit 17). Medieval.

55–57. Constans (three). *CHK* ii, 35, as 41, as 197
C X L (1) (three). Late Roman occupation-material.

58–61. Barbarous *Fel. Temp. Reparatio* (four). Fallen horseman type
C XVI Y I (19). Medieval pit.
C XVII Y III Part 3 (4). Medieval.
C X L I (1) (two). Late Roman occupation-material.

62. Valentinian I. *RIC* 24a
C XVI Y I (23). Medieval.

63–66. Valens (four). *RIC* 9b, 16b, Rev. illegible (two)
C XVI Y I (16). Late Roman dark earth.
C XVII Y III Part 3 (5). Pit. Late Roman.
C XVII Y III Part 3 (6). Destruction-layer of Roman building over lane.
C XIV M Pit 1. Medieval.

67–68.   Gratian (two). *RIC* 15, *CHK* ii, as 335
C XVI Y I (16). Late Roman dark earth.
C X L I (1). Late Roman occupation-material.

69—70.   House of Theodosius (two). Rev. *Victoria Auggg*, illegible
C XVII Y II Part 1 (10) (two). Destruction-layer of Roman building east of lane.

71.   Arcadius. Rev. illegible
C XIV N (5). Roman building-debris.

72–74.   Third or fourth century (three), illegible
C XIV M I (19). Roman building-debris.
C XIV M I (22) (two). Ash above third- or fourth-century floor.

75–76.   Fourth century (two), illegible
C XIV M III (8C). Charcoal deposit. Fourth century.
C X L II Pit 1. Late Roman.

77.   Henry II or III. Silver penny. 'Short-cross'
C XVI Y I (20). Medieval pit.

78.   Gui de Danipierre, Count of Flanders (1263–97). Silver sterling imitating penny of Edward I. *Chautard*, p. 5, no. 1
C XVII Y II Part 2 (4). Medieval.

79.   Anglo-Gallic Jetton of Edward I (1272–1307). Probably made in France
C XVII Y III Part 2 (18). Destruction-layer of Roman building over lane (intrusive).

80.   York penny. ? Edward III (1327–77)
C XVII Y III Part 4 (12). Medieval.

81.   Jetton. Fifteenth-century; roughly imitating a French plaque or blanc, perhaps of Franco-Flemish origin
C XIV M I (6). Occupation-layer below Period 2 floor in Room 3.

82–83.   Elizabeth I (two) sixpences.
C XVII Y IV (3) (two). Post-medieval.

84–85.   Nuremberg counters (two) *c.* 1580–1600.
C XVII Y III Part 1. Unstratified.
C XVII Y III Part 4 (2). Post-medieval.

86–119.   Unidentified (thirty-four).

VII. COINS FROM C XV SITE X: BUS STATION SITE

1. Commodus, *sestertius*. Rev. illegible
    C XV X I (21). Sixth- or seventh-century layer.

2. Postumus, *antoninianus*. *RIC* 331
    C XV X III (18). Pit cut through Roman levels.

3. Victorinus, *antoninianus*. *RIC* 71
    C XV X III (18). Pit cut through Roman levels.

4–6. Tetricus I, three *antoniniani*. *RIC* 86, 87, illegible
    C XV X I Pit 6 (two). Sixth century.
    C XV X III (11). Late Roman dark earth.

7. Radiate. Rev. illegible
    C XV X III (18). Pit cut through Roman levels.

8. Constantine II (Caesar). Rev. *Gloria Exercitus*
    C XV X I Pit 8. Medieval.

9. Constans. Rev. *Fel. Temp. Reparatio*
    C XV X I Pit 6. Sixth century.

10. Valentinian II. *RIC* IX p. 133, No. 64a
    C XV X I (23). Fouth-century brown earth.

11. Henry II (1154–89). Short-cross penny (*c.* 1180–89)
    C XV X V (1). Occupation layer, twelfth century.

12. ?Edward I (1272–1307). Halfpenny
    C XV X III (8). Make-up for late thirteenth-century floor.

13–20. Unidentifiable.

B. THE SMALL OBJECTS
By Sally Stow

A. OBJECTS OF BRONZE

(a) THE BROOCHES (Fig. 61)

1. One-piece brooch. The straight bow, circular in section, is sharply angled from the spring. C XXVIII C XX Pit 15 (p. 102). *c.* A.D. 300–350.

2. Annular brooch or buckle with seating for loop of pin. C XIV Q I (10). Fifteenth-century destruction debris (p. 59).

3. Unusual disc brooch[70] made of a single sheet of bronze decorated with a central boss and four surrounding bosses, all filled with glass pastes. In between the bosses are pellets formed by punching (repoussé); the whole brooch is surrounded by a zone of plain beading. The design and repoussé technique indicate that the brooch is Frankish and of early sixth-century date. It is possibly an import, but perhaps more likely was made locally. The closest parallels[71] in Britain are from Howletts Grave 26, Long Wittenham Grave 108 and St. Peter's Street, Northampton (*Northampton*, Pl. 47, pp. 248 ff.). C X D Trench A. Medieval earth above Roman wall (p. 27).

4. Ansate brooch[72] of the eighth century. The bow, the underside of which is hollow, is curved longitudinally. The central part is plain, but at each end is a not-quite circular flat plate decorated with grooves forming a cross set within two diamond-shapes. The grooves are open and X-ray examination indicated that they never had a filling of niello or like substance. Beneath one plate are two pierced lugs between which a pivot was fixed for mounting the head of the pin which was of iron, the tension being provided not by a spring but by the thickness of the clothing held between brooch and pin. Beneath the other plate is the catch-plate; both this and the lugs were cast in one piece with the bow.

---

70. Dr. Rupert Bruce-Mitford examined this brooch and provided the first two parallels quoted.
71. But these are all composite brooches.
72. Thanks are due to the late Gerald Dunning for examining this brooch.
73. *Berichten van de Rijksdienst voor het Oudheidkundig Bodemonderzoek,* v (1954), 65–9, Pls. XV-XVII..

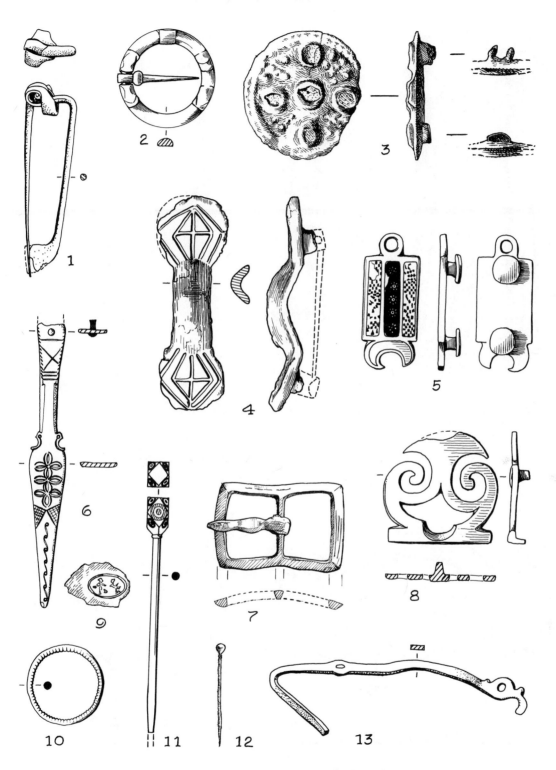

Fig.   61.   Objects of Bronze. Scale 1 : 1

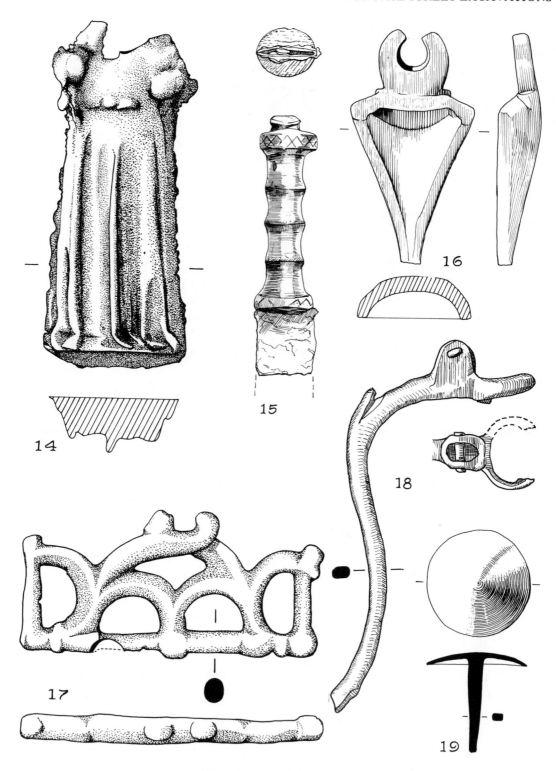

Fig. 62. Objects of Bronze. Scale 1 : 1

This type of brooch is very rare in England, the closest parallel being an example with ring and dot pattern from Totternhoe, Beds. (*Dunstable Museum Report*, 1925–26, p. 7, fig. 9). They are common in the Low Countries[73] and in Northern France and this brooch is probably an import. C XX C I (5). Medieval loam floor above late Saxon deposit (p. 94).

(b) OTHER OBJECTS OF BRONZE (Figs. 61–62)

5. Belt- or apron-mount decorated with three enamelled strips; the central one is blue with red and yellow flowers, and the outside ones are mottled yellow and black. One end is crescent-shaped, the other contains a central perforation. There are two studs on the underside for attachment. For a similar example cf. *O.R.L.* 32, *Zugmantel*, Pl. X, No. 48. C XIV M III (4). Occupation-layer (p. 117). *c.* A.D. 280–320.

6. Strap-end decorated with floral and linear motifs. There is a small stud at the top for attachment. C XV R IV (4). Dark soil above north—south street (p. 70). A.D. 420–460.

7. Rectangular buckle. C XXVIII C XX (3). Early seventeenth-century chalky soil (p. 103).

8. Pelta-shaped strap-mount. Flat ridge along bottom and one central stud for attachment. Cf. *O.R.L.* 32, *Zugmantel*, pl. XII, No. 8. C XV R. In rubbish pit beneath Woolworth's (p. 74).

9. Intaglio set in a bronze ring of late second-century type.[74] Dimensions: Ring *c.* 23 mm. in external diameter. Intaglio, oval 12 mm. by 8 mm. C XVII Y IV (8). Medieval black earth (p. 124).

   Dr. Martin Henig writes: 'The subject is a cupid holding (?) a bunch of grapes and about to spring away towards the left. He is being watched by a cock which stands beside him (and is shown to the same scale). There can be little doubt that he is mischievously taunting the bird, and indeed this theme of Cupid playing with pet birds and animals is frequently found on intaglios.[75] There are close parallels to this gem from Aquileia (although Cupid was mistaken for Pan in the publication)[76] and a gem found at Jagsthausen but now lost depicts a standing Cupid confronting a cock.[77] A jasper intaglio said to depict 'a cock chasing Cupid' and thus presumably resembling the type of the Canterbury gem has been found in Leicester[78] but cannot now be located. Cocks were clearly considered to be auspicious birds and are often shown by themselves on gems. Thus two cornelians (from Chesters fort and Slayhill Saltings near Upchurch, Kent)

---

74. F. Henkel. *Die römischen Fingerringe der Rheinlande* (Berlin 1913), Nos. 1196–7 and 1206–9.

75. Cupid is shown with a goose on a garnet from Colchester, and playing with a hare on a green jasper in the Bath cache.

76. G. Sena Chiesa, *Gemme del Museo Nazionale di Aquileia* (Aquileia 1966), Nos. 429–430.

77. Henkel, *op. cit.* (note 74), No. 2162; cf. also A. Furtwangler, *Beschreibung der Geschnittenen Steine* (Berlin 1896), No. 6787, and, with another bird, 6788; with two cocks cockfighting, Nos. 6789 ff.

78. Leicester City Museum 279. 1961.

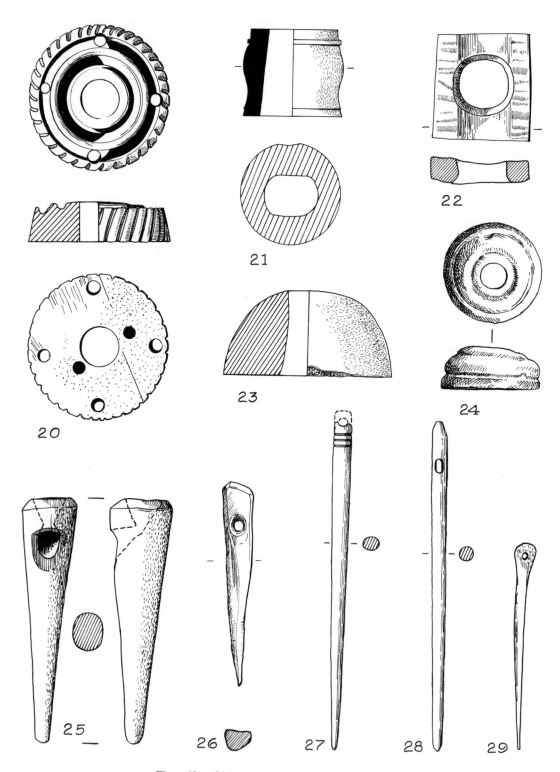

Fig. 63. Objects of Bone. Scale 1 : 1

represent a cock together with ears of wheat,[79] and a cock is depicted with a cornucopia on an onyx from Silchester.[80] A jasper from Binchester shows a cock confronting a snake and must refer to the warding off of evil powers.[81] Cupids are also common on gems, and were again believed to bring good luck.'[82]

10. Finger-ring with grooved decoration on inside edge. C X J I (1). Dark earth (p. 53). A.D. 270–350.

11. Pin with faceted head decorated with concentric circles which probably contained red and yellow enamelling. C XIV Q I (31). Pre-fourteenth-century occupation-layer (p. 58).

12. Small spherical-headed pin. C XI N II Pit 2. Saxon (p. 66).

13. Thin strip, rectangular in section, with two perforations and one end hooked, the other broken. Possibly part of a small handle. C XV R V Pit 1. Medieval (p. 74).

14. Part of a statuette of a draped female, cast in an open mould. The head and neck are missing and the arms short and stumpy. The back is flat suggesting that perhaps the figure was attached to the side of a shrine. The rather crude finish may indicate local manufacture. C XV R IV Pit 8. Medieval (p. 74).

15. Tubular knife-handle with four finger-grips. There is a small squarish knob at the top and below this a moulding decorated with zig-zags; a similar moulding at the bottom. Part of the iron knife remains. C XV S II (24). Loam floor (p. 43). A.D. 190–220.

16. Attachment for bucket-handle. Cf. *O.R.L.* 32, *Zugmantel*, Pl. XIII, No. 14. Caudebec des Elbeuf, *O.R.L.* 32, p. 93, fig. 13. *Richborough* iii, Pl. XIV, No. 52. C X L II Pit 1. Late Roman (p. 113).

17. Open-work fitting. C XV R I Pit 8. Medieval (p. 74).

18. Jug-handle with attachment for lid. Cf. *Richborough* iii, Pl. XIV, No. 49. C XIV M III (4). Occupation-layer (p. 117). *c.* A.D. 280–320.

19. Stud with large flattish head and rectangular-sectioned shank. C XIV Q I (41). (?) Roman pit (p. 58).

B. OBJECTS OF BONE (Figs. 63–65)

20. Decorated circular fitting with central perforation, probably a gaming piece. The upper surface is decorated with incised circles and cut through the outermost circle are four not-quite symmetrically-placed small holes. The outside edge is notched. The base is flat

79. *Arch. Ael.*[1], iii (1844), 144–5, fig. 3 (Chesters) and F.H. Marshall *Catalogue of Finger Rings* (1907), No. 1165 = H.B. Walters, *Catalogue of Engraved Gems* (1926), No. 2473 (Slayhill).
80. Gough's Camden i (1806), 205.
81. *Arch. Ael.*[4], xxxix (1961), 34, No. 42 and Pl. 6 No. 12.
82. On Cupid cf. G.M.A. Richter, *Metropolitan Museum. Catalogue of Engraved Gems* (Rome 1956), 74–75. There were six Cupids in the Bath cache.

and cut into it are two small holes which do not penetrate the whole thickness of the object; these were possibly for fastening it to the lathe. C X M I (12). Layer of ash sealing pit (p. 78). *c.* A.D. 130–150.

21. Turned cylinder with ridge at each end. Possibly a hinge-spacer (cf. *Verulamium* i, fig. 54, No. 192) or a toggle. C X L I (8). Street-silt (p. 111). Late second to third century.

22. Rectangular plaque with wide central groove containing perforation. C X C II (5). Medieval pit (p. 27).

23. Plain spindle-whorl made from femoral head. C XXVIII C XX (17). Oven (p. 104). (?) Fourteenth century.

24. Spindle-whorl decorated with concentric circles. C XV X II (4). Brown earth (p. 139). Sixteenth century.

25. (?) Peg, perforated through top and one side. C XIV M III (10). Ash above hearth (p. 117). Late second century.

26. Small bodkin with circular eye. C XXVIII C XX (28). Fifteenth-century brown soil in cess-pit (p. 104).

27. Needle with three incised grooves below almost circular eye. C XIV M II (13). Pre-third-century occupation earth (p. 116).

28. Needle, stained green, with oblong eye. C X M I (8). Floor (p. 79). A.D. 180–230.

29. Small needle or bodkin with rounded head and circular eye. C XXIII C I (8). On Saxon floor (p. 88).

30. Tapering rod with two collared grooves at each end; one end shows much greater signs of wear than the other. Probably a spindle. C XVI Y I (21). Medieval (p. 124).

31. Polished thread-picker tapering towards each end. C XVI Y I (20A). Medieval pit (p. 124).

32. Pin with two incised grooves below pointed head. Crummy Type II. C X M I (14). Loam (p. 78). A.D. 100–130.

33. Pin with three incised grooves below sharply-pointed head. Crummy Type II. C XIV M II (13). Pre-third-century occupation-earth (p. 116).

34. Pin with knobbed head. Crummy Type III. C X C II (12). Hypocaust filling (p. 33). *c.* A.D. 360.

35. Pin with very irregular shank and unshaped head. Probably unfinished. C XXVIII C XX Pit 15 (p. 102). Fourth century.

36. Part of a rectangular plaque with two perforations at end. One side is decorated with a leaf motif, the other is scored and was presumably stuck to something. C XV X III (1). Post-medieval dark earth (p. 139).

37. Part of double-edged comb. C XV S II (1). Early medieval dark earth (p. 49).

38. Die with fairly large, rather irregular incised markings. Six opposite one, five opposite two, and four opposite three. C XVII Y II Part I (1). Early seventeenth-century pit (p. 130).

39. Knife-handle made of two strips of bone set on either side of a thin iron tang and held in position by four irregularly-spaced rivets. Blade missing. C XVII Y II Part I (2). Late sixteenth- to early seventeenth-century yard metalling (p. 130).

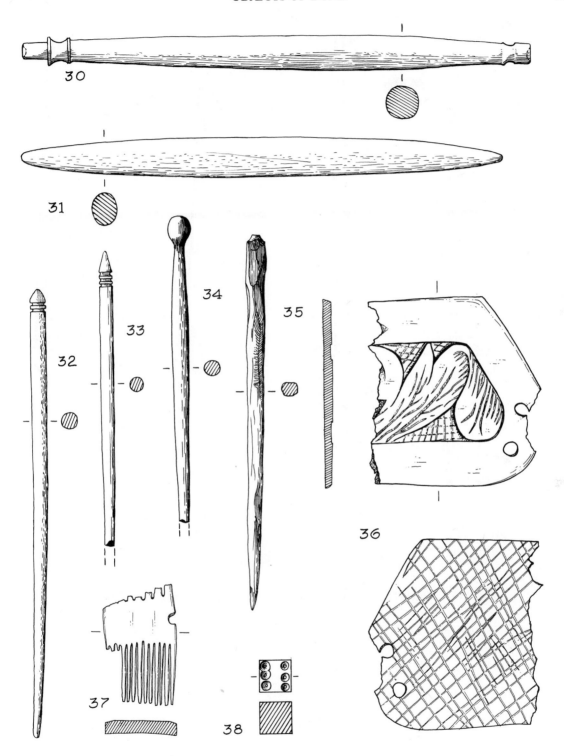

Fig. 64. Objects of Bone. Scale 1 : 1

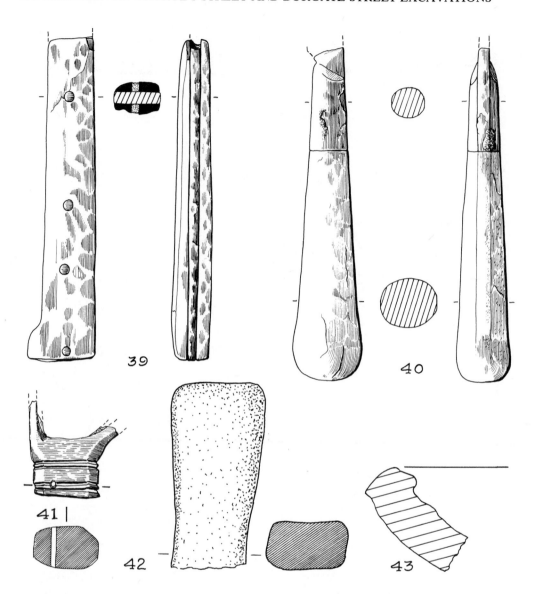

Fig.   65.   Objects of Bone (39–40), Jet (41), Stone (42) and Bronze (43). Scale 1 : 1

40. Knife-handle made of single piece of bone hollowed out to receive thin circular iron shank which secured blade (a small part of which survives) to handle. C IX B II (2). Pit. Seventeenth or eighteenth century (p. 53).

C. OBJECT OF JET (Fig. 65)

41. Part of an object, possibly the leg from a casket, decorated with four incised grooves. There is slight wear on the base and a small hole through one of the grooves. C XXVIII C XX Pit 15 (p. 102). Fourth century.

D. MISCELLANEOUS OBJECTS (Fig. 65)

42. Part of a hone of medium-grained sandy limestone. C XXVIII C XX Pit 12 (p. 103). Late Saxon.

43. Large piece of bronze residue from the base of a crucible. C XV R V Pit 1 (p. 74). Medieval.

E. PIPE-CLAY FIGURINES[83] (Pls. XXXII and Fig. 66)

44. (See Pl. XXXIIA) Figurine of Mother-Goddess seated on a high-backed chair, nursing two infants.[84] A similar example comes from Austin Friars, London, cf. Wheeler, *London in Roman Times*, pl. XXI, No. 5. C XVII Y III Part 3 (6). Burnt material in western wall-trench of timber-framed building (p. 122) c. A.D. 390–400.

45. Fragment of horse, probably a mare.[85] The head and legs are broken off and only the right side of the body remains (Pl. XXXIIB). The object is of white clay and made in a two-piece mould. Similar horses are common on the Continent, cf. E. Tudot, *Collection de Figurines en argile, Oeuvres premières de l'Art gaulois* (Paris, 1860), Pl. 59. There are several parallels from England, from Wroxeter,[86] the site of the Church of All Hallows by the Tower, (London) and Newstead.[87] C X L II (4). Burnt daub. Third century (p. 111).

---

83. Thanks are due to Dr. F. Jenkins for examining these objects.
84. Cf. F. Jenkins, 'The Cult of the Dea Nutrix in Kent', *Arch. Cant.,* lxxi (1957), 38 ff.
85. This object has been published fully by Dr. F. Jenkins in 'The Horse Deity of Roman Canterbury', *Arch. Cant.*, lxxvii (1962), 142 ff.
86. *Wroxeter* iii, p. 34 and Pl. XXIII, fig. 2.
87. Curle, *Newstead*, Pl. LXXIII.

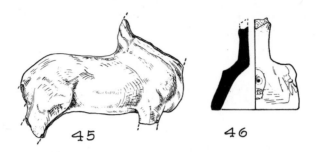

Fig. 66. Pipe-clay figurines. Scale 1 : 1

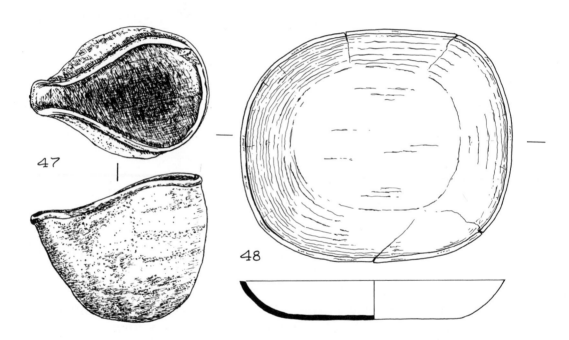

Fig. 67. Pottery crucible and wooden dish. Scale 1 : 2

46. Base of figurine with skull in centre (Pl. XXXII c). Rising from the base is a vertical stem the top of which is broken. This object was unstratified: there are no Romano-Gaulish parallels and the fabric which is smooth and waxy would be unusual in the Roman period. It is probably part of a medieval crucifix; the skull and bones at the base of a crucifix are paralleled on medieval paintings. Cf. M. Rickert, *Painting in Britain in the Middle Ages* (1954), Pl. 154 (date 1383–1384), Pl. 167 (early fifteenth century). C XV R unstratified.

F. CRUCIBLE (Fig. 67, Pl. XXXIIIA)

47. Granular grey ware, smoked near spout. C XI P I Pit 1 (p. 55). A.D. 1050–1150.

G. OBJECT OF WOOD (Fig. 67)

48. Wooden dish (Pl. XXXVB) (?) Ash. C XX C II. Well (p. 92). Fourteenth century.

H. OBJECTS OF IRON (Fig. 68)

49. Socketed chisel. Cf. Curle, *Newstead*, Pl. LIX, Nos. 7, 8. C XXVIII C XXI (20). Medieval floor (p. 107).
50. Spatula with long handle of square section. Probably used for cooking. C XXVIII C XX Pit 3A. Fifiteenth-century cess-pit (p. 105).
51. Bucket handle: semicircular rod with hooked ends. C XXIII C V A (5). Late Saxon floor (p. 96).
52. Right-angled hook, square in section, one end pointed. Probably a door-fastening, the door being fixed by dropping loops or rings over the hook. Cf. H. Cleere, 'Roman Domestic Ironwork, as Illustrated at the Brading, Isle of Wight, Villa', *Bulletin of the Institute of Archaeology, London*, i (1958), 55 ff. C XXIII C V A (13A). Destruction-layer from Roman Period II clay-walled house (p. 86). c. A.D. 290.
53. Part of a key. C XXVIII C XX Pit 3A. Fifteenth-century cess-pit (p. 105).

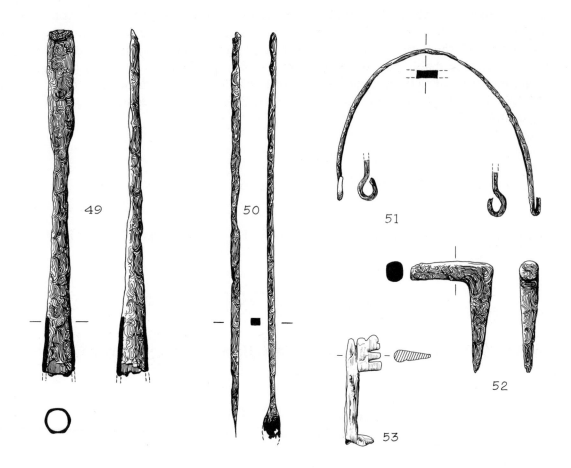

Fig. 68. Objects of Iron. Scale 1 : 3

I. OBJECTS OF CLAY (Figs. 69–71)

1. Griddle fragment in buff clay, partly smoked, consisting of parts of three bars, and either a handle or a foot at right angles to them. C XV S II Pit 5, A.D. 120–150 (p. 49).
2. Fragment of small tile in bright reddish clay with mixed sand and chaff, made in a sand mould. The top has been recessed by drawing a wooden implement across, and the sides trimmed with a knife. Several of these, together with larger pieces of *tegula* size with wood-grain impressions, three of them burnt as if from a hearth, were found in C XXII C V A 4, Saxon occupation and floors, c. A.D. 850–950 (p. 96). They may be re-used Roman, or else Saxon tiles (p. 325).
3. Saxon loomweight in baked clay, C XXII C I 8, Saxon occupation and floors, c. A.D. 850–950 (p. 89).

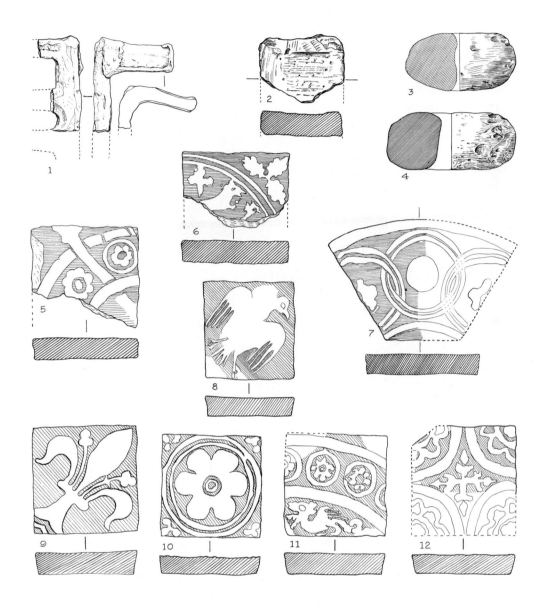

Fig. 69. Clay griddle, loom-weight and tiles. Scale 1 : 4

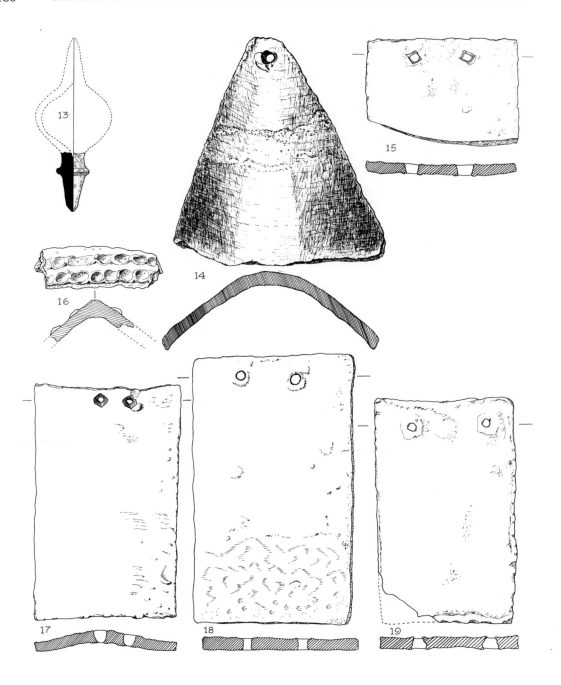

Fig.   70.   Medieval roof-finial and roofiing-tiles. Scale 1 : 4

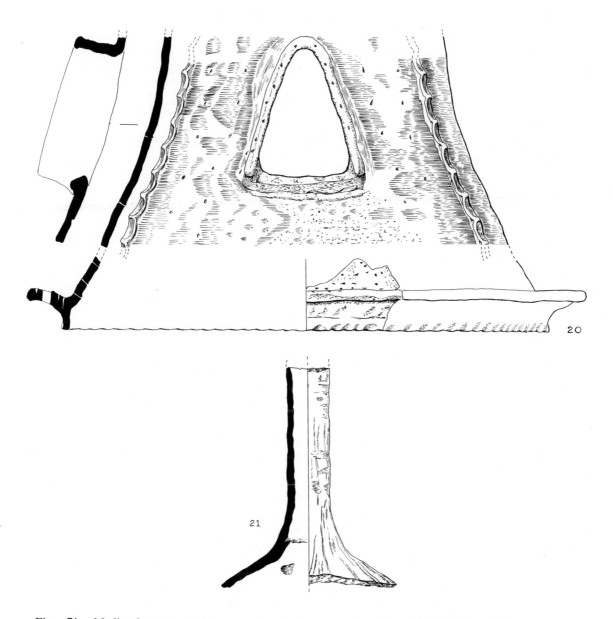

Fig. 71. Medieval pottery roof-louver and sixteenth-century bottle-shaped distilling vessel. Scale 1 : 4

4. As No. 3, C XXII C IV 14, one of sixteen fallen from a loom on to a cobbled floor (p. 89).

Nos. 5–12: medieval glazed floor-tiles, with pattern in 'printed' style in white slip (showing yellow under glaze); probably made at Tyler Hill, Canterbury. Fourteenth century, probably after 1325.

5. Floral motif, white slip on red clay with grey core, probably second half of fourteenth century. C XIX Z II 1 (p. 57). Seventeenth-century layer.

6. Dog and oak leaves, as No. 5, C XIX Z III Pit 1, post-medieval pit (p. 58).

7. Interlaced circles, yellow on orange-green background. C XIV M I 10. Late thirteenth- to early fourteenth-century chalky loam floor (p. 115).

8. Eagle on mainly green background (worn). C XVII Y II 3 (6). Fourteenth-century mortar floor (p. 125).

9. Fleur-de-lys, yellow on brown background. C XVII Y III 3 (2). Fourteenth-century loam floor (p. 125).

10. Floral motif, as No. 9. *Ibid.*

11. Dragon and floral motifs, colour as No. 9. C XVII Y III 3 (2A). Fourteenth-century loam floor (p. 125).

12. Central cross with floral corners, one cut diagonally, colour as No. 9. C XVII Y IV 1. Modern make-up (p. 125).

13. Medieval roof finial (reconstruction after G.C. Dunning). Reddish clay with grey core, with some thin glaze, orange-green, above the collar. The point would be slotted into the end of a ridge tile. C XXII C II 11. Gravel metalling of doorway in Building A, late medieval (p. 93).

14. Triangular terminal tile from the descending ridge of a gable, in granular red-brown clay; made flat on a gritty surface and then bent. C XV R III Pit A, second half of the thirteenth century (Fig. 23).

15. Roof-tile fragment with square peg-holes set diagonally, mortared lower surface. C XIV M I 3. Make-up of Period III (p. 116).

16. Ridge-tile fragment in coarse grey clay with flint grit, reddish surface, with two thumbed strips on one side, one strip on the other. C XVII Y II 2 (4). Late thirteenth to early fourteenth century (p. 130).

17. Roof-tile with hexagonal peg-holes, in hard reddish clay with some shell grit on lower surface; two, in good condition. C XV R IV Pit 11 which contained fourteenth-century pottery and one fifteenth-century sherd (p. 74).

18. Roof-tile with circular peg-holes and thin glaze on lower part; two. C XVI Y I base of Period 2 Drain (p. 125). Fourteenth century.

19. As No. 18, unglazed. C XVII Y III 2 (13). Eighteenth-century floor (p. 127).

20. Roof louver fragment showing a triangular aperture with sides surrounded by a projecting canopy with squared outer edge, not extending along the base of the aperture. Vertical thumbed strips have been applied between the apertures. A flange has been added above the base, pierced by peg-holes 1.5 cm. in diameter (one found) through which pegs would have secured it to a platform on the roof. Hard finely granular reddish to grey clay with

grey core, with stab-marks over much of the surface, especially on the flange. Dark green to orange glaze, over traces of buff slip, partly covers the surface but does not extend to the flange.[88] C XV R IV Pit 2, late thirteenth or early fourteenth century.

21. Neck of a bottle-shaped vessel used for distilling (cf. *Medieval Arch.*, xvi (1972), 118 fig. 33, nos. 7 and 9), in hard light reddish to grey clay. It is broken at the top of the neck and just below the junction with a bulbous body. C XV R I 17. Infilling of sixteenth-century cellar containing sixteenth- to seventeenth-century pottery (below, Nos. 219–240).

J. OBJECTS OF STONE (Figs. 72–73)

1. Donkey mill. Fragment of upper stone, diameter 48.7 cm., made of Kentish ragstone. C X J (p. 53).

Nos. 2–4. Roman or Saxon querns in Mayen lava

2. Upper stone, diameter 47.6 cm., with worn grinding surface. C XXII C II 19, Saxon dark earth (p. 88). *c.* A.D. 850–950.

3. Upper stone. C XXVII R XI 8. A.D. 90–120. Concrete floor in St. Margaret's Street baths (vol. v).

4. Upper stone. C XIII T III Pit 2, medieval pit (p. 133).

Nos. 5–6. Medieval querns in Mayen lava

5. Pendelmühl ('oscillating') quern.[89] Upper stone with ring-hole on left; there is a shallow hole 10 cm. from this. The grinding surface is worn smooth with traces of grooving remaining. C XIV M I 8. Phase 3 of bakery (p. 115). Fourteenth century.

6. Pot quern. Upper stone with rectangular slot on left in which a fragment of iron is wedged, secured by lead; there is a circular hole, 9.5 cm. from this and 5.5 cm. deep, tapering at the bottom, for a wooden handle. C XIII T II 2. Eighteenth-century pit (p. 133).

7. Cresset lamp with slight hole near centre, perhaps for the wick, in limestone, smoke-blackened. C XXIII C V D Pit 5 (M 10). Second half of thirteenth century (p. 91).

88. Drawing after G.C. Dunning. Cf. *idem*, 'A Pottery Louver from Great Easton, Essex', *Medieval Archaeology*, x (1966), 74–80.
89. *Antiquity*, xxix (1955), 69, Fig. 1, No. 4; cf. references cited there.

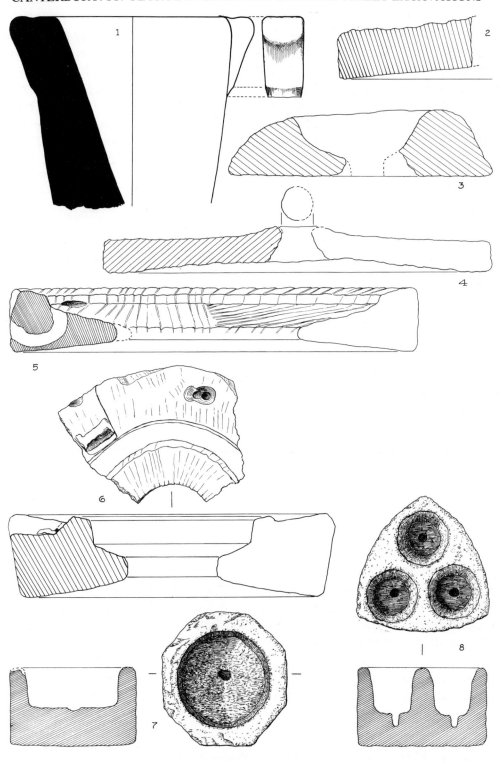

Fig. 72.   Objects of Stone. Scale 1 : 4

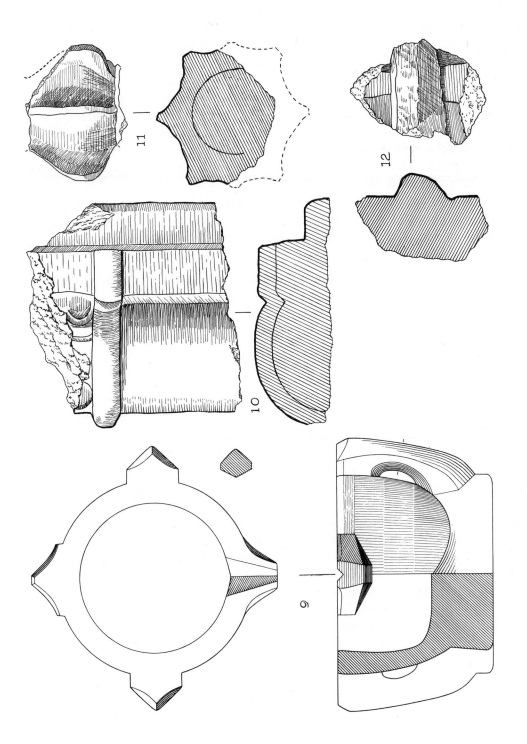

Fig.   73.   Medieval mortar of Caen stone. Scale 1 : 6 (*Drawn by G.C. Dunning*) Architectural fragments. Scale 1 : 3 (*Drawn by M.G. Wilson*)

8. Cresset lamp in limestone, with holes for the wick in each of the three compartments. C XXVIII C XX 28, cess-pit with fifteenth-century pottery (p. 104).

9. Caen stone mortar [90] with four lugs at rim-level spaced equally around the edge. The lugs are triangular in plan and the front one has a V-shaped groove cut in the top which is wider and deeper on the inside than on the front of the spout. The handles, of irregular diamond-shaped section, are long, extending from the rim almost to the base; they project some distance beyond the side of the bowl and each is pierced with a small elongated hole. Caen stone mortars of this type have been found at a number of sites along and close to the south and south-east coast of England from Southampton to King's Lynn. A close parallel comes from Dover Castle, see *JBAA* (3rd Series), xxxii (1969), fig. 11, S.7. Drawing by G.C. Dunning. C XXII C II 13, among timber and chalk blocks from the collapse of the well-top (p. 93). Fourteenth century.

10. Fragment of Romanesque attached column in Purbeck marble, probably late twelfth century. The miniature scale of the piece suggests that it came from a decorative feature rather than from an actual architectural element. Unstratified, C XV Area R.

11. Small octagonal fluted finial of cretaceous greensand. C XV R I 23.

12. Part of octagonal or semi-octagonal colonnette of cretaceous limestone, possibly chalk. C XV R I Pit 9.

K. SLATE ROOFING-TILES (Fig. 74)

1, 2. Medium grey, with two and one peg-holes. C XIV Q I Pit 1. Cut through burnt daub (1). Early fourteenth century (p. 59).

3. Rather light grey with single peg-hole; a large number, light to medium grey. C XIV Q I 10. Fifteenth century or later (p. 59).

4. Medium grey with two peg-holes. C XVII Y III 3 Pit 1. Probably fourteenth century (p. 123).

These slates have been submitted to the Geological Survey and Museum, London, but it has proved impossible to determine their source. Slate can vary very greatly even within one quarry. Although a Cornish origin might seem probable, a Welsh origin cannot be ruled out, for surface workings near the coast could have existed long before the main quarries were developed in the nineteenth century. Cf. similar uncertainty over a thirteenth-century slate from Rose Lane (*Arch. Cant.*, lxviii (1954), 142 and fig. 24, No. 9), which was examined both at the Geological Survey and by Mr. J. Setchell of the

90. For a discussion of Caen stone mortars cf. note by G.C. Dunning in A.M. Cook, D.C. Mynard and S.E. Rigold 'Excavations at Dover Castle', *JBAA* (3rd Series), xxxii (1969), 82–4. See also Dunning in H. Clarke and Alan Carter, *Excavations in King's Lynn 1963–70* (Society for Medieval Archaeology Monograph Series No. 7, London 1977), 331 ff.

Fig. 74. Medieval slate tiles. Scale 1 : 4

Delabole Slate Company of Cornwall. In *Sussex Archaeological Collections*, ciii (1965), Dr J.W. Murray suggests a south Devon origin for similar slates found on a number of sites in Sussex. For a survey of the trade in slate, see E.M. Jope and G.C. Dunning, *Antiq. Journ.*, xxxiv (1954), 209–17.

L. ROMAN RELIEF-PATTERNED FLUE-TILES (Fig. 75)

All the relief-patterned tiles from the 1946–56 excavations are published together here. The classification follows that of A.W.G. Lowther, *A Study of the Patterns on Roman Flue-tiles and their Distribution* (Research Papers of the Surrey Archaeological Society, No. 1, Guildford, 1948). The majority of the fragments, most of which were identified by A.W.G. Lowther, were found residually in late Roman, Saxon or medieval deposits, or else unstratified. The exceptions are two fragments of Die 16 dated to A.D. 90–120, and one of Die 43 dated to the late first or early second century. This evidence of date conforms with that from elsewhere.

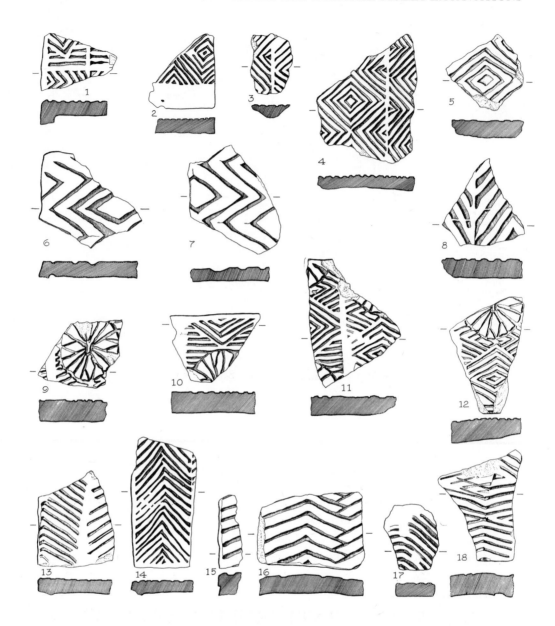

Fig. 75. Roman relief-patterned flue-tiles from various sites in Canterbury. Scale 1 : 4

DIE 4

1. C XXII F V 2A. Marlowe Avenue Car Park. Mid to late second-century rubbish deposit.

GROUP 5 PATTERN, PERHAPS DIE 15

2. C XXIV Castle II 5C. Medieval floor.

DIE 16

3. C XXVIII Castle XI 1. Roman defensive bank (with much residual pottery). A.D. 270–290.
4. C XV R III 3. Medieval layer (p. 74).
   Others (not figured) from this die from C VII L 3. Occupation over Belgic Ditch near Rose Lane (*Arch. Cant.*, lxviii (1954), 102). A.D. 90–120.
   C VII K 3 Pit R 2. Roman rubbish pit on NE side of Rose Lane (*Arch. Cant., ibid.*) Late first to early second century.
   C XXIII K I 8A St. Mildred's, south-west of the Tannery (report forthcoming).

DIE 18

5. C XXII H I Pit 1, medieval. St. Peter's Lane.
   Others (not figured) from C XXVIII Castle XI 1. Roman bank (with much residual pottery) A.D. 270–290.
   C XIII S II 5, medieval. Building south of St. Margaret's Street Baths.

GROUP 5 PATTERN, PERHAPS DIE 22

6,7. C XXXII S (unstratified). Simon Langton School yard.
   Another (not figured) from C IX A I Pit 7, medieval. St. George's Street Baths.

DIE 29

8. C VI II 6, modern rubble. Butchery Lane Building.
   Another (not figured) from C XIII CW 33. A.D. 240–260. Occupation beneath Roman rampart-bank.

DIE 32

9. C XIII Q V 4. Saxon earth above Roman debris, St. Margaret's Street Baths.
10. C XXVII R X (unstratified). St. Margaret's Street Baths.
11. C XXVII R IX Pit 7. Medieval robber trench, St. Margaret's Street Baths.
12. C XII Q II 5, modern make-up. St. Margaret's Street Baths.
    The following from St. Margaret's Street Baths, are not figured:
    C XII Q I 6 (voussoir tile). Above main filling of Period II cold bath, end of second century.
    C XII Q II 2. Roman debris, late fourth century.
    C XIII Q V 4. Saxon earth above Roman debris; and another unstratified from this trench.
    C XIII R III B1 (stamped on two adjacent sides), medieval earth.
    C XIII R IV 6, two. Black earth, A.D. 370–450+.
    C XXVII R VI 5. Medieval robber-trench.
    C XXVII R IX. Medieval robber-trench; and Pit 7, medieval.
    C XIII R IVA 5, A.D. 400+. St. Margaret's Street.

    Other examples of Die 32, not figured, came from:
    C XII R Y III 5. Medieval robber-trench and *ibid*. 1 (stamped on two adjacent sides). Post-Roman dark soil. Rose Hotel yard.
    C XXV E XV VI 2. Medieval earth. East of the Marlowe Theatre.

DIE 41

13. C VIII J 2 Pit 3 (M5). Medieval pit. Rose Lane, see *Arch. Cant.*, lxviii (1954), 103, fig. 1.

DIE 42

14. C XIII R IV 18, A.D. 160–200. Pit below floor, St. Margaret's Street Baths.
    Another from C XXVII R, unstratified (not figured).

DIE 43

15, 16. C VII F 9 (stamped on adjacent sides). Butchery Lane, builders' debris associated with first phase of the west wing. Late first to early second century.

DIE 45

17.   C XXIX E XX C 3. Dark soil, A.D. 330–370. Rose Lane.

GROUP 8 PATTERN, PERHAPS DIE 46

18.   Whitehall Field. Unstratified above Belgic cremation 2.

C. THE POTTERY
By Marion Wilson

The mortaria have been examined by Mrs. K.F. Hartley and her date-range for each type and her attribution of source are recorded in brackets in each entry. This is normally followed by the context of the vessel and its date. Sherds of Black-burnished wares where possible are referred to J.P. Gillam's type-series (see Gillam in the List of Abbreviations) and his dates (as later revised) are quoted immediately following. Other dates given are those assigned to the context of each vessel or group. These dates have been arrived at by a careful study of the various contexts in which each type occurs.

For some medieval pottery from Canterbury it is convenient to use the classification of the groups discussed in *Arch. Cant.*, lxviii (1954), 128 ff. The dating of these has been adjusted slightly and is now considered to be as follows:

Group I	*c.* 975–1025
Group II	*c.* 1050–1100
Group III	*c.* 1080–1150
Group IV	*c.* 1250–1300

I. BATH BUILDING (Figs. 76–79)

A. ROMAN

Nos. 1–4: Pottery from C IX A IV 4 gully. c. A.D. 150–200

1. Hard pink-buff ware, white grits (A.D. 140–200, local).
2. Hard red-grey rather finely granular ware, burnished.
3. Hard light grey-buff slightly granular ware, burnished. Similar to Gillam Type 137 (A.D. 180–250) but in local ware.
4. Light grey-buff burnished ware.

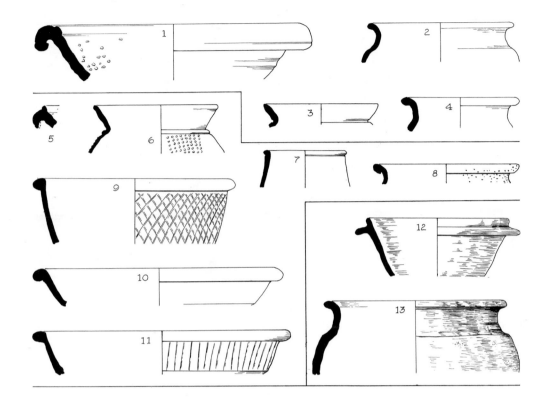

Fig. 76.   Roman pottery from the St. George's Street Baths. Scale 1 : 4

Nos. 5–11: Pottery from C IX D III 1. Pre-building grey earth. c. A.D. 170–220

5. Probably local: second half of second century.

6. Hard burnished light grey ware.

7. Imitation colour-coated beaker in hard burnished grey ware. Such local copies are common in Canterbury in the third century.

8. Hard rather granular grey ware.

9. Black-burnished 2 ware; cf. Gillam Type 222, A.D. 150–210.

10. Black-burnished 2 ware; Gillam Type 313, A.D. 190–240.

11. Hard burnished light grey ware; cf. Gillam Type 312, A.D. 190–240.

12. Coarse grey ware, uneven burnished surfaces, C IX A V 20. *c* A.D. 360.

13. Coarse granular dark grey ware, uneven burnished surface, C IX D III 3. *c.* A.D. 360.

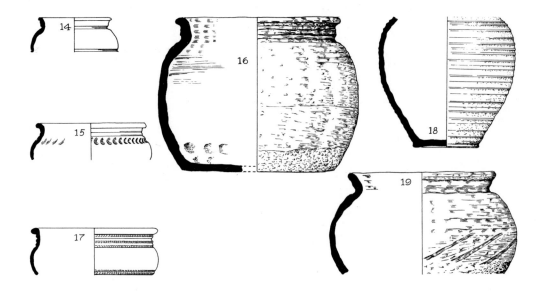

Fig. 77. Roman Pottery from the St. George's Street Baths. Scale 1 : 4

Nos. 14, 15: Pottery from C IX A IV 1. Drain filling. A.D. 360–370

14. Finely granular burnished grey ware.

15. Fine reddish paste, orange-red coating with stamped demi-rosettes; Oxfordshire, Young's Type C 78.4, dated A.D. 340–400.

16. Very coarse granular reddish to light grey ware, roughly burnished; slight indications of being wheel-shaped, but certainly hand-finished, and closely resembling other late fourth-century hand-made vessels from Canterbury (cf. vessels from the Rose Hotel Yard).[91] Also an everted rim of a smaller jar in this ware.
C IX A V 14, rubble on second-period hypocaust floor in Room 1.

17. Fine reddish paste, orange-red coating, rouletted; Oxfordshire, Young's Type C 75.10, dated A.D. 325–400. C X C II 6, rubble A.D. 370–390.

Nos. 18, 19: Pottery from C IX A V 5. Rubble. A.D. 370–390

18. Granular grey-brown ware with rough surface and regular rilling.

91. *The Archaeology of Canterbury*, v, 'Excavations in the Marlowe Car Park and associated Areas' (forthcoming).

19. Hand-made in very coarse granular grey-brown ware, upper part unevenly burnished, with burnished diagonal lines on body. Cf. No. 16.

B. SAXON AND MEDIEVAL

20. Hand-made in coarse black chaff-tempered ware with uneven surface, burnished. Sixth to seventh century. C IX A V 8. Dark earth above collapsed wall.
21. Hard rather finely granular grey ware, ninth or tenth century. C IX A V 13. Gravel floor.

Nos. 22–25: Pottery from C IX A V Pit 1: pit through Room 4. Early twelfth century with earlier sherds

22–23. Hard rather finely granular light grey ware, uneven darker surface, with vertical knife-trimming and burnishing. Late Saxon or medieval Group 1, ? early eleventh century.[92]
24. Hard rather finely granular reddish ware, thick grey core. This is a medieval fabric, comparable to medieval Groups II and III. Also a Group III cooking-pot rim of *c.* 1070–1150.
25. Hard granular dark grey ware with uneven surface, of late Saxon character, though lacking the knife-trimming of Group I. cf. No. 28.

Nos. 26–27: Pottery from C X C II Pit 2: through Room 8

26. Hard rather finely granular grey ware with irregular surface, knife-trimmed, with some vertical strokes and burnishing; apparently hand-made. Late Saxon, cf. Group 1.
27. Wire-cut base in hard finely granular grey ware. Late Saxon, cf. Hamwih Class 15, from northern France.[93] See Appendix III.
     The pit also contained cooking-pot rims of medieval Groups II, III, IV ranging in date from the mid eleventh to the late thirteenth century. It is probable that the filling of two pits was not distinguished.

92. Groups I-IV refer to the classification of Canterbury early medieval pottery published in *Arch. Cant.*, lxvii (1954), 128–38. Group I is dated *c.* 975–1025. Group II is dated *c.* 1050–1100. Group III is dated *c.* 1080–1150. Group IV is dated to the second half of the thirteenth century.
93. Information from Dr. Richard Hodges.

28. Hard rather finely granular light grey ware, knife-trimmed and smoothed, vertically on shoulder. Medieval Group I, ? early eleventh century. C X C II Pit 1: through Room 8. Also from this pit two Group III rims, dated ? first half of the twelfth century.

Nos. 28–29: Pottery from C IX A V (Extension) 1.
Black earth over Rooms 1–2.

29. Hard granular light grey ware, red-grey uneven surface. cf. No. 25. Late Saxon.
30. Ware as No. 28 but more irregular, partly smoothed with some vertical tooling on neck.

31. Hard granular dark grey-brown ware with irregular surfaces, trimmed smooth on rim and shoulder. Late Saxon. C IX A I Pit 7 (Fig. 2, Pit M 7). The pit also contained a rim similar to No. 36, and one of Group III.

Nos. 32–33: Pottery from C IX A I Pit 6 (Fig. 2, Pit M 6)

32. Hard rather finely granular light grey ware. Ninth to tenth century.
33. Hard granular grey-brown ware; two. Medieval Group II dated 1050–1100.

Nos. 34–37: Pottery from C IX A II 3, pit cutting drain on NE side of baths

34. Hard rather finely granular grey-brown ware with uneven surface, smoothed near base. Late Saxon. Also a ninth- to tenth-century rim.
35. Hard granular grey-buff ware; two. Group III, ? first half of twelfth century.
36. Coarse light grey-brown shell-tempered ware.
37. Hard granular reddish ware with trace of shell-grit on surface.

Nos. 38–41: Pottery from C X C II Pit 5: through Room 8. Thirteenth century

38. Hard granular light grey to reddish ware with shallow incised decoration, covered with thin glaze, orange and green; two.
39. Coarse brown ware with thick shell-grit, with finger-impressions on rim. The rim form suggests a date between medieval Groups III and IV.
40. Ware as No. 39, probably earlier than Group IV.
41. Ware as No. 39, cf. medieval Group IV, second half of thirteenth century.

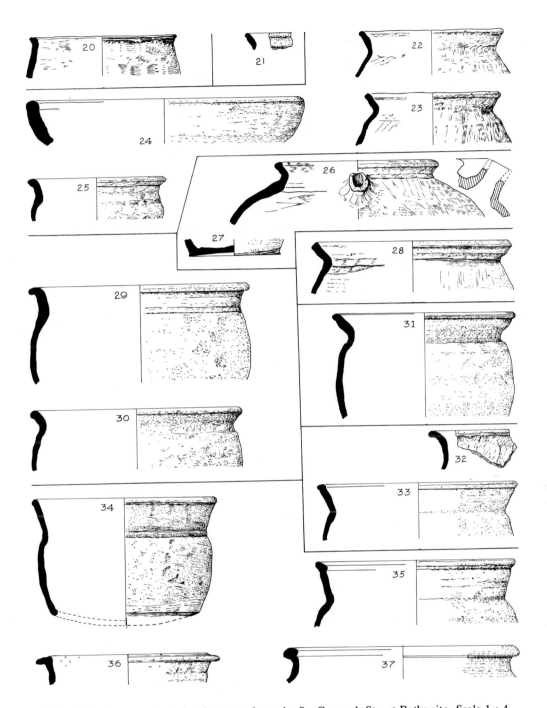

Fig. 78. Saxon and medieval pottery from the St. George's Street Baths site. Scale 1 : 4

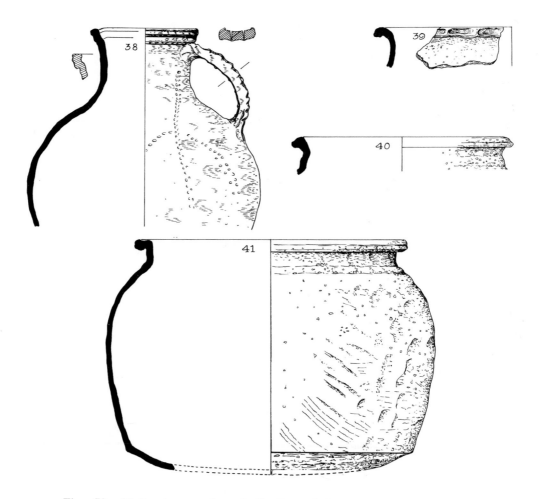

Fig. 79. Medieval pottery from the St. George's Street Baths site. Scale 1 : 4

II. THE APSED BUILDING (p. 41), Figs. 80–82

A. PRE-BUILDING

Nos. 42–58: Pottery from C X G V Pit 1 (Fig. 8), pre-dating masonry house. The pit yielded Neronian-Flavian samian (Dr. 18, 18R, 27), but the coarse ware is mainly of the second century. *c.* A.D. 100–130.

42–43.   Fine hard burnished grey ware.

44.   Fine hard burnished light grey ware with panels of barbotine dots.

45.   Ware as No. 44, with diagonal scored lines (small sherd).

46–47. Hard granular grey ware. 47 is first-century.

48. Coarse granular grey ware with incised shoulder-decoration, furrowed body; burnished on rim and neck.

49. Burnished grey-brown ware.

50. Ware as No. 48. First-century.

51. Coarse granular grey ware with pitted surface, lightly burnished; another larger jar.

52–54. Hard granular light grey ware.

55. Hard granular grey ware with darker surface.

56–57. Hard granular grey ware.

58. Coarse granular light grey ware, uneven dark surface, partly burnished; two. First-century.

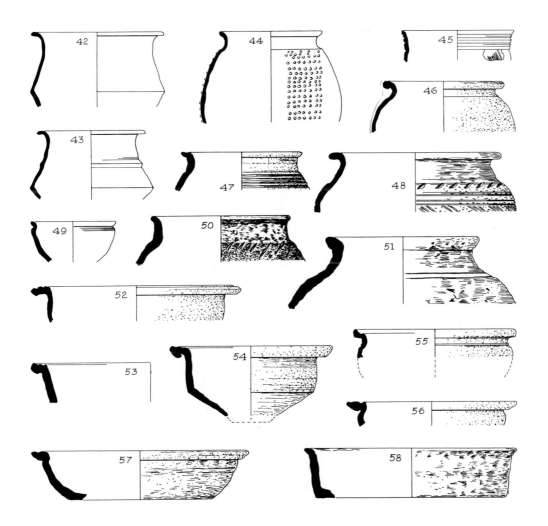

Fig. 80. Roman pottery from the Apsed Building. Scale 1 : 4

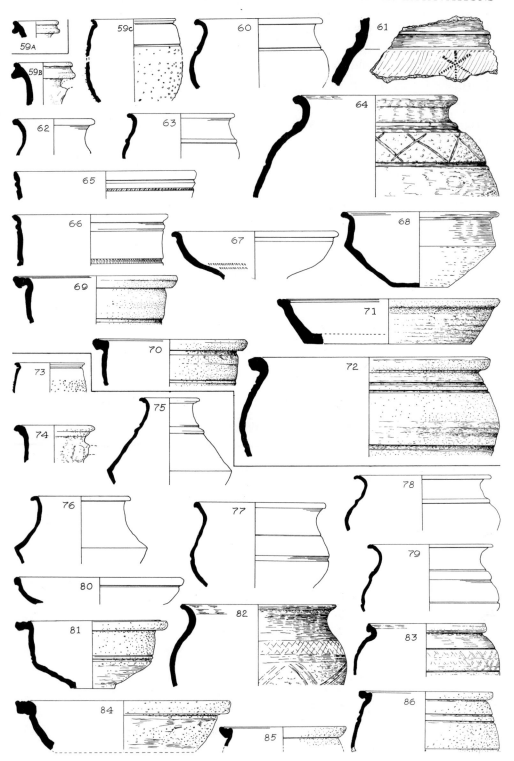

Fig.   81.   Roman pottery from the Apsed Building. Scale 1 : 4

59A.   Flagon in finely granular red-buff ware, grey core, C XV S II Pit 5, A.D. 120–150. There was also a clay griddle fragment (Fig. 69, No. 1).

Nos. 59B–72: Pottery from C XV S II Pit 4. Below floor of Period I timber building. The pit yielded many sherds of Flavian-Trajanic samian and one of Trajanic Dr. 37; no Black-burnished 2 ware was present. Date of deposit *c.* A.D. 110–130.

59B.   Hard finely granular buff ware, smoothed.

59C.   Rough-cast beaker in fine hard orange-buff paste, dark red-brown coating.

60.   Fine hard burnished grey-buff ware; four.

61.   Storage jar sherd with deeply incised star probably made by the end of a small bone.

62.   Fine hard grey ware, dark burnished surface.

63.   Fine hard burnished grey ware.

64.   Very coarse granular grey-buff ware, roughly burnished rim and neck, with burnished lattice on shoulder; two.

65.   Fine hard grey ware, darker burnished surface, with rouletted line.

66.   Fine hard burnished grey ware, with rouletted groove.

67.   Fine hard grey ware, dark burnished surfaces, rouletted band inside.

68.   Hard finely granular grey ware, upper part roughly burnished.

69(two)–70.   Hard granular grey ware; also four other reeded rims.

71.   Hard rather granular light grey ware, partly smoothed; two.

72.   Hard granular grey ware, partly smoothed.

Nos. 73–86: Pottery from C X G IV 4 Pit. c. A.D. 130–160

73.   Rough-cast beaker in fine hard orange-buff paste, red-brown coating.

74.   Flagon in rather granular light grey-brown ware, orange-buff surface.

75.   Fine hard burnished grey ware.

76.   Fine grey to reddish ware, black surfaces, burnished outside.

77–79.   Fine hard burnished light grey ware.

80.   Reddish ware with burnished surface or slip; two.

81.   Hard granular light grey ware.

82–83.   Coarse granular grey-buff ware, unevenly burnished above burnished lattice.

84(two)–86(two).   Hard granular grey ware.

87.   Black-burnished 1 ware of Gillam Type 329, dated 190–340. S I 4. Loam floor of Period I. *c.* A.D. 190–220.

88.   Hard finely granular buff ware, white and grey grits (local, probably third century). S I 6. Period I floor below Room 4.

89. Hard finely granular light buff ware, yellow-brown slip, translucent grey-white grits (A.D. 150–250, probably Lower Germany). S I 1 (Pit 2) pre-dating wall of Room 1; another sherd in S I 3 (Pit 1).

B. FLOORS OF BUILDING

90. Finely granular deep buff ware, smoothed. S II 21. Primary concrete floor in Room 2. *c.* A.D. 240–260.

    Nos. 91–94: Pottery from S II 20. Occupation on concrete floor. c. A.D. 250–300

91. Hard granular grey ware.
92. Hard granular grey ware, burnished on lip and shoulder.
93. Poppy-head beaker rim in fine hard burnished brown ware.
94. Black-burnished 2 ware, cf. Gillam Type 312, dated 190–240.
95. Colour-coated beaker sherd in hard finely granular orange-buff paste, brown coating, with part of deeply stamped rosette and rouletted line. S II 14. Last floor in Room 2 (not in Section). Another sherd in 13 destruction. *c.* A.D. 300–340.

C. CONTEMPORARY LAYERS OUTSIDE BUILDING

Nos. 96–99: Pottery from S II 37. Yellow-brown loam. c. A.D. 240–360

96. Hard granular orange-red ware, grey core (local, imitating Nene Valley type; late third, or fourth century).
97. Imitation colour-coated beaker in fine hard grey ware, burnished between rouletted zones. Late third-century type.
98. Finely granular dark grey ware, rather unevenly burnished.
99. Hard rather finely granular grey ware.

Nos. 100–102: Pottery from S II 9. Occupation earth. c. A.D. 240–350.

100. Grey paste, yellow colour-coating inside, orange-buff outside, rouletted.
101. Very fine white paste, glossy 'metallic' dark silver-grey coating, with barbotine tendril.
102. Fine hard burnished dark grey ware (reconstructed from two similar beakers).

Nos. 103–104: Pottery from S II 8. Black occupation-earth. c. A.D. 320–360

103. Hard rather finely granular light grey ware, burnished on rim and base inside.
104. Hard orange-buff paste with some white chalky inclusions, grey 'metallic' colour-coating, with barbotine scale-pattern between indentations; one sherd in layer 4 above (destruction).

D. DESTRUCTION LAYERS OF APSED BUILDING

Nos. 105–106: Pottery from S II 12. c. A.D. 360–400

105. Coarse grey-brown ware, uneven burnished surfaces.
106. Hard orange-buff paste, brown colour-coating, rouletted.

Nos. 107–108: Pottery from S II 30. c. A.D. 360–400

107. Coarse granular grey ware, unevenly burnished lip.
108. Hand-made sherd in coarser ware than No. 107 with burnished lattice (reconstructed after a similar jar found in Canterbury Lane); cf. No. 299 below.
    Also a flanged bowl in hard whitish paste, dark grey 'metallic' coating, cf. Gillam Type 230, dated 360–400 (not figured).

E. SAXON AND MEDIEVAL

109. Hand-made Saxon sherd in hard finely granular grey ware with irregular bosses pressed out by the thumb. The surface is uneven, with patchy burnishing in all directions. C XV S II 7. Black earth above destruction layers. Similar sherds from a jar were found on a Saxon floor in Canterbury Lane dated to the ninth or early tenth century (No. 324).

Nos. 110–112: Pottery from C XV T II 9. Lowest cobbled surface. Eleventh century

110. Hard rather finely granular grey ware with uneven surface, smoothed near base. Late Saxon.
111, 112. Hard rather finely granular red-buff ware, grey core, with rather uneven surface. Late Saxon. Cf. No. 28.

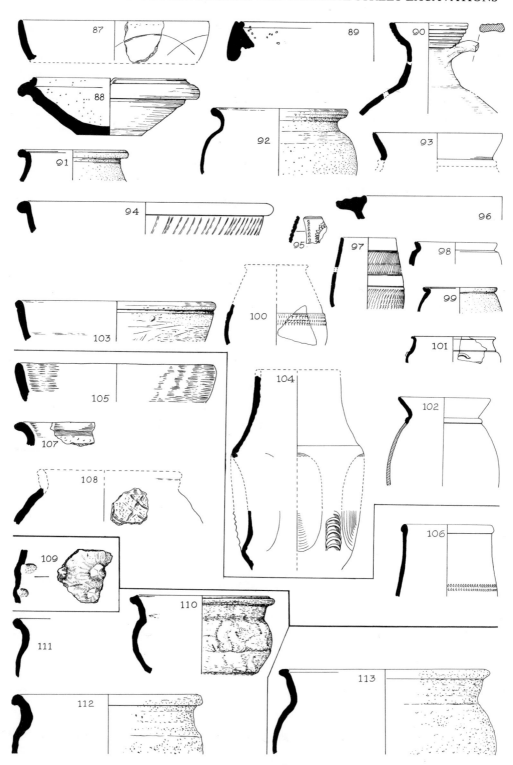

Fig. 82.   Roman, Saxon and medieval pottery from the Apsed Building site. Scale 1 : 4

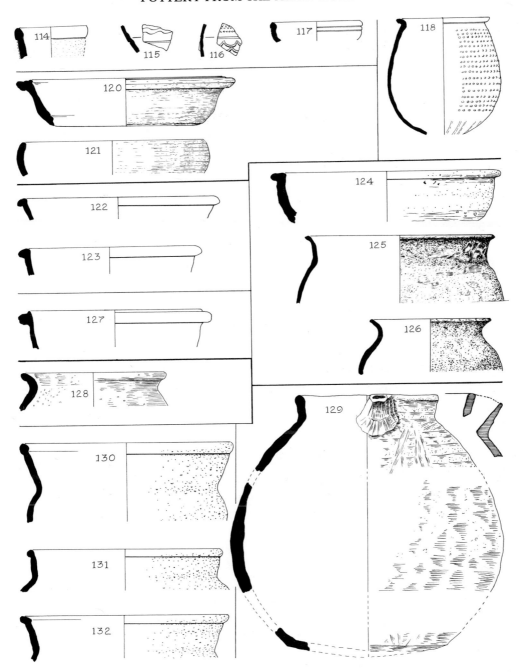

Fig. 83. Roman, Saxon and medieval pottery from minor sites on the south side of St. George's Street (C X Site J (Nos. 114–121), C XI Site O (Nos. 122–126), C XI Site P (Nos. 127–132)). Scale 1 : 4

113. Hard granular grey ware, rather uneven surface. Medieval Group II dated 1050–1100. Also two other cooking-pots usually found in association with Group II (not figured). C XV T II 5. Top cobbled surface.

III. POTTERY FROM MINOR EXCAVATIONS IN ST. GEORGE'S STREET (pp. 51–67)

(c) C X SITE J: South side of St. George's Street (Fig. 83)

Nos. 114–117: Pottery from C X J 3C and 3B, lower and upper filling of sleeper trench.
Third century

114. Hard red-buff paste, grey core, red-brown colour-coating (surface flaked off below the rim) (3C).
115. Hard orange-buff paste, black colour-coating outside with white painted wavy line.
116. Hard red to grey paste, dark grey colour-coating outside, with applied scales below rouletting.
117. Hard burnished dark grey ware.

118. Fine hard burnished grey ware with panel of applied dots, and vertical burnished lines below, C X J I 6. Occupation on gravel floor. c. A.D. 160–220.
119. (Fig. 84) Very coarse granular red to dark grey ware, unevenly burnished rim and neck, incised shoulder decoration above rilling, C X J I 5A. Hollow to south of sleeper trench. Probably second-century.

Nos. 120–121: Pottery from C X J I 5A, in filling of storage jar No. 119, derived from Pit 1

120–121. Finely granular buff ware, partly smoothed. No. 120 residual second-century; No. 121 c. A.D. 200–250.

(d) C XI SITE O: South side of St. George's Street (Fig. 83)

122–123. Hard burnished grey ware, Pit 1, c. A.D. 180–250.

Nos. 124, 125: Pottery from Pit 2. Ninth to tenth century, Saxon.

124. Hard finely granular grey-brown ware with some shell grit, red-brown surfaces, smoothed near base.

125. Hard very granular dark grey ware with irregular surface, with some knife-trimming.

126. Hard granular grey ware, sooted. A flat knife-trimmed base probably belongs to this pot. Ninth to tenth century. C XI O Pit 3.

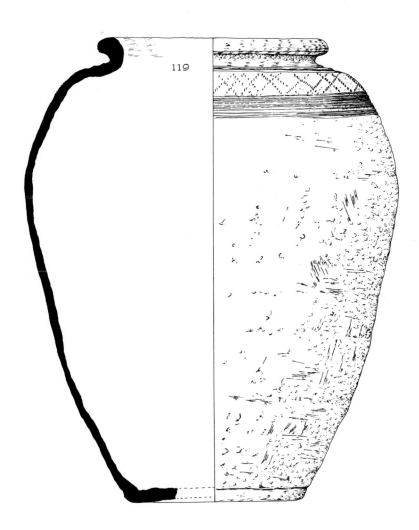

Fig. 84. Roman storage jar from C X Site J. Scale 1 : 4

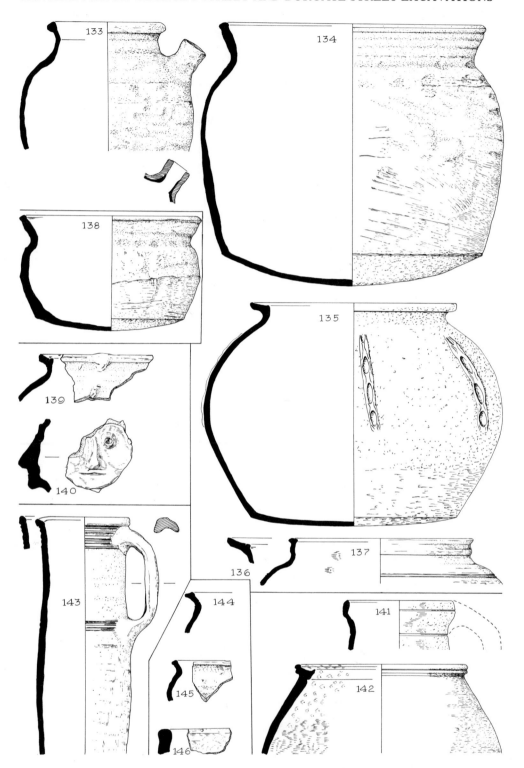

Fig.   85.   Medieval pottery from the south side of St. George's Street (C XIX Site Z). Scale 1 : 4

C XI SITE P: South side of St. George's Street (Fig. 83)

127. Rather coarse grey ware, reddish surfaces, burnished outside, C XI P I Pit 2. *c.* A.D. 270–350.
128. Coarse grey ware with fine calcite grit, burnished; A.D. 360–400. Also a colour-coated dish rim in white paste, red coating. C XI P I Pit 3.
129. Saxon pitcher sherds (top incomplete) with a bar spout having a circular perforation through the wall of the pitcher and widening to a rounded rectangular opening at the mouth; hand-made in hard grey sand-tempered ware, with uneven burnished surface. Cf. *Richborough* iii, No. 362 with lugs and handle, dated to the (?) second half of the eighth century. C XI P I Pit 5.

Nos. 130–132: Medieval pottery from C XI P I Pit 1. c. A.D. *1050–1150.*

130. Hard granular light grey ware, sooted; three. Medieval Group II, A.D. 1050–1100.
131. Hard granular light grey to reddish ware. Cf. Group III, (?) first half of twelfth century.
132. Ware as No. 131; three. Group III.

(e) C XIX SITE Z: South side of St. George's Street (Fig. 85)

Nos. 133–137: Pottery from Z I 2. Medieval cess-pit

133. Hard rather finely granular grey ware, uneven surface, with tubular spout. Insufficient remained to show the position of the handles. Probably eleventh century.
134. Hard light grey granular ware, irregular red-brown surface, smoothed near base. Medieval Group II, A.D. 1050–1100 (for this see Introduction, p. 24). Also another cooking-pot rim of this date.
135. Hard granular red-grey ware with applied finger-impressed strips. Cf. Medieval Group IV (second half of thirteenth century) or a little later. There were three other cooking-pot rims of this date, and many pots and dishes dating from the eleventh to the late thirteenth centuries.
136. Hard rather finely granular grey ware with pierced rim. Fourteenth century.
137. Hard rather finely granular grey-brown ware, splashed with transparent glaze inside. Fourteenth century. Cf. a somewhat similar jar from the well in Canterbury Lane, No. 457.

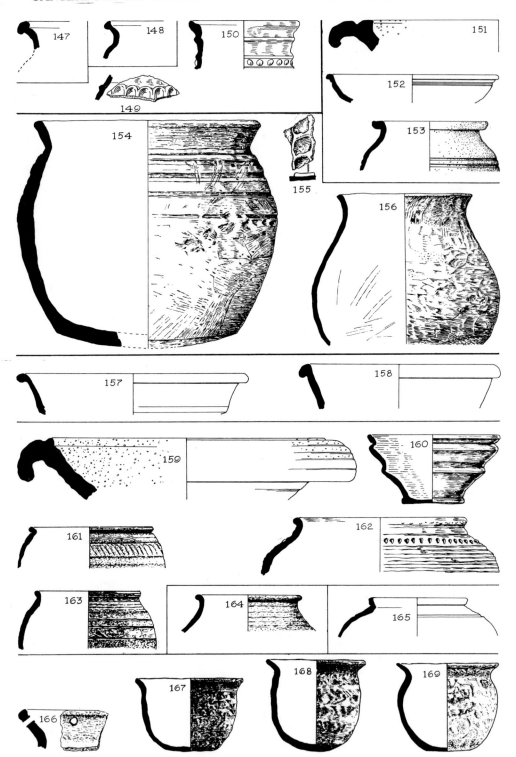

Fig. 86. Roman, Saxon and medieval pottery from sites on the north side of St. George's Street (C XIV Site Q (Nos. 147–150), C X Site K (Nos. 151–156) and C XI Site N (Nos. 157–169). Scale 1 : 4

138. Hard grey granular ware with uneven surface, knife-smoothed on lower part. The ware is late Saxon rather than medieval, though the form foreshadows Medieval Group II, suggesting a date in the second quarter of the eleventh century. Z II 5. Burnt daub and charcoal on loam floor.

Nos. 139–140: Pottery from Z I Pit 4. Fourteenth century.

139. Cooking-pot with pierced rim and applied strip, in hard rather finely granular red-buff ware with light grey surface.
140. Face-mask from a jug in hard rather finely granular reddish ware, grey core, with good transparent glaze, mottled light and dark green. There are traces of an underlying light slip.

Nos. 141–142: Pottery from Z I Pit 3. Fourteenth century.

141. Hard granular dark grey-brown ware, some transparent glaze, orange-green. Cf. No. 413 from the well in Canterbury Lane.
142. Hard finely granular reddish ware, dark grey surface, transparent glaze, orange-green, thickening lower down.

143. Hard rather finely granular red-brown ware, body smoothed. Cf. No. 417 from the fourteenth-century well in Canterbury Lane, although these baluster pitchers were also made in the late thirteenth century (cf. No. 869). Z I 3. Phase 1 loam floor.

Nos. 144–146: Pottery from Z I 1. Phase 1 earth floor. (?) Second half of fourteenth century.

144. Cooking-pot sherd with pierced neck in hard rather finely granular reddish ware. Both ware and form suggest a late fourteenth-century date.
145. Jar sherd with fragment of lip, ware as No. 144, grey-buff.
146. Dish sherd in hard finely granular buff ware with fairly thin transparent glaze, dark and light green.

(f) C XIV SITE Q North side of St. George's Street (Fig. 86)

147. Cooking-pot sherd in hard granular grey ware; also a similar rim probably from a bowl, C XIV Q I 27. Occupation earth. Probably twelfth century.

148. Hard granular grey-brown ware, C XIV Q I 26. Primary gravel floor. Fourteenth century.

149. Jug sherd with applied finger-impressed decoration, in hard granular grey ware with patchy mottled green glaze. Fourteenth century. C XIV Q I 9. Period 2 gravel floor.

150. Hard finely granular light reddish ware, red-grey to buff surface, decorated with applied pellets of deep yellow on a brown ground, with a yellow band above; covered with transparent glaze. London made, imitating a Rouen type (London Museum, *Medieval Catalogue,* pl. LXIII, 1, dated to the fourteenth century) C XIV Q I 9A. On surface of gravel floor 9. Cf. No. 189. Fifteenth century.

(g) C X SITE K North side of St. George's Street. (Fig. 86).

Nos. 151–153: Pottery from C X K I Pit 2. c. A.D. *80–140*

151. Fine hard buff ware, grey and white grits (A.D. 80–150, probable import).
152. Hard grey ware, burnished especially inside.
153. Hard granular dark grey ware.

Nos. 154–156: Late Saxon pottery from Pit 1

154. Coarse brown ware with grey pitted surface, knife-trimmed and smoothed with some vertical strokes (worn). Cf. No. 351.

155. Sherd with applied thumb-impressed strip, grey-brown ware with dark grey surface, similar to No. 154 but with finer grit.

156. Hard finely granular dark grey ware, uneven knife-trimmed surface, burnished. Cf. No. 342 from the ninth- to tenth-century floor in Canterbury Lane. There was also a twelfth-century rim sherd in this pit, of Medieval Group III type.

(h) C XI SITE N North side of St. George's Street (Fig. 86)

157,158.   Hard grey ware with darker burnished surfaces, C XI N I Pit 1. c. A.D. 180–250.

Nos. 159–163: Pottery from C XI N II 9. Pit. c. A.D. *50–80*

159. Fine hard cream-buff ware (probably NE France; A.D. 55–85).

160. Rather coarse grey Belgic ware, darker burnished surfaces; residual.
161. Hard granular light grey ware with raised shoulder decoration.
162. Coarse granular grey ware, with incised shoulder decoration and furrowed body.
163. Ware as No. 162, with shallow girth grooves.

164. Hard granular light grey ware, C XI N II 3, post-hole packing. A.D. 80–120.
165. Fine cream ware with red slip, C XI N II Gully, perhaps for sleeper-beam.

Nos. 166–169: Pottery from C XI N II Pit 2. Saxon.

166. Perforated rim sherd in rather soft sand-tempered brown ware, grey core; perhaps eighth to ninth century.
167–169. Hand-made in hard granular grey ware with uneven burnished surfaces. Late sixth or seventh century.

IV. POTTERY FROM AREA R AND MINOR SITES WEST OF CANTERBURY LANE (pp. 69–80)

A. ROMAN from Area R (Fig. 87).

170. Butt beaker in smooth light red-grey ware, C XV R III 29. Surface 1 of north-east to south-west street. Also good quality *terra nigra* plate sherds and a coarse bead rim. Claudian.

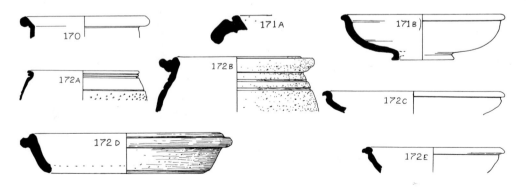

Fig. 87.   Roman pottery from Area R. Scale 1 : 4

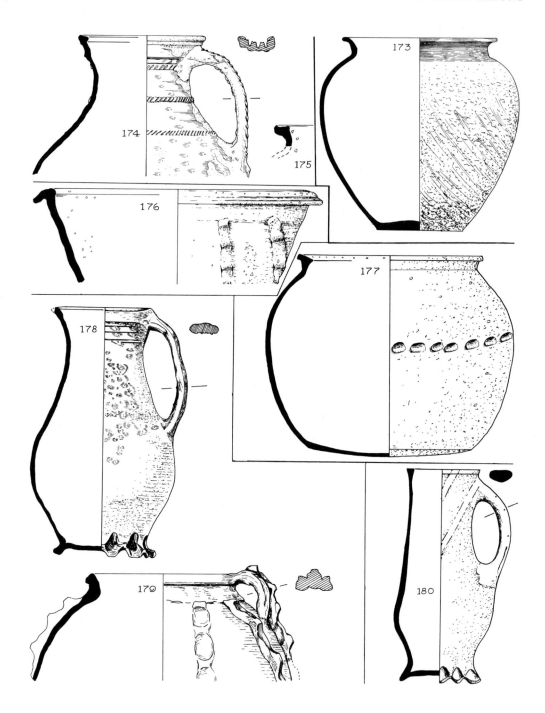

Fig. 88. Roman and medieval pottery from Area R. Scale 1 : 4

Nos. 171 A, B: Pottery from C XV R III 15. Silt from street. c. A.D. 45–160

171A.   Mortarium in finely granular cream ware, grey grits (A.D. 70–110, probably S.E. Britain).

171B.   Fine red-buff ware, grey core, reddish burnished surface or slip with fine mica. c. A.D. 110–160.

172A.   Fine hard pale red-buff paste, dark grey-brown coating, roughcast, C XV R V 24 = 23. Greenish road silt. c. A.D. 80–150.

172B.   Hard granular grey ware, C XV R IV Extension 1 layer 16. Occupation earth. c. A.D. 120–150.

172C.   Burnished buff ware, Ext. 1 layer 15. Occupation earth. c. A.D. 130–160.

172D.   Hard rather finely granular light grey ware, smoothed surface, Ext. 1 layer 14. Road silt. c. A.D. 125–160.

172E.   Finely granular grey ware, reddish buff core, butnished surface. C XV R I 35. Occupation layer, c. A.D. 110–140.

173.   Coarse granular grey-brown ware, burnished rim and neck, C XV R I Extension 1, timber slot in I 28. The rim may be compared with Gillam No. 127, dated A.D. 130–170. Although the surface was mainly flaked away on the lower part, there were no traces of decoration. c. A.D. 160–200 in mid third-century context.

B. MEDIEVAL from Area R (Figs. 88–89).

Nos. 174, 175: Pottery from C XV R I Pit 9. Second half of thirteenth century.

174.   Hard granular red-buff ware, grey core, with applied bands on neck, incised to represent cabling, and with pierced rim. On the shoulder the incisions were made directly onto the jug. The surface is partly covered with thin glaze, orange-green. Cf. *Arch. Cant.*, lxviii (1954), Fig. 20, No. 41, dated to the second half of the thirteenth century.

175.   Cooking-pot in coarse shell-tempered light red-buff ware, grey core, of the same date.

176.   Hard granular red-grey ware, some shell grit on surface, with applied finger-impressed strips; also another with upturned rim and a cooking-pot rim; cf. No. 177. C XV R III Pit 2. Second half of thirteenth century.

177   Hard granular reddish ware, with pierced rim and finger-tip impressions on body. CXV R III Pit A. Second half of thirteenth century.
        There was also a triangular terminal tile from this pit (Fig. 70, No. 14).

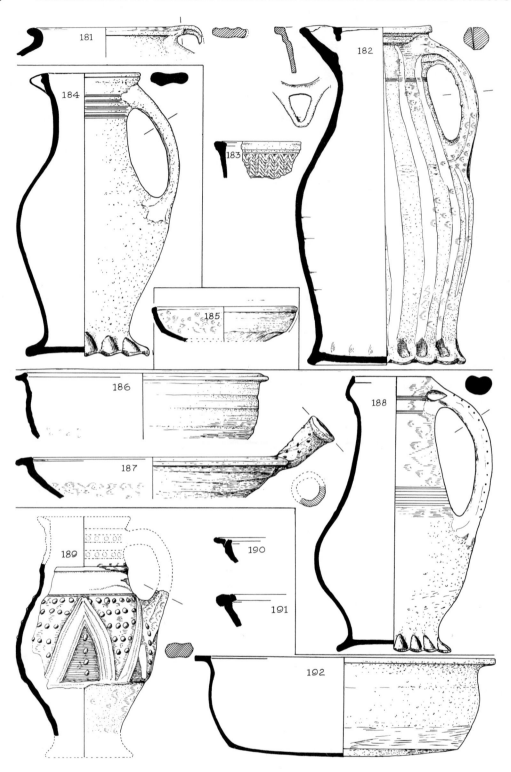

Fig.   89.   Medieval pottery from Area R. Scale 1 : 4

Nos. 178, 179: Pottery from C XV R IV Pit 2. late thirteenth or early fourteenth century.

178. Hard granular reddish ware with thin glaze on upper part, orange and green; there is a slight spout, and the handle is lightly pierced.
179. Hard finely granular grey ware with smoothed surface and applied thumb-impressed strips on body and handle; the rim has an applied collar, lightly pressed down.

180. Hard granular grey-buff ware, with diagonal bands of white slip, arched towards the top, C XV R V Extension 2, layer 2. Brown earth in ? pit. Probably late thirteenth century.

Nos. 181–183: Pottery from C XV R IV Pit 1. Fourteenth century.

181. Hard granular light grey-brown ware, burnished on rim and handle.
182. Hard granular reddish ware, with vertical stripes in yellow-buff slip, probably glazed (worn); bar spout and pierced handle.
183. Jug in hard granular reddish ware, with incised wavy line decoration on neck and on a separate body sherd; covered with transparent glaze, brownish green.

184. Hard granular reddish ware, with patches of transparent glaze below the spout; also a cooking-pot sherd, glazed inside as in the fourteenth century. C XV R III Pit 5. Fourteenth century.
185. Rather fine hard granular reddish ware, smoothed near base, with transparent glaze, orange-green, inside. This and other sherds appear to be in fourteenth-century ware, though there is also a fifteenth-century jug sherd with apple-green glaze. C XV R IV Pit 11. This pit also yielded some whole roof-tiles (Fig. 70, No. 17).

Nos. 186–188: Pottery from C XV R III Pit 6. Fourteenth century.

186. Hard finely granular grey-buff ware, partly smoothed, with some thin glaze, orange, inside; sooted.
187. Ware as No. 186, reddish, with thin transparent glaze near the base inside; there is a small opening where the pierced tubular handle joins the dish.
188. Hard granular reddish ware, grey core, with thin glaze on upper half, orange-green. Cf. No. 413 from the fourteenth-century well in Canterbury Lane.

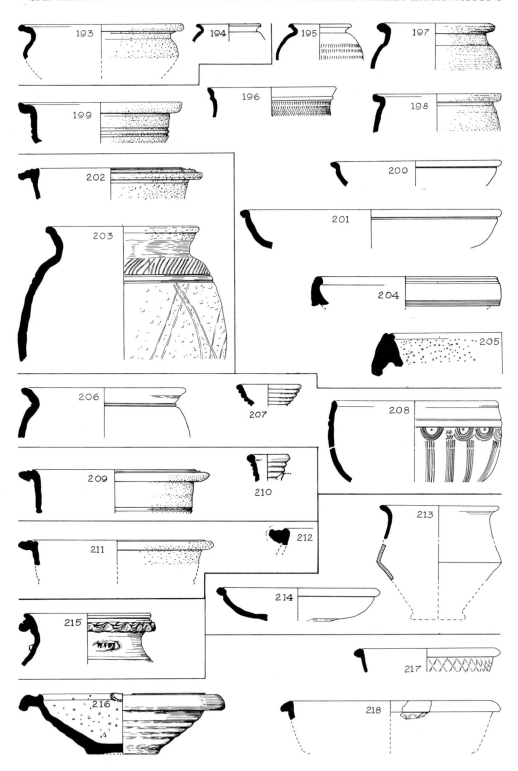

Fig.   90.   Roman pottery from the west side of Canterbury Lane (C X Site H, C X Site M). Scale 1 : 4

Nos. 189–192: Pottery from C XV R V Pit 1. Fourteenth century.

189. Hard finely granular grey-buff ware, pink core; the body is covered in brown slip which shows between the applied chevron and stud decoration which are in white slip (yellow beneath transparent glaze); the white/yellow neck cordon is also applied. London made, imitating a Rouen type cf. *London Museum Medieval Catalogue*, pl. LXIII, 1, dated to the fourteenth century. Cf. Nos. 150, 383.

190. Pierced dish rim in hard finely granular brown ware. Fourteenth century.

191. Pierced dish rim in hard granular ware; two. Fourteenth century.

192. Hard granular reddish ware with sparse shell, roughly knife-trimmed near base.

IVb. SITES C X H AND C X M (Fig. 90)

Nos. 193, 194: Pottery from C X H 14. Cultivation soil. c. A.D. 50–130.

193. Hard rather granular grey ware. *c.* A.D. 100–130.

194. Fine hard burnished grey ware. *c.* A.D. 100–130.

Nos. 195–201: Pottery from C X H 13. Dark soil below first metalling of side street. c. A.D. 100–140.

195, 196. Fine hard burnished grey ware, rouletted.

197, 198. Hard granular grey ware, red core.

199. Hard granular light grey ware.

200. Hard grey ware with darker surface, burnished inside and lip.

201. Smooth hard burnished grey ware.
      Also a bowl sherd; cf. No. 208.

Nos. 202, 203: Pottery from C X H 10. Street 2. c. A.D. 180–220.

202. Hard granular grey ware.

203. Coarse granular grey ware, burnished on rim and neck, with incised shoulder decoration, and burnished lattice on body.
      Also a mid to late second-century dish resembling *Verulamium* Type 963.

Nos. 204, 205: Pottery from C X H 2A. Street 3. c. A.D. *230–260.*

204.   Orange ware with grey core, cream slip (late second century or later, probably local).
205.   Hard whitish buff ware, smooth yellow surface with shallow fine grooves, translucent white-grey grits (A.D. 150–250, probably Lower Germany).

Nos. 206–208: Pottery from C X H 12. Dark soil at north end of Trench overlying Street 1. c. A.D. *180–240.*

206.   Smooth hard burnished light grey ware.
207.   Flagon in orange-buff ware.
208.   Smooth hard burnished grey ware, with incised and compass-drawn decoration, copying Dr. 37.

Nos. 209, 210: Pottery from C X H 9. Loam underlying occupation-earth 7. c. A.D. *140–170.*

209.   Hard granular grey ware.
210.   Flagon in finely granular buff ware.

Nos. 211, 212: Pottery from C X H 7. Occupation-earth from ? earlier timber structure. c. A.D. *170–200.*

211, 212.   Hard granular light grey ware.

SITE C X M

Nos. 213, 214: Pottery from C X M 15. Pit-filling below primary floor of timber building. c. A.D. *110–140.*

213, 214.   Hard burnished grey ware.

215.   Hard finely granular buff ware with frilled rim; widely-spaced applied strips on the neck have incisions that are repeated on the rim. C X M I 12. Layer of ash sealing pit. *c.* A.D. 130–150.

Nos. 216–218: Pottery from C X M 11. Primary floor. c. A.D. 150–180.

216.   Smooth buff ware, grey and white grits (mid second century, probably local).
217–218.   Black-burnished 2 ware. No. 218 may be compared with Gillam's Type 222, dated A.D. 150–210.

IVc. POST-MEDIEVAL POTTERY FROM AREA R
(Figs. 91–92)

Nos. 219–240: Pottery from C XV R I 17 and 11. Late sixteenth- to early seventeenth-century infilling of sixteenth-century cellar. Sherds of the same vessels occur in the lower filling (17) and the upper (11).

219.   Stoneware jug in hard finely granular light grey paste, salt-glazed mottled yellow-brown surface, some thin colourless glaze inside. (11). Another rim in 17, lower filling. Late sixteenth century. Frechen. (*Hurst 1964; Steinzeug*).

220.   Jug imitating stoneware form in hard very finely granular reddish ware, covered with good green glaze outside, and partly inside; another with dark green glaze.

221–223.   Hard finely granular light reddish ware; some thin glaze on No. 221 may be accidental.

224.   Hard finely granular reddish ware, nearly covered with orange-green glaze.

225.   Smooth hard very finely granular reddish ware, some thin glaze, orange-green to brown, inside.

226.   Ware as No. 221, grey core.

227.   Handled jar in hard finely granular bright reddish ware with trace of glaze on rim. (11). Probably from same production-centre as Nos. 222, 223.

228.   Hard rather finely granular red-buff to grey ware. A second jar had three deep finger-impressions to steady its sagging base.

229.   Hard finely granular grey ware, reddish core, with orange-brown glaze inside, especially on lower half. Coarser ware than No. 221.

230.   Hard finely granular red-buff ware, similar to No. 221, with rather thin glaze, orange-green on base, lip, and lower part inside.

231.   Ware as No. 230, red with grey tinge, nearly covered inside with rather thick brown glaze (less than half found).

232.   Hard very finely granular buff ware, inside covered with deep yellow glaze. Surrey ware.

233.   Hard finely granular dark reddish ware, partly covered inside with orange glaze; the outer surface is smooth, with a thin film of glaze in places; sooted. The feet have been pinched out with fingers and thumb. Perhaps Dutch.

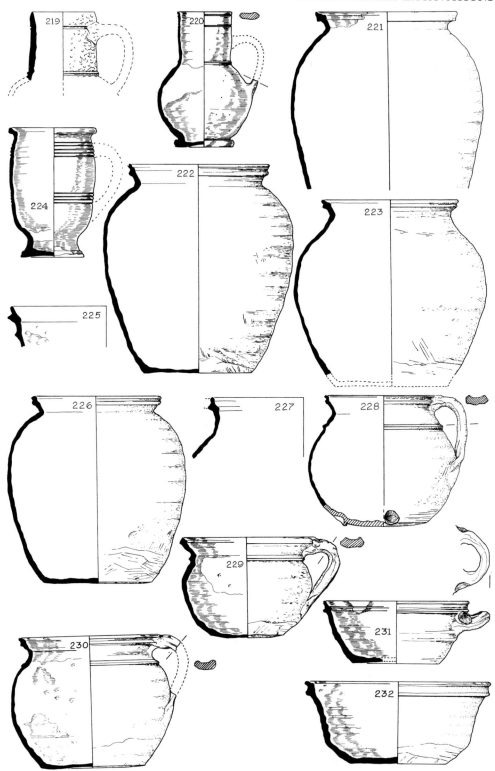

Fig. 91. Post-medieval pottery from Area R, cellar in Trench I. Scale 1 : 4

234. Hard finely granular red-buff ware, with yellow glaze on base and upper part outside, and on lip and lower part inside; single handle. Perhaps Surrey.

235. Pipkin in rather coarse hard finely granular grey-brown ware; also part of another base in finer ware, with good orange-brown glaze inside.

236. Tripod base sherd with zone of rilling outside, in hard very finely granular dark reddish ware, smoked. The upper surface outside, and base inside, are covered with good orange-brown glaze, thinly elsewhere.

237. Pipkin in hard finely granular red-grey ware, with some orange-green glaze, especially on the base inside.

238. Chafing dish with loop handle(s), one support found, in hard finely granular reddish ware, covered inside and partly outside with orange-brown glaze.

239. Flask in hard very finely granular buff ware.

240. Dish in finely granular dull buff ware.

241. Mug in fairly hard, rather finely granular bright reddish ware, surface covered with thin glaze, orange; also a stoneware sherd, cf. No. 219 for ware. C XV R I 9. Thick unsealed deposit of black soil, cut by cellar, containing medieval sherds ranging from the eleventh to the fourteenth century: this mug does not necessarily pre-date the cellar.

Nos. 242, 243: Pottery from C XV R I 2. Rubbly earth above filled-in cellar. Some sherds from this layer join some in 17 and 11.

242. Rather granular buff ware with some glaze, yellow and green, on rim and inside near the base.

243. Hard finely granular reddish ware, covered inside with yellow glaze (half of bowl found).

244. Hard finely granular light red-buff ware, grey core. C XV R I 3. Pocket of earth on top of 2.

For further post-medieval pottery from Area R, see Nos. 858–868.

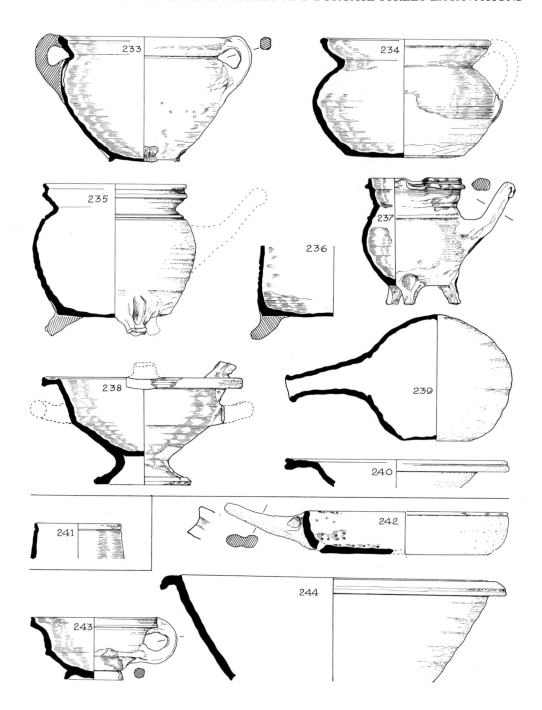

Fig. 92. Post-medieval pottery from Area R, cellar in Trench I. Scale 1 : 4

Va. POTTERY FROM EAST SIDE OF CANTERBURY LANE, C XX–C XXIV, SITE C (pp. 81–100)

A. ROMAN (Figs. 93–95)

Nos. 245–248: Pottery from C XV N I 10. Occupation on gravel floor. c. A.D. *150–210.*

245.   Grey ware, smoothly burnished dark surfaces with lattice.
246.   Hard smoothly burnished grey ware, copying Dr. 38.
247.   Hard rather granular light grey ware, burnished.
248.   Rather granular burnished grey ware.

Nos. 249, 250: Pottery from C XXIII C V A Pit XI, below primary floor. c. A.D. *43–90.*

249.   Hard granular grey ware, burnished on shoulder.
250.   Granular grey ware, burnished neck, furrowed body.

Nos. 251–259: Pottery from C XXIII C V A 15. Occupation on Phase ii floors. c. A.D. *150–210.*

251.   Hard light grey to buff burnished ware with wavy-line decoration.
252–255.   Hard granular grey ware.
256.   Hard burnished light grey-buff ware.
257.   Flagon in hard orange-buff ware, cream slip.
258.   Hard granular grey ware.
259.   Rouletted beaker sherd in fine hard grey ware, of a kind usually found in third-century contexts where, however, the rouletted beakers are normally less bag-shaped (cf. Nos. 262, 275–6).

Nos. 260–262: Pottery from C XXII C I 23. Gritty silt on Period II opus signinum floor. c. A.D. *260–280 but open until 360.*

260.   Black-burnished 2 ware, of Gillam Type 313, dated A.D. 190–240.

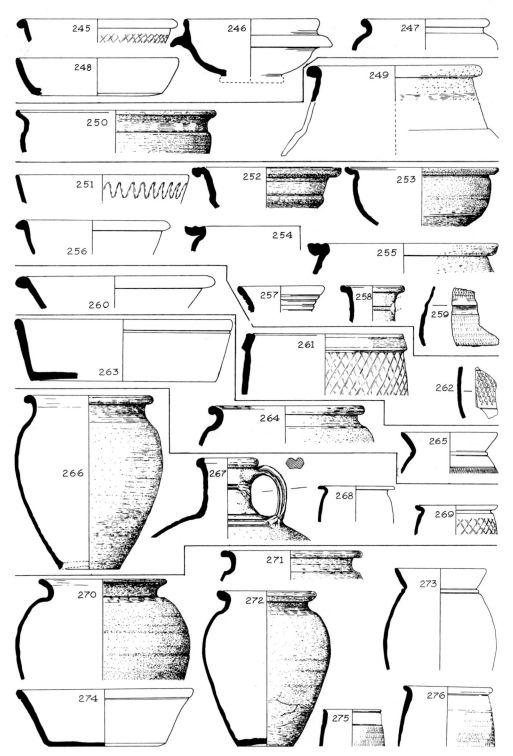

Fig. 93.   Roman pottery from the east side of Canterbury Lane (C XV Site N (Nos. 245–248) and C XX–
C XXIII Site C). Scale 1 : 4

261.   Finely granular light reddish ware with trace of cream slip, and burnished lattice. This type has been found at Verulamium (No. 2150) in two deposits dated A.D. 200–225.

262.   Rouletted sherd in hard burnished grey ware.

Nos. 263–265: Pottery from C XXII C I 23A. Silt in timber slot on north side of opus signinum floor. c. A.D. 280–290.

263.   Hard burnished dark grey ware; cf. Gillam Type 319, dated A.D. 200–350.

264.   Hard rather finely granular grey ware, with burnished lines on rim and shoulder.

265.   Rouletted poppy-head beaker in fine hard smoothly burnished dark grey ware. This type does not appear before *c.* 170–180 and occurs frequently in third-century contexts.

Nos. 266–269: Pottery from C XXIII C V A Pit X, in Period II secondary floor. c. A.D. 220–260.

266.   Hard finely granular grey-brown ware, smoothed rim and neck.

267.   Slightly granular reddish ware (rim incomplete).

268 .   Fine hard burnished grey ware.

269.   Ware as No. 268, with burnished lattice.

Nos. 270–276: Pottery from C XXIII C V A 13. Occupation and burnt debris on final Period II floors. c. A.D. 280–290.

270 (two)–272.   Hard granular grey ware with burnished lines on rim and shoulder.

273.   Fine hard burnished light grey ware.

274.   Burnished grey ware (burnt); two.

275–276.   Fine hard light grey, burnished above rouletting.

Nos. 277, 278: Pottery from .C XXIII C V A 12. Period II fallen wall-clay. c. A.D. 280–290.

277.   Coarse granular dark grey to brown ware, unevenly burnished rim and neck; though hand-made, it does not belong to the late fourth-century group such as Nos. 291–296, but is an interesting anticipation.

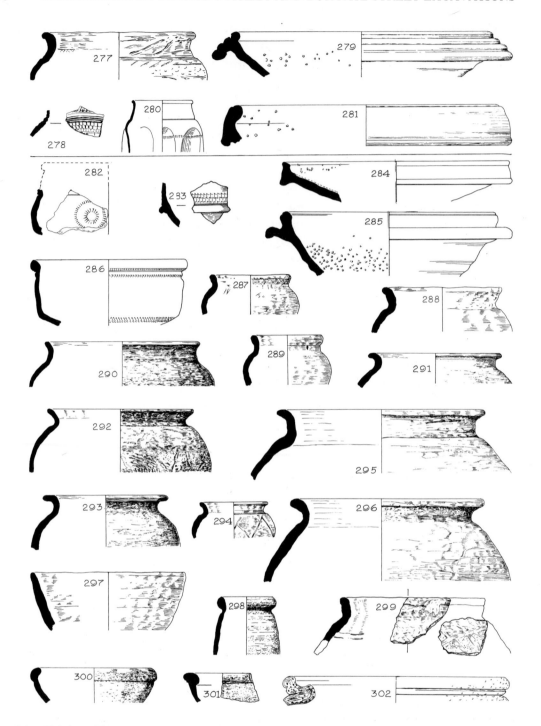

Fig. 94. Third- to fifth-century Roman pottery from the east side of Canterbury Lane (C XX–C XXIII Site C).
Scale 1 : 4

278.   Beaker sherd in fine reddish paste with brick-red colour-coating inside, 'metallic' grey-brown outside over scale-pattern rouletting; a third- to fourth-century type, probably imported.

279.   Buff ware with orange-buff surface, black ironstone grits (probably third century; Nene Valley). C XXIII C V A Pit 9. in final Period II floor. *c* A.D. 270–290.

Nos. 280, 281: Pottery from C XXIII C V C 7. Period II fallen wall-clay. A.D. 280–290.

280.   Rhenish ware in fine reddish paste with glossy 'metallic' green-grey colour-coating.
281.   Hard buff ware, cream slip, reddish and dark grey grits (A.D. 150–250, Lower Germany).

Nos. 282–302: Pottery from C XX-XXIII C I 9, 9A and C V A 7, 5. Black cultivation-soil above Period III destruction-level. c. A.D. *380 to fifth century.*

282.   Red colour-coated bowl with stamped rosette, in Oxfordshire ware, of Young's Type C 84.12, dated A.D. 350–400+.
283.   Hard reddish ware, orange-red coating, rouletted; cf. Young's Type C 53.2 (plain).
284.   Hard reddish ware, white slip, white quartz grits (probably third century, Kent).
285.   Hard buff ware, orange-buff colour-coating, red and white quartz grits; cf. Young's Type C 100.7, dated to the fourth century.
286.   Slightly micaceous reddish ware, grey core, worn red colour-coating; cf. Young's Type C 68.3, dated A.D. 300–400+. As noted previously, red colour-coated Oxfordshire bowls of types other than those imitating Dr. 31, and perhaps Dr. 38, do not seem to appear in Canterbury before *c.* A.D. 360.
287.   Hand-made in coarse grey ware with rather fine shell-tempering, unevenly burnished.
288.   Hand-made in coarse granular grey-brown ware, red core, unevenly burnished.
289.   Coarse granular grey ware, burnished buff surface and lip.
290–293.   Hand-made in coarse granular grey or grey-brown ware, unevenly burnished.
294.   Coarse hand-finished grey-buff ware, uneven burnished surface with burnished decoration.
295–296.   Coarse hard granular grey-brown ware, hand-finished and unevenly burnished.
297.   Hand-made in coarse granular grey-brown ware, unevenly burnished.
298.   Rather finely granular grey-buff ware, smoothed surface, dark grey inside.
299.   Hand-made in coarse grey-buff ware with sand and fine shell tempering, irregular burnished surface decorated with cross-burnished lines; perhaps Romano-Saxon in this ware. Another example had been published above (No. 108).

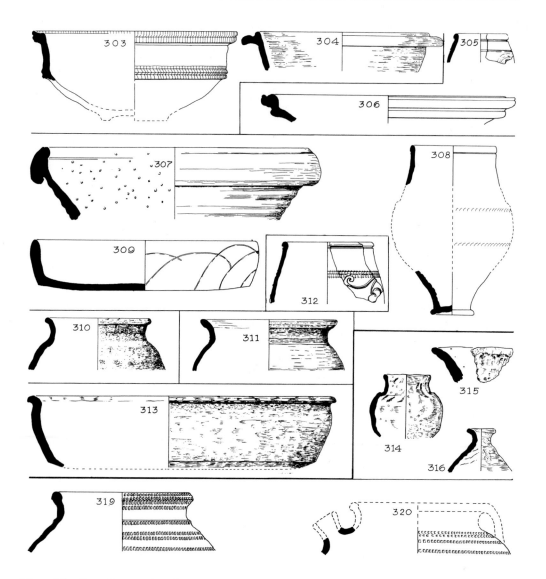

Fig. 95. Late Roman, late Saxon and Badorf-type pottery from C XX–C XXIII Site C. Scale 1 : 4

300.   Hard granular grey ware with black rather uneven surface, burnished lip, sooted.

301.   Granular whitish ware.

302.   Coarse grey-buff ware with large black grits, imported from the Rhineland, see *Britannia*, vi (1975), 176.

      The layer also yielded a flange from an *'à l'éponge'* vessel imported from the Poitiers region of Gaul. For the type see No. 608 below. Residual here.

Nos. 303, 304: Pottery from C XXII C I Pit R 4. c. A.D. *300–350.*

303. Smooth hard white ware with orange-brown paint on rim and cordon (reconstructed from another in a destruction-layer dated A.D. 340–360 in the St. Margaret's Street Baths). Oxfordshire: Young's Type P 24, dated A.D. 240–400+.

304. Hard granular grey ware, partly burnished.

Nos. 305, 306: Pottery from C XXII C II Pit 6. c. A.D. *350–400.*

305. Finely granular light buff paste, dark brown colour-coating, with trace of barbotine decoration.

306. Hard reddish ware and coating, cf. Young's Type C 42.1 copying Ludowici Tg.

Nos. 307–309: Pottery from C XXIII C V A Pit 2. c. A.D. *360–fifth century.*

307. Whitish-buff ware, white grits (A.D. 150–250, Lower Germany).

308. Orange-grey paste, brown colour-coating; local ware.

309. Black-burnished 1 ware, complete dish of Gillam's Type 329, dated A.D. 190–340.

310. Hand-made in coarse granular grey ware, with partly smoothed uneven surface, sooted. C XXIII C V A Pit R 13. *c.* A.D. 370–450.

311. Hard grey ware, partly burnished, C XXIII C V A Pit R 12. *c.* A.D. 380–fifth century.

312. Hard finely granular orange-buff paste, red inside, with barbotine leaf decoration and dark grey-brown 'metallic' coating; probably local. C XXII C I Pit R 3. *c.* A.D. 400–420.

313. Coarse granular grey ware, unevenly burnished dark surface. C XXI C I Pit R 5. *c.* A.D. 400–450.

B. SAXON POTTERY (Figs. 95–98)

314. Coarse shell-tempered grey-brown ware, roughly hand-made, showing finger-marks; burnished. C XV N 2. Daub and charcoal layer above late Saxon floor. The layer also contained a wheel-turned rim; cf. No. 342 as well as an intrusive late eleventh-century cooking-pot rim.

315. Smooth grey-black ware with sand and a few flint grits, uneven partly burnished surface; although hand-made, it is probably of ninth-century date. C XXII C I 9, trodden into late Roman cultivated soil.

Fig. 96.   Sherds of Pingsdorf ware from Canterbury Lane (C XX Site C). Scale 1 : 2

316.   Hard rather finely granular grey ware with uneven darker surface burnished with irregular horizontal strokes. Probably made in northern France (Hamwih Class 14, Black ware) a type probably dating from the seventh to the early ninth century.[94] Spiral marks on the inside suggest that the whole neck was twisted during manufacture. Cf. No. 325. C XXII C I 8D. Saxon cobbled floor. See Appendix III.

317.   Sherd in Pingsdorf ware in hard finely granular cream ware, grey core, with red-brown painted design. C XX C I 9A. Narrow oblique trench cut through the late Saxon occupation-layer and sealed by (1). Eleventh century.

318.   As No. 317, deeper yellow throughout. C XX C I 1, floor (?) with Group III cooking-pot sherds (first half of twelfth century) immediately below modern cellar floor.

Nos. 319–347: Pottery from C XX-XXII C I 8. Occupation on Saxon cobbled floor. c. A.D. 850–950.

319–321.   Sherds in Badorf-type ware, see Appendix III and Pl. XXXIII B. Note: No. 320 is a restoration of No. 321.

322.   Sherd in Badorf-type ware: smooth fine yellow-buff ware, grey core; applied ribs with roller-stamped decoration.
Another sherd from C V A 6 (not figured) *c.* A.D. 850–950.

323.   Sherd in granular light grey ware, with stamped cross decoration.

324.   Sherds of a large vessel with irregular bosses, in fairly hard and finely granular grey-brown ware, the surface cross-burnished with narrow stokes. Sherd of another in C V A 4. See also No. 109 above.

325.   Pitcher with strap handle attached to the rim, in granular grey ware with uneven surface, cross-burnished with narrow strokes. Probably made in northern France (Hamwih Class 14, Black ware), cf. No. 316. Two similar handles from other vessels were also present. Another intrusive in C XXII C II 9. See Appendix III.

94.   Gratitude is due to Dr. Richard Hodges for commenting on Nos. 316, 325 and 353. cf. *idem, The Hamwih Pottery* (CBA Research Report No. 37, London 1981), 21–4.

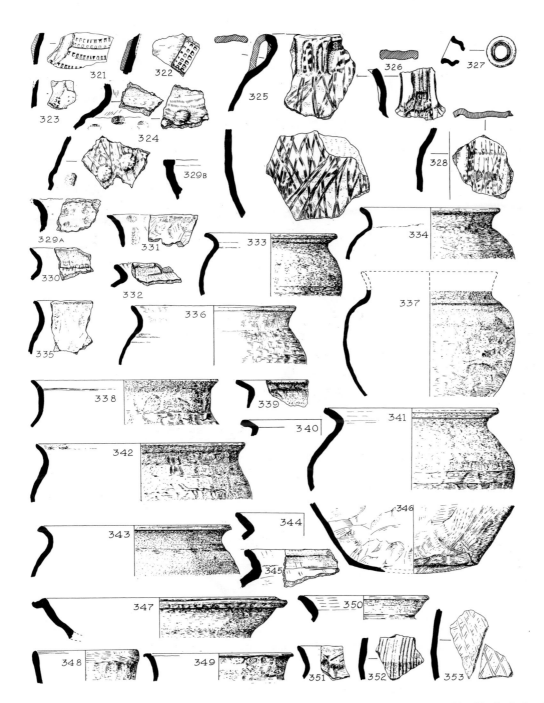

Fig. 97. Bardorf-type and late Saxon pottery from Canterbury Lane (C XX–C XXIII Site C). Scale 1 : 4

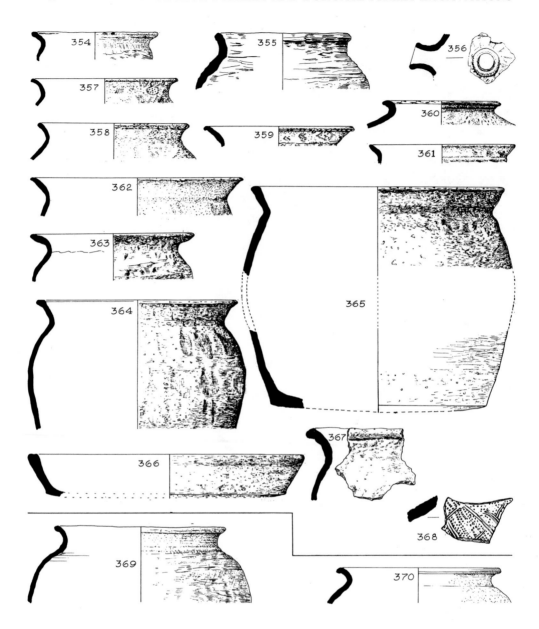

Fig.   98.   Late Saxon pottery from Canterbury Lane (C XX–C XXIII Site C). Scale 1 : 4

326. Strap handle, cf. No. 325, with dark surface; also dark cross-burnished sherds, and another handle in light grey ware.

327. Pitcher spout in fine slightly granular light grey ware; three. Cf. No. 356.

328. Sherd with vertical ridges converging towards the base, with a shallower horizontal ridge; in hard granular light grey ware, with narrow vertical burnishing (five sherds).

329A. Coarse dark grey ware with fine shell-tempering, irregular burnished surface.

329B. Rather coarse light grey-buff shell-tempered ware. Cf. No. 365.

330–344. Hard rather finely granular ware with a high proportion of sandy grit, the colour ranging from grey to grey-brown and dark grey, frequently with knife-trimmed surfaces. Thirty-six similar cooking-pot rims are not figured.

345. Hard rather finely granular light grey ware, knife-trimmed, with vertical burnishing. There is a resemblance to the Medieval Group I rims of later date.

346. Knife-trimmed base in hard rather finely granular grey-buff ware, with smoothed black surfaces.

347. Coarse granular grey ware, smoothed surfaces.

Nos. 348–353: Pottery from C XXIII C V A 4. Occupation and Saxon floors, as layer 8. c. A.D. 850–950.

348. Dark grey ware with fine grit, irregular smoothed surface.

349. Light grey ware with fine grit, smooth surface, perhaps imported. (?) Hamwih Class 13. Cf. Appendix III.

350, 351. Finely granular dark grey ware, partly burnished, with finger-impressions; also a sherd with a boss, cf. No. 324.

352. Hard finely granular grey-buff ware with regular vertical furrowing.

353. Cooking-pot sherd in hard finely granular light grey ware, rather smooth surface with burnished lattice. Northern France: Hamwih Class 13. Cf. Appendix III.

There were also present a number of fragments of Saxon, or re-used Roman, tiles (Fig. 69, No. 2).

Nos. 354, 355: Pottery from C XXII C II 9 and 7. Occupation and Saxon floors as layer 8

354. Hard rather finely granular grey-brown ware, knife-trimmed, and partly burnished (9).

335. Slightly granular grey-buff to grey ware, knife-trimmed; burnished surfaces (7). Also a strap handle cf. No. 325.

Nos. 356–366: Pottery from C XXIII C I 2. Saxon occupation as layer 8. c. A.D. 850–950.

356. Pitcher spout in hard finely granular grey-black ware. Cf. No. 327.

357 (two)–359. Hard rather finely granular light grey ware, red core, with traces of thin transparent lead glaze outside.

360–363 (two). Ware as No. 357, grey-black, unglazed.

364. Coarse dark grey-brown ware with plentiful shell-tempering, showing finger-impressions; sooted.

365. Ware as No. 364, lower part smoothed. Cf. No. 329B.

366. Rather coarse grey ware with plentiful shell-tempering.

367. Light grey finely shell-tempered ware with irregular surfaces. C XXII C II 30. Occupation on Saxon cobbled floor east of well. c. A.D. 850–950.

368. Rather coarse hard light grey ware with fine sand-tempering; pattern of roughly stamped lozenges bordered by grooves. Cf. a middle Saxon lugged pitcher from Ipswich, *Proc. Cambridge Ant. Soc.*, 1 (1957), 41, fig. 5, No. 1. C XXIV C VI 4. Dark soil over Saxon floor, which also contained three cooking-pot rims; cf. No. 362 etc.

Nos. 369, 370: Pottery from C XXII C II 19. Dark Saxon earth (not in section).
c. A.D. 850–950.

369. Hard rather finely granular grey-black ware, unevenly burnished body.

370. Ware as No. 369, light grey, unusually well made; also imported pitcher sherds as No. 325.

C. MEDIEVAL POTTERY (Figs. 99–100)

Nos. 371, 372: Pottery from C XXII C II 3. Early medieval dark soil over gravel floor 4 (Section P-Q).

371. Hard very uneven grey-black ware with fine shell-tempering, probably early eleventh century.

372. Hard finely granular light grey ware; sharply knife-trimmed, burnished with vertical strokes. Cf. medieval Group I.
Also a thirteenth-century cooking-pot sherd, probably intrusive.

Nos. 373, 374: Pottery from C XXIII C V A Pit 1 (M 6), sealed by chalk and gravel floor, layer 1.

373. Coarse reddish ware, grey core, with thick shell-tempering, thumbed rim, probably twelfth century.

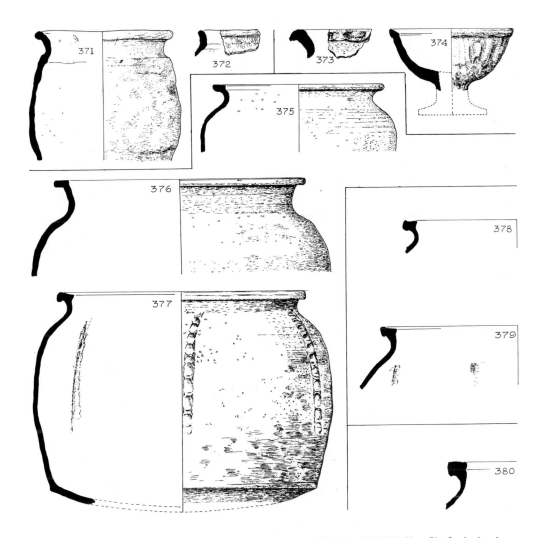

Fig. 99. Medieval pottery from Canterbury Lane (C XX–C XXIII Site C). Scale 1 : 4

374. Lamp in rather finely granular local reddish ware, grey core, roughly trimmed surface with irregular vertical grooves; smoked inside. Reconstructed after similar lamps from Thetford.

Nos. 375–377: Pottery from C XXIII C V C Pit 4. Black earth filling. Second half of thirteenth century.

375. Hard rather finely granular red-brown ware, with a little shell on surfaces.
376. Grey-brown shell-tempered ware.

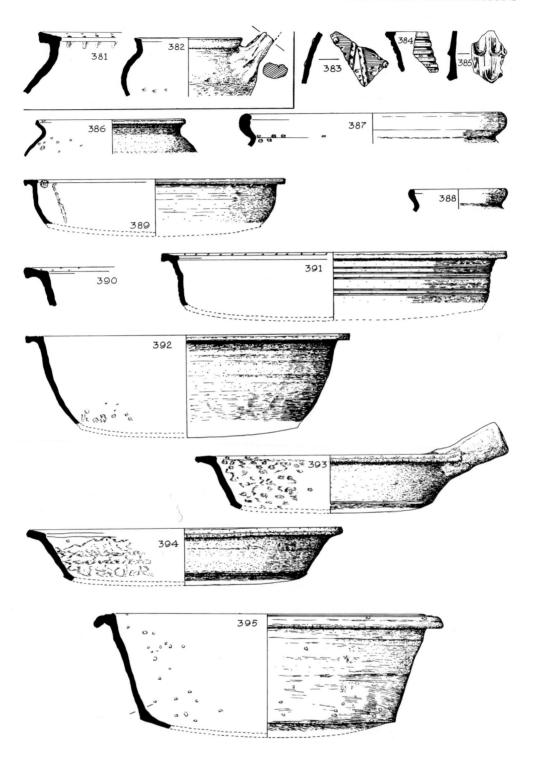

Fig. 100.   Medieval pottery from Canterbury Lane (C XX–C XXIII Site C). Scale 1 : 4

377.   Hard rather finely granular reddish ware, grey core, with some shell on surface; applied thumb-impressed strips.

Nos. 378, 379: Pottery from C XXIII C V C Pit 2 (M 7). Black earth and building debris.
Second half of thirteenth century.

378.   Hard granular reddish ware.

379.   Ware as No. 378, with applied strips; cf. No. 377.

380.   Hard reddish shell-tempered ware; also another cooking-pot as No. 377. C XXII C II Pit 5 (M 16). Sealed by chalk capping of well-shaft. Second half of thirteenth century.

Nos. 381, 382: Pottery from C XXII C III Pit 1. Ash, yellow loam, and earth tips.
Fourteenth century.

381.   Cooking-pot in hard rather finely granular red-brown ware, with pierced rim.

382.   Ware as No. 381 with splashes of thin glaze inside, sooted. Cf. No. 638.

Nos. 383–395: Pottery from C XXIII C V D Pit 2 (M 11). Early fourteenth century.

383.   Hard red-buff ware, grey core with applied chevron and studs in white slip, against a dark red-brown slip outside the chevron; covered by lustrous transparent glaze, showing yellow. Cf. No. 189, London imitation of a thirteenth-century Rouen jug.

384.   Granular red-brown ware, rilled neck, with some glaze, green-brown. Cf. No. 403.

385.   Finely granular red-brown ware with deep finger-impressions arranged horizontally, covered with good glaze, yellow-green. Cf. No. 401.

386.   Fine slightly granular reddish ware, with traces of glaze inside, sooted.

387.   Hard granular red-buff ware, smoothed surface, with traces of glaze inside.

388.   Finely granular reddish ware, sooted.

389.   Hard granular red-brown ware, grey core, smoothed surface, with trace of glaze inside; sooted.

390.   Hard rather finely granular reddish ware, pierced rim.

391.   Hard granular red-brown ware with deeply grooved body, smoothed surface, pierced rim; sooted.

392.   Ware as No. 391, reddish, with trace of glaze inside.

393.   Ware as No. 391, with thin glaze, brown, inside; tubular handle.

394.   Ware as No. 391 with thin glaze inside, orange; smoked.

395.   Hard rather finely granular red-brown ware, with a little shell throughout.

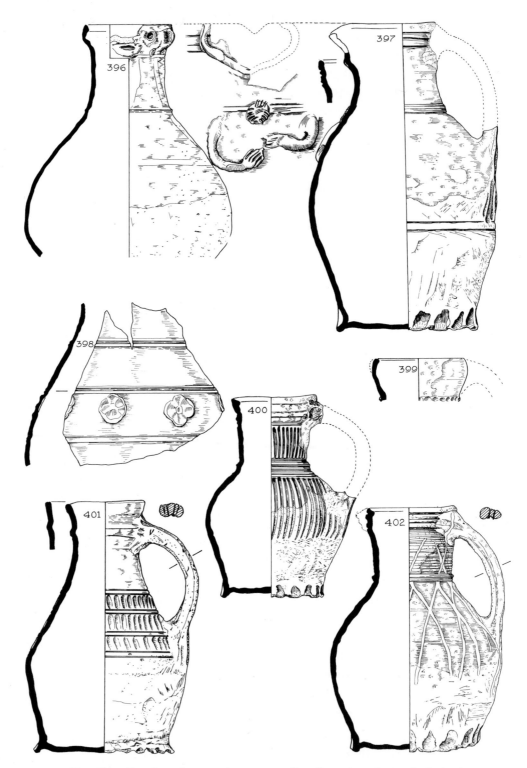

Fig. 101.   Jugs from fourteenth-century well at Canterbury Lane. Scale 1 : 4

D. POTTERY FROM FOURTEENTH-CENTURY WELL IN TRENCH C II (Figs. 101–108)

Nos. 396–438: Pottery from C XXII C II 14. Waterlogged material at the bottom of the well. All the jugs were made locally, in Tyler Hill ware.

396. Hard rather finely granular red-buff ware with part of crudely modelled face in central position; some light-coloured slip on upper part, covered with thin glaze, orange green; also sherds of another face-mask.

397. Ware as No. 396, reddish, with applied human arms and beard on body below the spout which represents the mouth; upper part glazed but without a slip.

398. Hard granular reddish ware, grey core with applied roughly stamped rosettes. Nearly covered with glaze, orange-green.

399. Ware as No. 398, grey-buff, decorated with finger impressions, perhaps on applied strip, with thin glaze, green-brown.

400. Hard rather finely granular red-grey ware decorated with vertical grooves; thin glaze, orange-green on upper part.

401. Hard granular grey-buff ware with impressed decoration, glaze as No. 400.

402, 403. Ware as No. 400, with rilled neck, decorated with lines of pale buff slip. This type of decoration has been found in a late thirteenth-century pit in Rose Lane (*Arch. Cant.*, lxviii, Fig 21, No. 48).

404(two), 405. Hard granular reddish ware decorated as No. 402, with thin glaze, orange.

406. Hard rather finely granular dark grey to red-buff ware, decorated with horizontal bands of white-buff slip, thin glaze towards the front, orange-green; two.

407. Ware as No. 406, with finely rilled neck, undecorated.

408. As No. 406, reddish ware.

409. Ware as No. 406, grey-buff, with vertical strips; spout broken off.

410. Hard rather finely granular grey-buff ware, covered with thin glaze, orange-green, on upper part, over traces of lighter slip.

411. Ware as No. 410, red-buff, with traces of horizontal lines of pale slip (worn), and vertical line on handle; spout broken off.

412. Hard granular reddish ware, with thin glaze, orange, on upper part towards the front.

413. Hard rather finely granular red-buff ware, glaze as No. 412; six.

414–416. Ware as No. 413, grey-brown and red-brown, with thin glaze, orange green.

417. Hard granular reddish ware; nineteen whole jugs and fragments of twenty more. These narrow, unglazed jugs are the most common type found in the well, as if they were primarily designed for drawing water; they tilt less on the hook than the round-bodied shapes.

418. Ware as No. 417 with thin glaze, orange-green, on upper part.

419. The same type as No. 417. Three whole jugs: one with letter H below the handle in white slip (419A), another with cross at base of handle (419B).

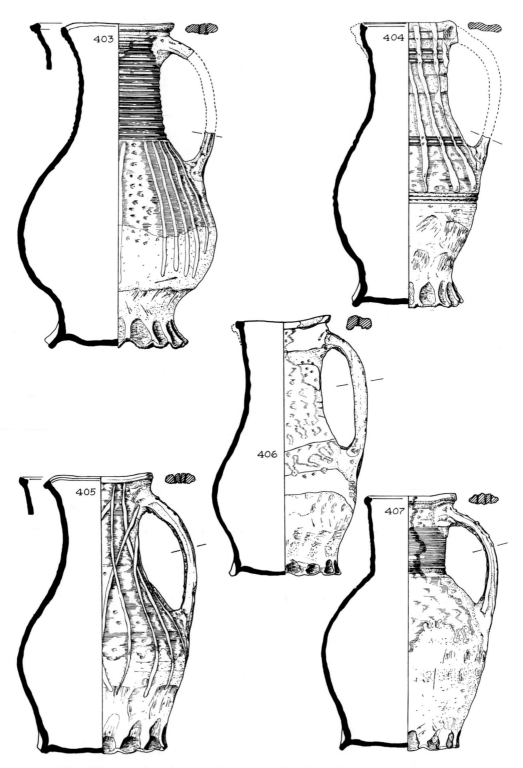

Fig. 102.   Jugs from fourteenth-century well at Canterbury Lane. Scale 1 : 4

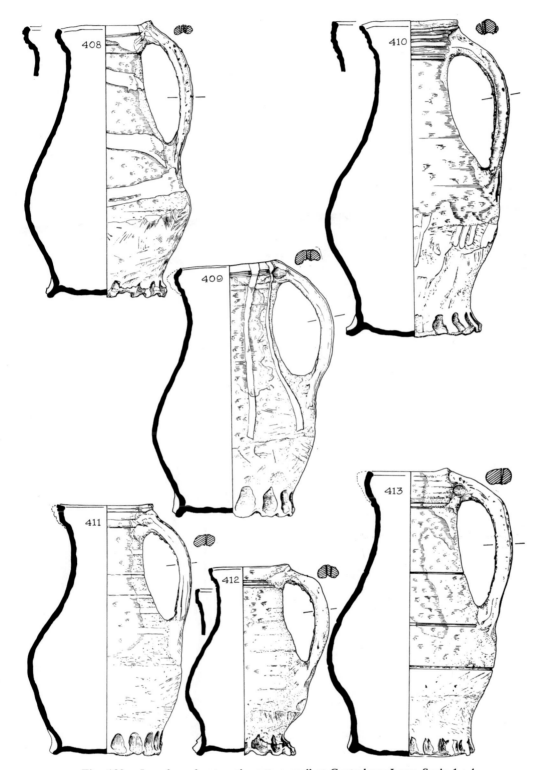

Fig. 103.   Jugs from fourteenth-century well at Canterbury Lane. Scale 1 : 4

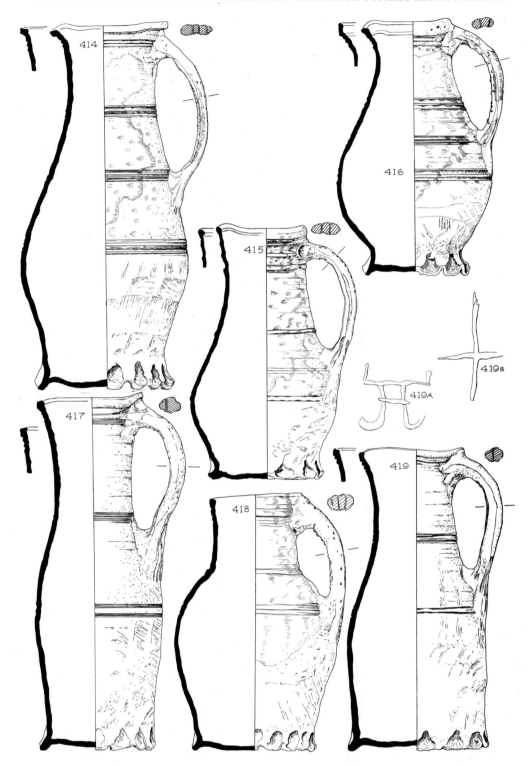

Fig. 104.   Jugs from fourteenth-century well at Canterbury Lane. Scale 1 : 4

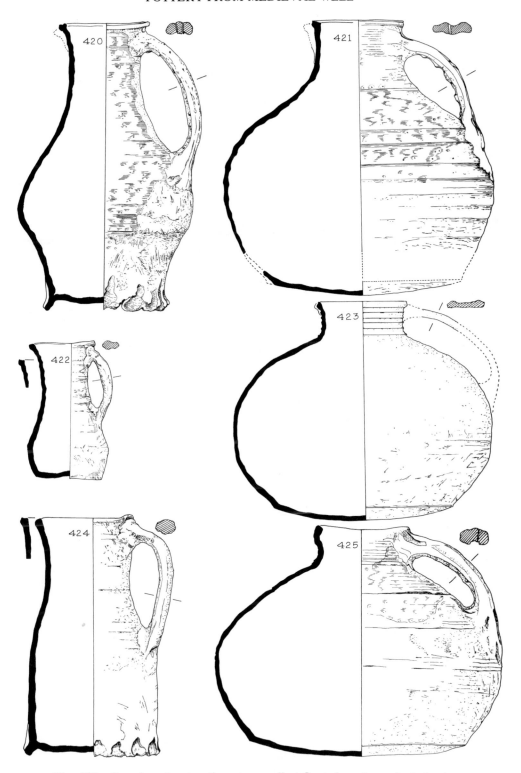

Fig. 105. Jugs from fourteenth-century well at Canterbury Lane. Scale 1 : 4

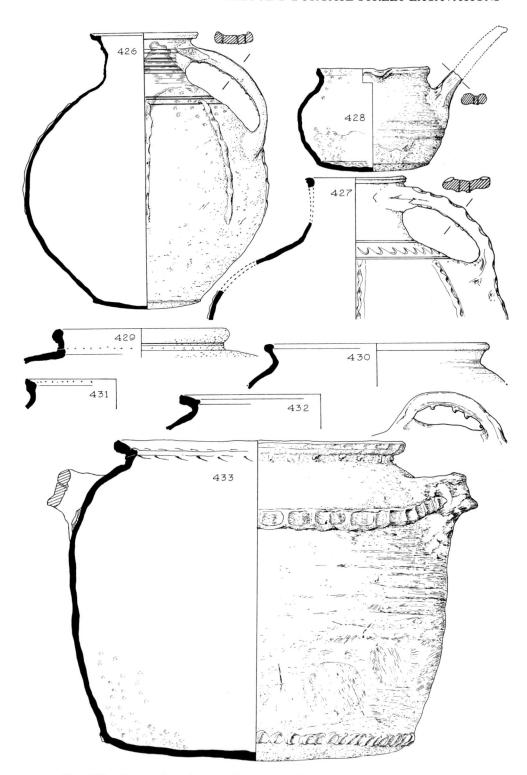

Fig. 106.   Pottery from fourteenth-century well at Canterbury Lane. Scale 1 : 4

420. Hard rather finely granular bright reddish ware, with thin glaze, orange, covering the upper part; spout broken off.

421. Hard rather granular grey-brown ware, grey core, smoothed surface, with thin glaze, green, on upper part; spout broken off.

422. Rather granular grey-buff ware, partly smoothed surface. This very small jug is complete and unchipped, and might have fallen in from the edge of the well.

423. Hard rather finely granular grey ware, brown inside, with rilled neck and slight spout.

424. Hard granular ware, bright reddish outside, grey inside, smoothed lower part; unglazed. Cf. Nos. 417, 419.

425. Hard granular buff ware, with traces of lighter slip on upper part, under thin glaze, orange-green (worn).

426. Hard granular grey ware with applied thumb-impressed strips; a little thin glaze, dark green, on neck.

427. Ware as No. 426 with the addition of a scored wavy line on the shoulder, and thumb impressions on the handle edges; the neck may have been rilled; unglazed.

In all, sixty-five complete jugs were recovered from the bottom of the well, together with at least forty-one broken jugs, in addition to a quantity of badly smashed pieces. In many cases the spout had been knocked off, presumably on the side of the well.

Nos. 428–438: Other vessels, lost or thrown into the well. Although these might all have been deposited as rubbish when the well was abandoned, similarities between the bulk of the pitchers make it unlikely that the well was dug before the fourteenth century.

428. Pipkin in hard rather finely granular red-brown ware, smoked outside; the base and lower part inside covered with thin glaze, orange.

429. Hard granular reddish ware, grey core, pierced neck.

430. Buff granular ware, perhaps under-fired.

431. Hard granular red-brown ware, grey core.

432. Ware as No. 431.

433. Hard granular grey-brown ware, with pierced rim, neck and handles (one broken), and applied thumb-impressed strip; sooted.

434. Hard granular red-brown ware with thin glaze, orange-green, inside; sooted.

435, 436. Hard rather finely granular bright reddish, and red-brown, ware, sooted.

437. Granular buff ware, grey core, with applied thumb-impressed strip, smoke-blackened; trickles of thin glaze inside.

438. Hard granular reddish ware, thin glaze, orange-green, inside, sooted outside; trace of handle.

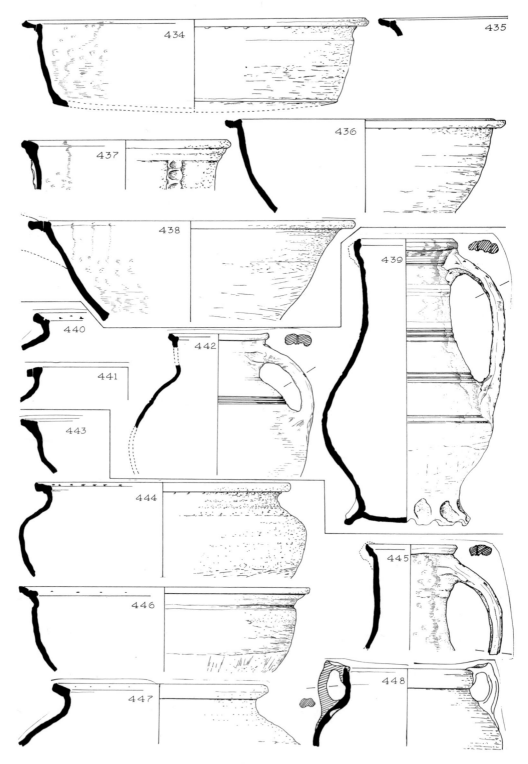

Fig. 107. Pottery from upper levels of the fourteenth-century well at Canterbury Lane. Scale 1 : 4

Nos. 439–442: Pottery from C XXII C II 13. Collapsed timber and chalk from well-head.

439.   Hard finely granular light reddish ware with rather thin glaze, orange-green, on upper part. This presumably is a pitcher lost in the well, covered with earth from layer 13, and if so will be among the latest types used in the well.

440, 441.   Hard rather finely granular light grey-buff ware, grey core, pierced rim.

442.   Finely granular buff ware, smooth surface (worn); unlike Tyler Hill ware.
Also a bowl sherd of the same type as No. 446.

Nos. 443–448: Pottery from C XXII C II 12. Dark soil, filling-in of well.

443.   Dish in hard finely granular brown ware, smoked.

444.   Bowl in hard rather finely granular light reddish ware, pierced rim.

445.   Hard rather finely granular grey-brown ware with some thin glaze, green-brown, especially in front.

446(two), 447.   Hard rather finely granular red-buff ware, grey core, pierced rim; sooted.

448.   Hard rather granular grey ware, uneven lighter surface (one handle found).

Nos. 449, 450: Pottery from C XXII C II 11. Dark soil, filling-in of well.

449.   Hard rather finely granular grey-brown ware, pierced rim.

450.   Hard finely granular red-buff ware, uneven surface, pierced rim; also part of a jug similar to No. 417.

Nos. 451–457: Pottery from C XXII C II 9. Dark soil in well above yellow loam.

451.   Hard granular grey to reddish ware, buff inside, with applied thumb-impressed strips; some thin glaze, green-brown, on upper part towards the front.

452.   Two-handled cooking-pot in hard rather finely granular reddish ware, grey core.

453.   Cooking-pot with horizontal strap handles and applied thumb-impressed strip as No. 433, in hard granular reddish ware with a little thin glaze, orange green.

454.   As No. 453, dark grey; diameter 24 cm.

455.   Hard granular reddish ware with smooth surface, pierced rim.

456.   Hard granular red to grey-buff ware, grey core, with some thin glaze, orange-green.

457.   Hard rather finely granular grey-brown ware, partly smoothed, with pierced neck.

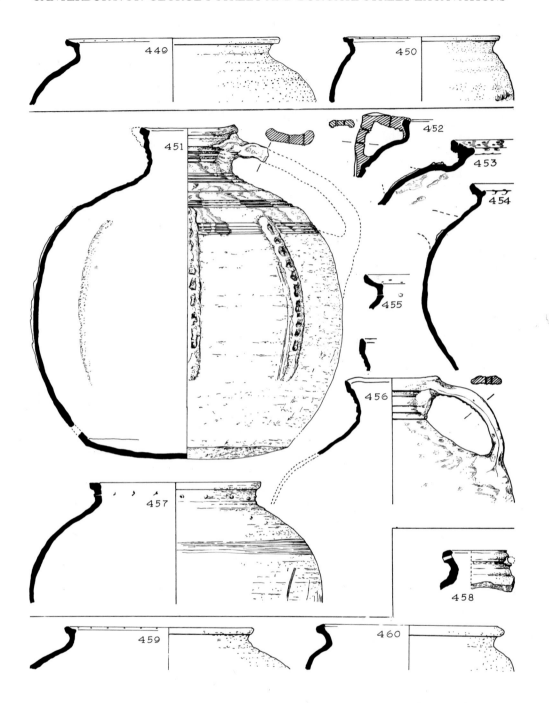

Fig. 108.   Pottery from the upper levels of the fourteenth-century well at Canterbury Lane. Scale 1 : 4

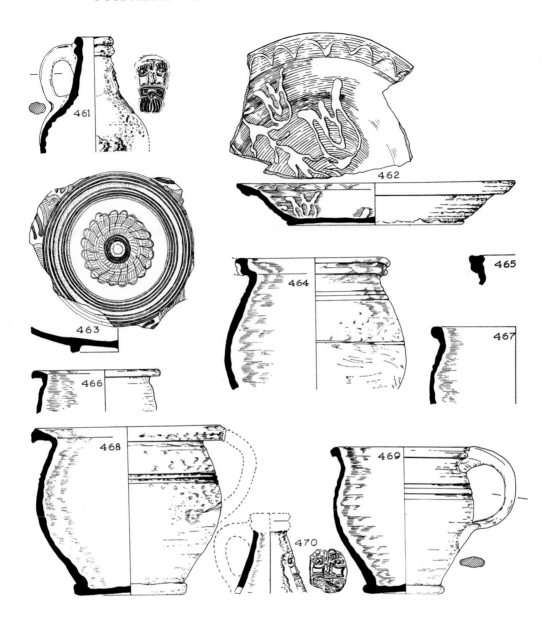

Fig. 109.   Post-medieval pottery from Canterbury Lane (C XX–C XXIV Site C). Scale 1 : 4

Nos. 458–460: Pottery from C XXII C II 3. Dark earth in the upper filling of the well.

458.   Cooking-pot in hard granular grey-brown ware, with perforated rim; splashed with glaze outside.

459, 460.   Hard finely granular reddish grey ware.

E. POST-MEDIEVAL POTTERY FROM C XX–C XXIV, SITE C (Fig. 109)

Nos. 461–469: Pottery from C XXII C II Pit 1, above well

461.   Bellarmine jug in hard rather dark grey stoneware with stamped face-mask, salt-glazed surfaces, thick closely mottled deep red-brown outside; rather roughly made. Cf. No. 470. Mid seventeenth century, Frechen. (*Hurst* (1977), 219–38).

462.   Slipware plate in hard finely granular reddish ware, with design in white slip inside, showing yellow under glaze against orange-brown background.

463.   Maiolica plate in very finely granular pinkish buff ware, with design inside in deep and medium blue, yellow, orange and green; covered inside with white opaque tin glaze, buff outside. South Netherlands, *c.* A.D. 1500.

464.   Pipkin with spout, and handle attached to the rim, in hard finely granular bright reddish ware, covered inside and on upper part outside with glaze, orange-brown.

465.   Hard finely granular reddish ware, both surfaces covered with glaze, orange-brown.

466.   Ware as No. 465, light reddish with rough surface; thin glaze, yellow-green, inside.

467.   Chamber-pot in ware as No. 465, covered inside with glaze, orange-brown.

468.   Chamber-pot in hard reddish ware, grey core, covered inside and on upper part outside with rather thin glaze, orange-green.

469.   As No. 468, in grey-brown ware, reddish core with internal glaze only.

Nos. 470, 471: Pottery from C XXII C IV 1. Loam floor of Building B

470.   Bellarmine jug as No. 461, mid seventeenth century, Frechen. (*Hurst* (1977), 219–38).

471.   (Not figured: for type see No. 905 below). Posset pot in hard finely granular buff ware with pattern in brown slip; surfaces covered in smooth glaze, yellow. Staffordshire, mid to late seventeenth century.

Vb. POTTERY FROM CANTERBURY LANE, C XXVIII
SITES C XX AND C XXI (pp. 101–8).

A. ROMAN (Figs. 110–111)

Nos. 472–474: Pottery from C XXVIII C XX 47. Occupation on loam floor. c. A.D. 160–190.

472.   Fine hard burnished grey ware.
473.   Smooth cream ware.
474.   Coarse granular grey-brown ware, uneven burnished surface and lip.

475.   Fine hard burnished grey ware with three rouletted bands on rim. C XX 52. Loamy soil at south end of trench. *c* A.D. 200–240.

Nos. 476, 477: Pottery from C XX 63. Loamy soil similar to layer 52. c. A.D. 200–240.

476.   Black-burnished 1 ware, cf. Gillam Type 329, dated A.D. 190–240.
477.   Black-burnished 2 ware.

Nos. 478, 479: Pottery from C XX Pit 13 cut into secondary floor. c. A.D. 180–210.

478.   Hard cream-white ware, white grit (A.D. 140–190, probably local).
479.   Black-burnished 2 ware. Not in Gillam.

480.   Hard cream ware, white grit (late second or third century, probably an import). C XX 46. Hearth debris sealing layer 47 and Pit 14. *c*. A.D. 200–220.
481.   Hard finely granular cream ware, buff core, white and grey grits (A.D. 130–180, probably local). Also a third-century mortarium rim fragment in local ware (not figured); C XX 61. Occupation-layer, *c*. A.D. 200–240.

Nos. 482–484: Pottery from C XX 62. Chalk, loam and gravel floor cut by Pit 15.
c. A.D. 180–220.

482.   Fine hard orange-buff paste, 'metallic' dark grey-brown colour-coating, with white (discoloured) barbotine decoration below shoulder groove.

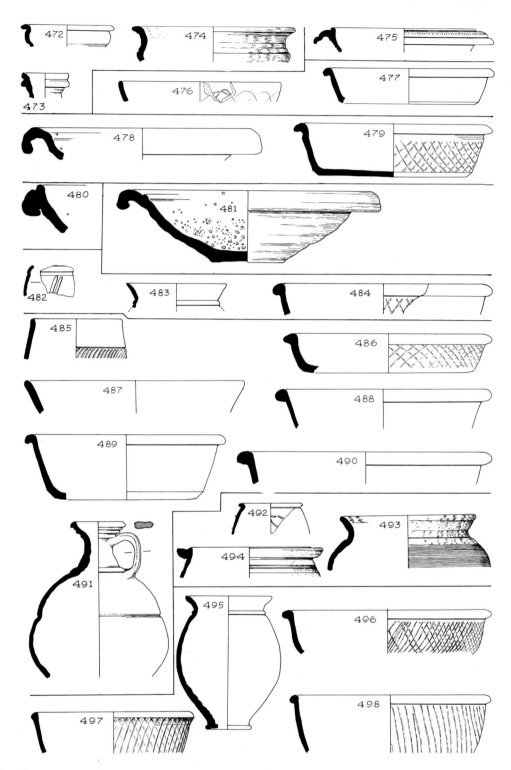

Fig. 110. Roman pottery from the north end of Canterbury Lane (C XXVIII Sites C XX and C XXI). Scale 1 : 4

483.   Poppy-head beaker in fine hard burnished grey ware.
484.   Black-burnished 2 ware, cf. Gillam No. 222, dated A.D. 150–210.

Nos. 485–491: Pottery from C XX 51. Thick occupation-earth below Saxon floor.
c. A.D. 230–270.

485.   Fine hard burnished grey ware, rouletted.
486.   Black-burnished 2 ware.
487–490.   Hard mottled grey and grey-buff burnished ware.
491.   Buff ware with burnished orange-buff surface or slip (worn).

Nos. 492–494: Pottery from C XXI 37. Gravel pit-filling cut through chalk and loam floor.
c. A.D. 190–220.

492.   Fine white paste, 'metallic' grey on orange colour-coating, with barbotine foliage, of a
        type dated A.D. 145–220 at Verulamium (No. 556).
493.   Coarse granular grey-brown ware, burnished on lip and shoulder, finely rilled below.
494.   Hard finely granular light grey ware.

Nos. 495–498: Pottery from C XXI 36. Gravel and occupation-material. c. A.D. 190–225.

495.   Fine hard grey ware with lighter slip.
496.   Black-burnished 2 ware; another in layer 35 above.
497, 498.   Hard mottled grey ware with burnished lattice.

Nos. 499–514: Pottery from C XXVIII C XX Pit 15. c. A.D. 300–350.

499.   Fine hard buff paste, orange-buff colour-coating.
500.   Ware as No. 499, with indentations made by narrow scored lines.
501.   Fine hard buff paste, dark grey-brown colour-coating outside, red-brown inside, with
        narrow scored indentation below rouletted band.
502.   Fine hard buff paste, dark grey-brown colour-coating, with alternating round indent-
        ations and scored lines which have cracked the sides; two whole beakers, and part of
        another in finer orange-buff paste with orange-brown coating.

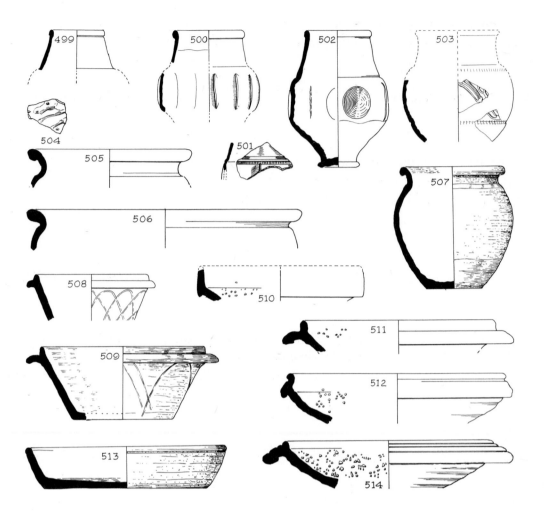

Fig. 111.   Roman pottery from a pit dated A.D. 300–350 at Canterbury Lane (C XXVIII C XX Pit 15).
Scale 1 : 4

503.   Fine hard grey paste, dark grey 'metallic' coating, with barbotine foliage, a type dated
at Verulamium (No. 1527) to A.D. 250–315+.

504.   Hunt cup sherd with large barbotine hound, in fine white paste, slate-grey coating; cf.
Gillam Type 89, dated A.D. 210–260.

505.   Hard finely granular dark grey ware.

506.   Ware as No. 505, grey, burnished.

507.   Ware as No. 505, partly burnished.

508, 509.   Black-burnished 1 ware, cf. Gillam Type 228, dated A.D. 290–370.

510.   Red colour-coated ware (burnt), quartz grits, of Young's Type C 97, dated A.D. 240–
400+.

511.   Hard whitish ware, quartz grits (burnt), of Young's Type M 17, dated A.D. 240–300.

512.   Hard brick-red ware with trace of white slip, white quartz grits (third century, probably late, Oxfordshire).

513.   Hard rather finely granular light grey ware, burnished on base inside.

514.   Hard pale buff ware, orange-brown slip, black ironstone grits (late third or fourth century, Nene Valley).

B. SAXON (Figs. 112)

515.   Hard rather finely granular light grey ware, partly burnished, cf. *Proc. Cambridge Ant. Soc.*, xlix (1956), 61, Fig. 6, 6 etc. St. Neot's-type ware. C XX 53, occupation below Saxon chalk floor. Tenth century.

516.   Hard finely granular dark grey ware with uneven surfaces and some knife-trimming, similar to Nos. 330–344. C XX 41. Occupation on Saxon chalk floor. *c.* A.D. 850–950.

Nos. 517–519: Pottery from C XX 36. Occupation-layer (not in Section). *c.* A.D. 850–950.

517, 518.   Ware as No. 516.

519.   Dark grey-brown ware, with a more granular surface than No. 516.

520.   Hard rather finely granular light grey ware, sharply knife-trimmed, with vertical burnishing on shoulder; perhaps *c.* A.D. 975–1025 (medieval Group I). C XX Pit 8.

C. MEDIEVAL (Fig. 112)

Nos. 521–525: Pottery from C XX Pit 11. Cut through Saxon building and ruins.
Eleventh century with residual Saxon sherds.

521.   Hard finely granular dark grey ware, sharply knife-trimmed leaving a polished surface.

522, 523.   Ware similar to No. 521 but with less knife-trimming.

524.   Hard rather finely granular dark grey ware with uneven surface, showing some knife-trimming or smoothing.

525.   Hard rather finely granular light grey-buff ware, sooted. Probably first half of the eleventh century; also a cooking-pot rim of Medieval Group II, second half of the eleventh century (not figured).

526.   Jug handle in hard finely granular grey-buff ware, grey core, orange-buff inside, with

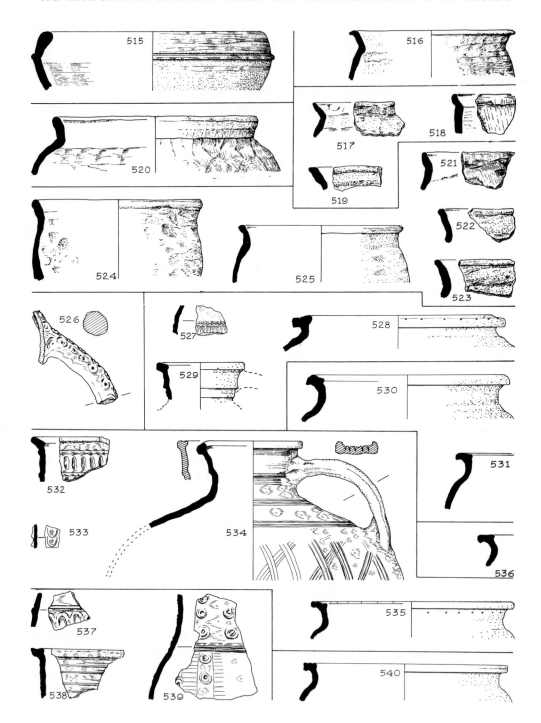

Fig. 112. Saxon and medieval pottery from the north end of Canterbury Lane (C XXVIII Sites C XX and C XXI). Scale 1 : 4

applied deeply stamped circles with central hole; some transparent glaze, brown and dark green. A body sherd has the same stamped pattern. Cf. No. 539 from the same or a similar jug. Late thirteenth or fourteenth century. C XX 22, gravel and loam floor with oven.

Nos. 527–529: Pottery from C XX 16 and 13. Filling of cellar. Fourteenth century.

527. Jug sherd in hard finely granular pale orange-red ware, with two rouletted bands; covered with glaze, yellow-green (16).

528. Hard granular red-brown ware, with some shell on surface.

529. Hard granular light red-buff ware, late thirteenth or fourteenth century; also a dish of the same type as No. 394 though with less internal glaze apparent; fourteenth century.

Nos. 530, 531: Pottery from C XX Pit 7. Second half of thirteenth to fourteenth century.

530. Hard rather finely granular reddish ware, grey core.

531. Ware as No. 530.

Nos. 532–535: Pottery from C XXI 23. Building III gravel and loam floors. Late thirteenth to early fourteenth century.

532. Hard granular red-brown ware, dark grey core, with impressed decoration; glaze on neck, green.

533. Jug sherd in fine hard buff ware with vertical applied scale pattern, good green glaze ouside, yellow inside. From Normandy, probably late thirteenth century.

534. Hard granular red-grey ware with scored lattice on body, some transparent glaze, orange-green. Late thirteenth or fourteenth century.

535. Hard finely granular reddish ware, pierced rim. Late thirteenth to fourteenth century.

536. Hard rather finely granular reddish ware. Late thirteenth century; also three other cooking-pot rims of this date. C XXI 18. Make-up for Building IV floors.

Nos. 537–539: Pottery from C XXI 14. Gravel floor of Building IV Phase 3. Fourteenth century.

537. Jug sherd in hard finely granular grey-brown ware with thumb-impressed decoration,

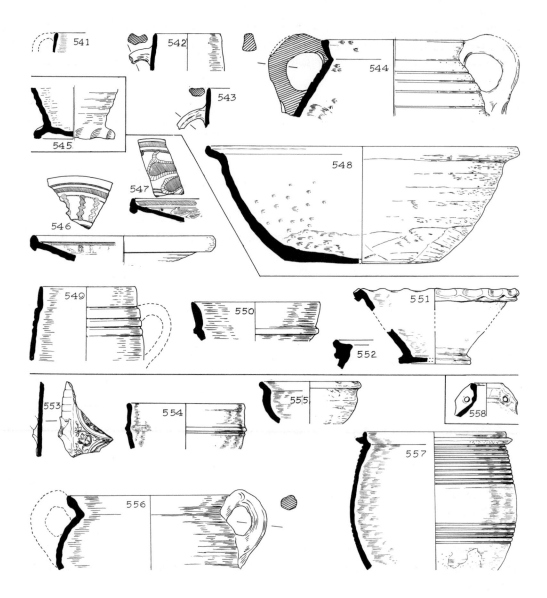

Fig. 113.   Post-medieval pottery from C XXVIII Site C XX. Scale 1 : 4

transparent glaze, orange-green. Cf. No. 385, fourteenth century, and decoration of No. 537 in local ware, of the same date.

538. Hard rather finely granular red brown ware, with some glaze, orange-green.

539. Hard finely granular grey-brown ware, similar to No. 536, bright orange-buff inside, with applied stamped circles, covered by vertical lines of yellow-buff slip on body; some transparent glaze, orange-green. Cf. No. 525. Late thirteenth or fourteenth century.

540. Hard rather finely granular reddish ware. Late thirteenth to early fourteenth century. Also a jug rim and neck similar to No. 534. C XXI 21. Black soil to east of Phase 2 wall-slot of Building IV.

D. POST-MEDIEVAL POTTERY FROM CXXVIII SITE C XX. (Fig. 113)

Nos. 541–544: Pottery from C XXVIII C XX 28. Brown soil in stone-walled cess-pit.
Fifteenth century.

541. Hard finely granular white-buff ware covered with good green glaze, mottled light and dark. Fifteenth century, ? French. Also a stoneware sherd in Siegburg ware, common in the fifteenth century (*Steinzeug*).

542. Hard rather dark grey stoneware, buff core, smooth grey salt-glazed surface with brown lip. Langerwehe, fifteenth century. (*Hurst* (1977), 219–38).

543. As No. 542 but grey throughout, with red-brown surface, underfired.

544. Hard rather gritty buff ware, a little thin glaze, yellow, inside. There was also a stone cresset lamp (Fig. 72, No. 8) in this pit.

545. Base in hard grey stoneware, uneven yellow-brown salt-glazed surface continuing under base, thinner glaze inside. Langerwehe, fifteenth century (*Hurst* (1977), 219–38); also other fifteenth-century sherds. C XX Pit 3. Filling of second stone-walled cess-pit.

Nos. 546–552: Pottery from C XX 3. Chalky soil sealing Pit 3 and loam floor on chalk make-up 5. Early seventeenth century.

546, 547. German slipware plates in hard finely granular buff ware, covered inside and on rim with white slip, with design in green and red-brown, glazed: the background shows pale yellow under the glaze. Also, not figured, another plate and two dish sherds in this ware. No. 546 is in Weser Ware. Late sixteenth to early seventeenth century (*Plymouth*).

548.   Hard finely granular reddish ware, with some thin glaze, orange-green, on base inside.

549.   Hard finely granular reddish ware, covered with thin glaze, brownish green.

550.   Hard finely granular grey ware, covered with glaze, dark orange-green.

551.   Smooth hard red-buff ware covered with glaze, deep yellow.

552.   Hard very finely granular bright reddish ware, covered inside with glaze, orange-brown. There was also a base sherd of a seventeenth-century drug jar in blue and white maiolica (not figured).

Nos. 553–557: Pottery from C XX Pit 2. Late sixteenth century.

553.   Tankard sherd in fine hard light grey stoneware with applied stamped decoration with name in small letters ? DAVID at bottom right; slightly saltglazed soapy surfaces. Siegburg, second half of sixteenth century (*Steinzeug*).

554.   Hard finely granular bright red to grey ware, covered with glaze, orange-green (incomplete: could have handle).

555.   Hard very finely granular red-buff ware, covered inside with glaze, orange-yellow.

556.   Hard very finely granular red-brown ware, covered with glaze, orange (patchy on handle).

557.   Hard finely granular bright reddish ware, nearly covered with glaze, dark yellow-brown. In Pit 4 there was a stoneware jug sherd in sixteenth to early seventeenth century ware (not figured).

558.   Costrel with flat pierced handles, squarely trimmed, in hard very finely granular reddish ware, partly glazed orange-green; also a jar rim as No. 552. C XX 2. Gravelly deposit sealing Pits 2 and 4.

VI (a) POTTERY FROM C X SITE L (Figs. 114–115)

559.   Base of Belgic pedestal jar in finely granular grey ware, C X L I 35, Belgic pit.

Nos. 560–562: Pottery from C X L I 32 and 24. Occupation-deposit on earliest floors of Period I Building. c. A.D. 100–130 with much residual material.

560.   Native copy of Gallo-Belgic plate in slightly granular grey ware, burnished inside. First century, residual.

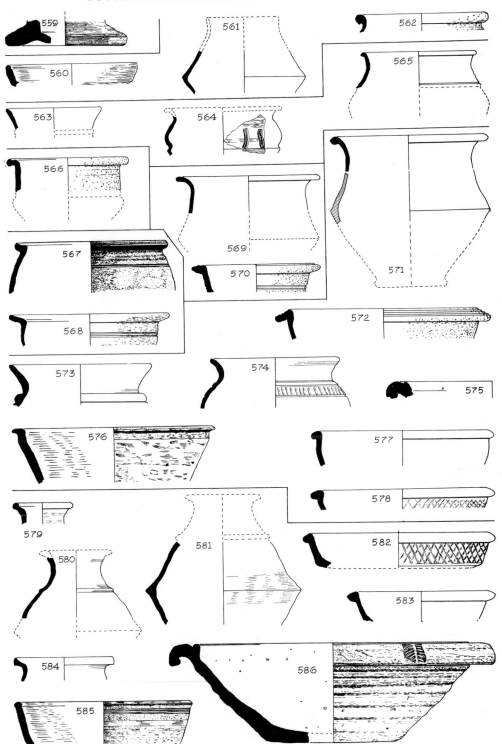

Fig. 114. Roman pottery from the south side of Burgate Street (C X Site L). Scale 1 : 4

561.   Carinated beaker sherd, and rim of another (of the type figured) in fine hard burnished grey ware.

562.   Hard slightly granular grey ware.

Nos. 563–565: Pottery from C X L I 31. Burnt layer in Period I Building. c. A.D. *120–140.*

563.   Poppy-head beaker in fine light grey ware, darker partly burnished surface.

564.   Fine smooth grey ware with horizontal burnished lines and incised decoration.

565.   Fine smooth burnished grey ware.

566.   Granular dark grey ware, C X L I 30. Period II primary loam floor. *c.* A.D. 130–150.

Nos. 567, 568: Pottery from C X L I 22. Occupation-material on Period II primary floor. *c.* A.D. *140–170.*

567.   Hard slightly granular dark grey ware.

568.   Ware as No. 567, grey.

Nos. 569–570: Pottery from C X L I 20. Occupation-material on Period II secondary floor. *c.* A.D. *150–180.*

569.   Fine hard burnished light grey ware.

570.   Granular light grey-brown ware with darker surface.

Nos. 571–578: Pottery from C X L I 16 and II 6. Debris-layer above Period II Building. *c.* A.D. *180–220.*

571.   Fine hard grey-buff ware with dark grey burnished surface: reconstructed with a carinated sherd from a second beaker of this type.

572.   Hard granular grey ware.

573.   Hard burnished grey ware (late type of poppy-head beaker); also the rim of a smaller beaker of this type (not figured).

574.   Hard burnished grey ware with burnished shoulder decoration.

575.   Mortarium in rather granular orange-buff ware with grey grit (A.D. 140–200, probably local).

576.   Coarse light grey-brown ware, burnished inside and on lip.
577.   Burnished dark grey ware with lighter grey-brown core.
578.   Burnished grey-brown ware, with burnished lattice.

Nos. 579–586: Pottery from C X L I 15 and II 5. Charcoally occupation-layer above Period II debris. c. A.D. 200–230.

579.   Hard grey ware, partly burnished.
580.   Fine hard burnished grey ware.
581.   Ware as No. 580 but with smooth surface, burnished near the carination.
582.   Grey-brown ware with darker burnished surface, and burnished lattice. Cf. Gillam's Type 310 (with diagonal lines) dated A.D. 170–210.
583.   Grey-brown ware with darker burnished surface.
584.   Fine hard burnished blue-grey ware with lighter core.
585.   Rather coarse and granular grey-brown ware, burnished inside and partly outside.
586.   Fine hard buff ware possibly with a cream slip, with white quartz grits and herring-bone stamp (A.D. 135–170; Kent, perhaps Canterbury).

Nos. 587, 588: Pottery from C X L I 14. Gravel spread below Period III primary floor. c. A.D. 200–230.

587.   Slightly granular dark grey ware, lighter core, burnished outside and on lip.
588.   Coarse grey-brown ware, partly burnished from rim to shoulder; also a jar rim of the same type as No. 589.

589.   Rather granular dark grey ware, lighter core, C X L I 13. Period III primary floor. Another rim noted from layer 14 (see under No. 588). The type can be dated c. A.D. 180–240.

Nos. 590–597: Pottery from C X L I 3 and 11. Occupation-layer on Period III primary floor. c. A.D. 240–280.

590.   Hard cream paste, dark brown colour-coat outside, light red-brown inside. Also the base of a red colour-coated bowl, not earlier than the late third century (not figured).
591.   Hard grey-black burnished ware with lighter grey-brown core.
592.   Hard rather granular grey ware with burnished lines on lip and shoulder, red-brown core.

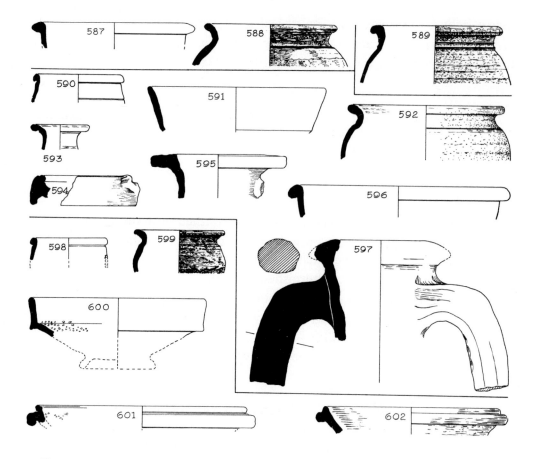

Fig. 115.   Roman pottery from the south side of Burgate Street (C X Site L). Scale 1 : 4

593.   Smooth hard grey ware with burnished lines on lip and shoulder.

594.   Mortarium in fairly smooth whitish ware (A.D. 150–250, probably Lower Germany).

595.   Flagon with single handle in red-buff ware with cream slip.

596.   Black-burnished 2 ware, cf. Gillam's Type 225, dated A.D. 200–250.

597.   Hard buff ware; Dressel form 20 (Spanish).

Nos. 598–602: Pottery from C X L I 1. Thick occupation-deposit above Period III secondary floors. c. A.D. 350–400.

598.   Hard orange-red paste and colour-coating, with trace of comb-stamped decoration, Oxfordshire ware of Young's Type C 37.2.

599. Coarse slightly granular grey-brown ware with irregular smoothing on upper part, probably hand-made; also four rims of larger jars in this ware.

600. Orange-red paste and colour-coating, grey quartz grits, Oxfordshire ware of Young's Type C 97, dated A.D. 240–400.

601. Fine hard yellow-buff ware, grey quartz grits, Oxfordshire ware of Young's Type M 22, dated A.D. 240–400.

602. Coarse grey ware with darker surface, burnished inside and to flange outside.

VI (b). POTTERY FROM C XIV SITE M (Figs. 116–117)

A. ROMAN

Nos. 603–606: Pottery from C XIV M I 26. Pit with chalk blocks cut through lower floors. c. A.D. 240–270.

603. Colour-coated beaker in hard orange-buff paste, grey-brown coating outside, red-brown inside, with white barbotine decoration below rouletted groove. Cf. *Verulamium* ii No. 1860 there dated *c.* 280–340. Probably British.

604. Very fine grey Rhenish ware, 'metallic' dark brown-grey coating.

605. Smooth hard grey burnished ware, lighter core.

606. Hard rather finely granular light grey ware, partly burnished on rim and shoulder.

Nos. 607–608: Pottery from C XIV M I 25. Yellow loam sealing Pit (26). c. A.D. 270–300.

607. Hard finely granular cream-buff ware, brown and grey quartz grits, Oxfordshire. cf. Young's Type M 17.2, dated A.D. 240–300.

608. Hard yellow-buff paste, orange colour-coating burnished outside, with darker mottling '*à l'éponge*'; import from Poitiers region of Gaul. Another sherd was found in Canterbury Lane, C XXII C I 9 (see above under No. 302). Cf. *Antiq. Journ.*, xxvii (1947), 171, fig. 12, Nos. 1–4; M. Fulford in D.P.S. Peacock (ed.), *Pottery and Early Commerce* . . . (London, 1977), 45; *Gallia*, xxxviii (1980), 265–78. There was also present a beaker sherd, cf. No. 603.

609. Colour-coated beaker sherd in hard orange paste, dark grey-brown coating, matt inside, with white barbotine decoration. Cf. *Verulamium* i (No. 1136) there dated *c.* 230–300. C XIV M I 22. Ash on *opus signinum* floor. Probably British. *c.* A.D. 300–330.

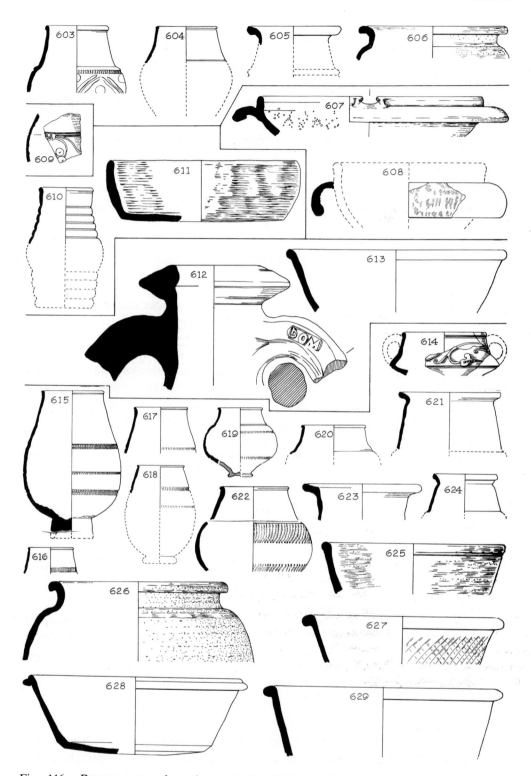

Fig. 116.   Roman pottery from the south side of Burgate Street (C XIV Site M). Scale 1 : 4

Nos. 610–611: Pottery from C XIV M I 19. Black earth with building-debris. c. A.D. *340–400.*

610.   Rhenish beaker in very fine reddish paste, grey core, 'metallic' brown-grey coating. Trier ware. Stanfield, 'Unusual forms . . .', *Arch. Journ.*, lxxxvi (1929), form 31. Probably residual.

611.   Coarse granular grey-brown ware with uneven burnished surfaces, hand-made.

Nos. 612–613: Pottery from C XIV M II 11. Loam floor with tiled hearth. c. A.D. *215–235.*

612.   Finely granular buff ware with pink-buff core, stamped **DOM** (Callender No. 552 there dated *c.* 140–180?). Dressel form 20. South Spanish.

613.   Finely granular grey-brown burnished ware.

Nos. 614–629: Pottery from C XIV M III 4 and 2. Occupation-material on loam floor.
c. A.D. *280–320.*

614.   Hard light reddish paste with small white inclusions, barbotine foliage, covered with 'metallic' silver-grey coating. Sherds from a second cup have a double rouletted groove below the carination. Central Gaulish; second century, residual.

615.   Fine reddish paste, silvery 'metallic' coating continuing below the base; two.

616.   Fine reddish paste, 'metallic' dark grey coating. Rhenish, third century.

617.   Fine orange-red paste, 'metallic' dark silver-grey coating; two. The form is similar to No. 616. Rhenish, third century.

618.   Fine reddish paste, 'metallic' grey-black coating. Rhenish, third century.

619.   Fine red and grey paste, 'metallic' dark silver-grey coating, reconstructed with the base of a second beaker of this type. Cf. Gose 209 but without indentations. There was also a second rim, and a base with indentations as Gose 209. Rhenish, third century.

620.   Fine red and grey paste, 'metallic' dark silver-grey coating. Rhenish, third century.

621.   Fine hard whitish-buff ware, burnished buff surface and lip.

622.   Hard burnished grey ware with rouletted zones.

623.   Flagon in finely granular buff ware with orange-buff slip.

624.   Fine hard burnished grey-buff ware.

625.   Hard granular dark grey ware, partly burnished.

626.   Hard granular grey ware, burnished on rim and shoulder.

627.   Black-burnished 2 ware, cf. Gillam Type 225, dated A.D. 190–240.

628.   Hard grey ware with rather dark burnished surfaces.

629.   Hard slightly granular dark grey burnished ware.

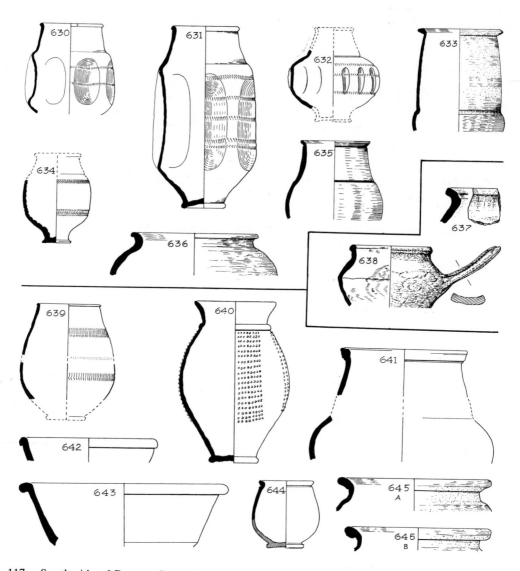

Fig. 117. South side of Burgate Street. Nos. 630–638 from C XIV Site M; Nos. 639–645 from C XIV Site N. Scale 1 : 4

Nos. 630–636: Pottery from C XIV M III 8 and 1. Charcoal deposit above hearth and sleeper-beam trench. c. A.D. *315–330.*

630. Fine brick-red Rhenish ware, grey core, with 'metallic' dark silver-grey coating. Third century.

631. As No. 630 with dark grey-brown coating, of Gillam's Type 46, dated A.D. 220–260. Rhenish.

632. Ware as No. 631, of Gillam's Type 45, dated A.D. 190–250. Probably Trier ware.

633. Local beaker. Hard finely granular grey ware, partly burnished.

634. Fine orange Rhenish ware, grey core, with 'metallic' grey-brown coating, cf. Gose form 209 (but without indentations) which is dated A.D. 100–250.

635. Local beaker. Hard burnished light grey ware.

636. Hard grey ware, unevenly burnished.

B. POST-ROMAN

637. Hard rather finely granular dark grey ware showing fine wheelmarks. Late Saxon cf. Medieval Group I *c.* A.D. 975–1025. C XIV M I 15. Stony layer sealing post-Roman gravel surfaces.

638. Pipkin in hard granular red-brown ware, smoothed surface, with thick glaze inside, orange-green; the handle tapers from 5 cm. to 2.5 cm. at the end. With the internal glaze it is more likely to be fourteenth than thirteenth century. C XIV M I 5. Make-up covering Oven 2. Cf. No. 382.

IVc. POST–MEDIEVAL POTTERY FROM AREA R

639–645: Pottery from C XIV N. Roman pit. c. A.D. *270–300.*

639. Fine reddish Rhenish ware, 'metallic' dark silver-grey coating; a type found at Nijmegen in levels dated ± 180–250.

640. Fine hard burnished grey ware with panels of barbotine dots. This type of poppy-head beaker extends from *c.* 160 throughout the third century.

641. Hard burnished buff ware, red-buff core.

642. Hard buff paste, dark brown colour-coating.

643. Hard finely granular grey ware, burnished mottled surfaces.

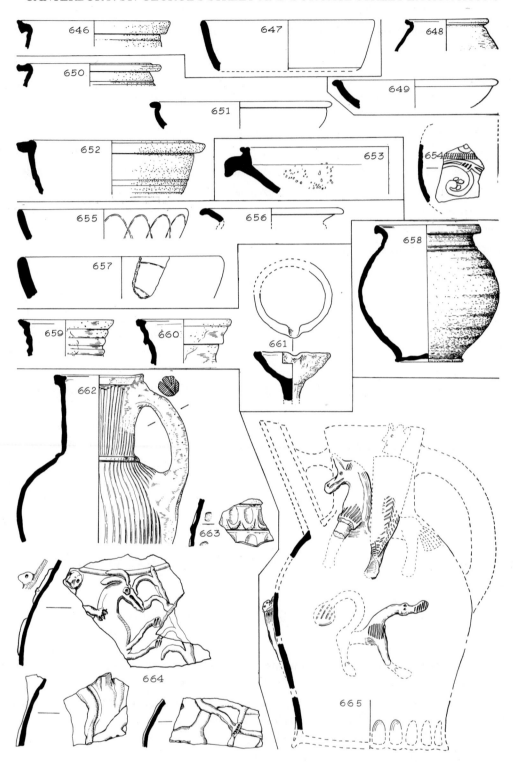

Fig. 118.   Roman and medieval pottery from Area Y, south of Burgate Street. Scale 1 : 4

644.   Fine hard burnished grey ware (reconstructed with base of a second beaker); imitating a colour-coated form such as Gillam's Type 86, dated 180–230.

645A, B.   Hard rather finely granular grey ware, partly burnished.

VI (d). POTTERY FROM AREA Y (pp. 120–130).

A. ROMAN (Fig. 118)

Nos. 646–647: Pottery from Y III 3 (26) Occupation earth below metalling of north-south lane. c. A.D. 130–170.

646.   Hard granular dark grey ware. The type itself can be dated c. A.D. 130–180.

647.   Hard burnished grey ware. This type of dish at Canterbury mainly belongs to the third century and later; its earliest dated appearance elsewhere in the city is c. A.D. 150–180.

Nos. 648–649: Pottery from Y III 2 (28). Occupation-layer on primary floor of timber building. c. A.D. 140–170.

648.   Hard finely granular grey ware, smoothed surface.

649.   Fine hard light grey ware, smoothly burnished.

Nos. 650–652: Pottery from Y III 3 (24). Gritty dirt on primary metalling of north-south lane. c. A.D. 140–180.

650.   Hard granular grey ware.

651.   Fine hard burnished grey ware.

652.   Hard granular grey ware.

653.   Hard finely granular cream ware, pink core, translucent white, brown and light grey grits (after A.D. 250, Oxfordshire). Y III 2 post-hole 2.

654.   Beaker sherd in fine light red-buff paste, micaceous orange-red coating, with rouletted band and white-painted design; Oxfordshire ware, Young's Type C 27, dated A.D. 270–400+. Y III 2 (18). Destruction-layer of timber-framed building. c. A.D. 390–400.

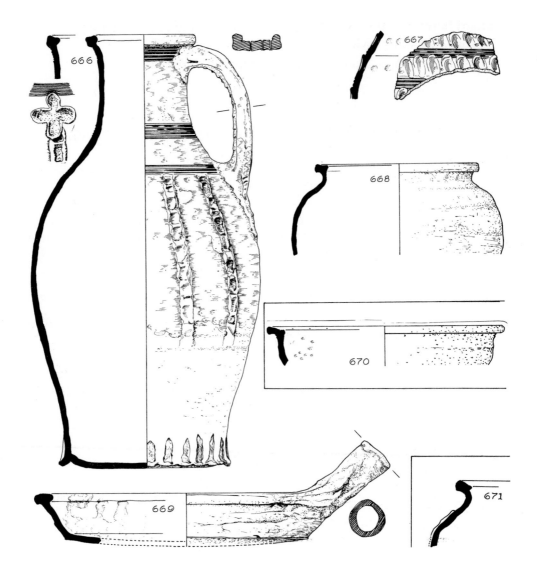

Fig. 119. Medieval pottery from Area Y. Scale 1 : 4

Nos. 655–657: Pottery from Y III 3 (6). Burnt material in western wall-trench of timber-framed building. c. A.D. 390–400.

655. Black-burnished 1 ware, cf. Gillam's Type 329, dated A.D. 190–340.

656. Black-burnished 1 ware, cf. Gillam's Type 147, dated A.D. 290–370.

657. Rather finely granular grey ware with burnished decoration; burnished inside, smoothed outside.

658.　Rather granular grey ware. Y I (34). Occupation-material on a loam floor of timber-framed building on west of the lane. Second century.

B. MEDIEVAL (Figs. 118–119)

Nos. 659–661: Pottery from Pit 16 (Y II 3, Pit 3). Fourteenth century.

659, 660.　Jugs in hard rather finely granular reddish ware, grey core, partly covered by thin glaze, orange, over some buff slip; also another jug-sherd in this ware with scored vertical lines on body, cf. No. 662 though with horizontally rilled neck (not figured).

661.　Cresset lamp roughly made in granular grey-brown ware, smoked round the projecting lip.

Nos. 662–664: Pottery from Pit 17 (Y III 3, Pit 3). Fourteenth century.

662.　Hard granular reddish ware with scored vertical lines, continuous from the neck downwards, partly covered with thin glaze, orange-green. Cf. No. 400 from the Well in Canterbury Lane.

663.　Ware as No. 662, red-buff, with horizontal rows of thumb-impressions and some worn buff slip under thin glaze. Cf. No. 401 from the Well in Canterbury Lane.

664.　As No. 665, in hard finely granular bright orange-red ware, grey core, with plastic decoration of one animal riding another (legendary beasts?) with a tree (right); two other sherds from this jug, that on the right showing the hand and arm of another animal; the outer surface covered with glaze, orange with green mottling.

665.　Knight jug in finely granular buff ware, smooth inside, with applied plastic fragments of two horses, shield, and two hounds, covered outside in good green glaze (reconstruction by G.C. Dunning). Made at Nottingham or Scarborough at the turn of the thirteenth and fourteenth centuries. See G.C. Dunning, 'The trade in medieval pottery around the North Sea', *Rotterdam Papers* i (Rotterdam, 1968), 41–2. Y I (1).

Nos. 666–669: Pottery from Pit 29 (Y V Pit 4) sealed by pitched tile hearth. Fourteenth century.

666.　Hard rather granular grey ware, with applied thumb-impressed strips on body, one with a cross at the top, and thin glaze, dark green, on upper part.

667.　Hard granular grey ware, buff inside, with rows of deep thumb-impressions, nearly covered with glaze, yellow-green with darker mottling; cf. No. 401 from the Well in

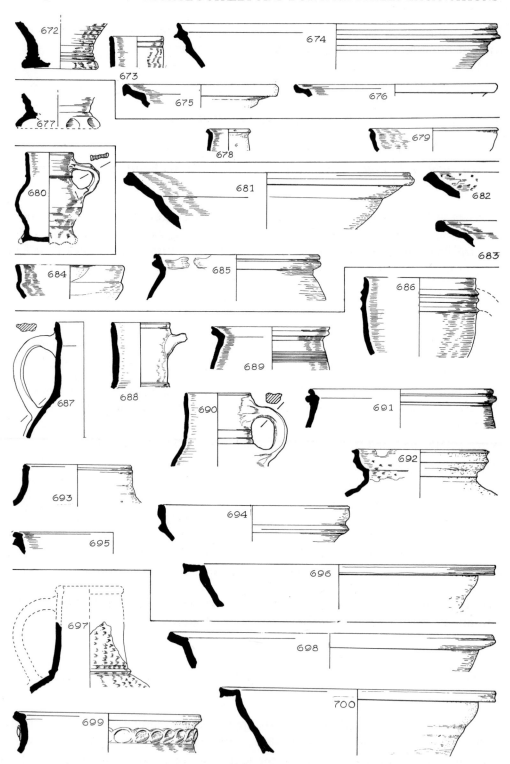

Fig. 120. Post-medieval pottery from Area Y. Scale 1 : 4

Canterbury Lane. The pit also contained the lower half of a large jug with sagging base, and scored wavy line decoration.

668. Hard granular grey-buff ware, smoked.

669. Hard granular reddish ware, grey core, smoothed near base, with tubular handle-socket; the base inside is covered with glaze, orange-green, which extends more thinly up the sides.

670. Hard granular grey-buff ware, with splashes of thin glaze inside; also two other dish rims, and the rim and handle fragment of a jug of the same type as No. 413 from the Canterbury Lane Well. C XVII Y II 1 (7). Black occupation-earth above cobbled floor of timber building. Fourteenth century.

671. Hard granular red-brown ware, with applied thumb-impressed strip, and some shell grit on the surface. Second half of thirteenth century. C XVII Y II 1 (8). Cobbled floor of timber building.

C. POST-MEDIEVAL (Figs. 120–121)

Nos. 672–676: Pottery from Y II 3 and 4 (1). Building 1, gravel basis for Period III chalk floor. Late sixteenth to early seventeenth century.

672. Stoneware jug base in hard rather granular light grey ware, surface covered in salt glaze, mottled golden brown. Frechen, second half of sixteenth century.

673. Hard grey stoneware covered in salt glaze, mottled dark brown outside, plain golden brown inside. Frechen, seventeenth century.

674. Smooth hard reddish ware.

675. Plate in hard very finely granular buff ware, covered with deep yellow glaze inside.

676. Plate in hard finely granular pale buff ware, covered inside with yellow-green glaze.

Nos. 677–679: Pottery from Y II 3 (3). Building 1, pebbly earth layer, latest floor of Period I in S-W room. Early sixteenth century.

677. Stoneware jug base in hard grey ware, covered outside with light grey salt glaze tinged with orange-brown, plain orange-brown inside. Langerwehe or Raeren, late fifteenth to early sixteenth century.

678, 579. Hard very finely granular reddish ware, covered inside with orange glaze.

680. Hard rather light grey stoneware, surface and neck inside covered with light grey-buff salt glaze, finely mottled with yellow-buff in places. Raeren, early sixteenth century; two. Y III 1 (1) Rubble filling of cistern.

Nos. 681–685: Pottery from Y II 1 (1). Pit sealed by Building 2, Period II rebuilding of Wall E.
Early seventeenth century.

681, 682. Hard very finely granular pinkish-buff ware with orange-buff surface, covered inside by smooth yellow-green glaze.

683. Ware as No. 862 but with deep yellow glaze inside.

684. Fine hard orange-buff ware, covered inside by smooth green glaze, with some yellow glaze outside (rim incomplete).

685. Fine hard reddish ware with some glaze, orange-green, on inner lip; a narrow base, glazed inside, may belong to this jar. There was also a stoneware sherd (not figured) in Langerwehe ware, fifteenth century and a base in Frechen ware, late sixteenth century.

Nos. 686–696: Pottery from Y II 2 (1). Earthy rubble, latest layer of yard-metalling, between
Buildings 1 and 2 corresponding to Y II 1 (2). Late sixteenth to early seventeenth century.

686. Hard finely granular reddish ware covered with thick (reduced) dark brown glaze; two.

687. Bellarmine jug in hard finely granular light grey stoneware, covered outside with salt glaze, closely mottled golden brown; plain light grey glaze inside the neck. Frechen, early seventeenth century.

688. Hard light grey stoneware, covered with light greenish-grey salt glaze outside, plain light grey glaze inside. Frechen, late sixteenth to early seventeenth century.

689. Hard finely granular reddish ware with finely rilled shoulder, covered with smooth glaze, orange-brown.

690. Hard light grey stoneware, covered with grey salt glaze tinged with golden-brown. Langerwehe or Raeren, fifteenth to early sixteenth century.
Also a stoneware sherd with applied decoration, of the mid-sixteenth century (Fig. 136, No. 12).

691. Hard finely granular reddish-grey ware.

692. Granular grey-buff ware with thin glaze, yellow-green, on inner lip.

693. Finely granular red-grey ware.

694. Smooth hard finely granular bright reddish ware, with a trace of thin glaze outside.

695. Hard reddish ware, inside and lip covered with thin glaze, orange-brown.

696. Ware as No. 694, unglazed.

Nos. 697–700: Pottery from Y II 1 (2). Deposit of earth, tiles and flints against NW side of Wall
E, sealing drain. Second half of sixteenth to early seventeenth century.

697. Stoneware jug neck with mottled golden-brown salt glaze outside, plain buff inside;

Frechen, second half of sixteenth century. Also (not figured) two thumbed bases; Raeren, early sixteenth century.

698. Hard very finely granular light reddish ware.

699. Ware as No. 698, with applied thumb-impressed strip on neck under rather 'metallic' brown glaze.

700. Ware as No. 698, bright reddish.

Nos. 701–704: Pottery from Y III 2 Pit 1 (post-medieval pit partly entering SW corner of Trench: not shown on plan). Fifteenth to sixteenth century.

701. Cup handle in hard grey stoneware, with finely mottled golden-brown salt glaze outside, plain grey inside. Langerwehe, fifteenth century.

702. Smooth hard very finely granular light reddish ware.

703. Ware as No. 702, with some glaze, orange-brown, on both surfaces.

704. Hard rather finely granular red-brown ware, covered inside with glaze, orange-brown.

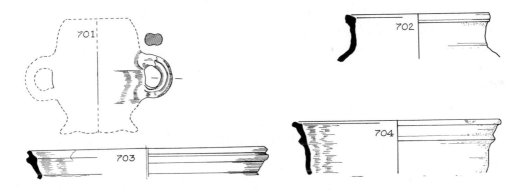

Fig. 121.   Post-medieval pottery from Area Y Trench III 2, Pit 1. Scale 1 : 4

VI (e). POTTERY FROM C XIII SITE T (pp. 130–133)

A. ROMAN, SAXON AND MEDIEVAL (Fig. 122)

Nos. 705–709: Pottery from C XIII T II 9. Black garden soil c. A.D. 340–400.

705. Red-buff paste, brown colour-coating with 'metallic' gold surfaces, rouletted. Uncertain origin.

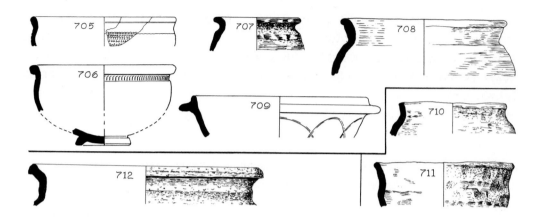

Fig. 122.   Roman, Saxon and medieval pottery from north side of Burgate Street (C XIII Site T). Scale 1 : 4

706.   Hard reddish paste, micaceous red coating, rouletted, Oxfordshire ware, Young's Type C 75, dated A.D. 325–400.

707.   Rather coarse granular grey ware, partly burnished.

708.   Coarse granular grey ware (burnt red), probably hand-made though the burnishing inside is unusually smooth.

709.   Black-burnished 1 ware, cf. Gillam's Type 228, dated A.D. 290–370.

Nos. 710–711: Pottery from C XIII T III 4. Post-Roman black soil.

710, 711.   Hand-made Saxon jar and bowl in finely granular dark grey ware with pitted surface, knife-trimmed and partly burnished; sixth or seventh century. A fifth-century Jutish sherd was found in III Pit 4 (published with other Jutish pottery in *The Archaeology of Canterbury*, v, Marlowe Car Park volume (forthcoming), No. 61).

712.   Cooking-pot in dark grey shell-tempered ware, late twelfth or early thirteenth century; also a rim of Medieval Group III type, dated to the first half of the twelfth century. C XIII T II 6. Burnt deposit with iron slag.

B. POST-MEDIEVAL (Fig. 123)

Nos. 713–716: Pottery from C XIII T II 3. Loam floor sealing large pit.
Early seventeenth century.

713. Jug in hard finely granular red-buff ware, grey core.

714. Hard red to grey ware, bright red core, covered inside with glaze, orange-brown.

715. Smooth hard pale buff ware, covered inside and on rim, and thinly outside, with mottled apple-green glaze.

716. Ware similar to No. 715 though less smooth and deeper colour, covered inside with smooth yellow glaze flecked with green.

Nos. 717–722: Pottery from C XIII T II 2. Plaster and demolition-debris over loam floor.
Probably *c.* 1730–50.

717. Spanish maiolica dish in buff ware with pattern in pale copper lustre on a cream ground (J.G Hurst, *Medieval Archaeology*, xxi (1977), 68–105.

718. Maiolica drug jar in very finely granular buff ware with pattern in medium blue on opaque white surface, tin-glazed; probably London, seventeenth century.

719. Maiolica plate in very finely granular yellow-buff ware, with pattern in deep, medium and pale blue on white surface, tin-glazed, pale buff outside.

720–722. As No. 719, in buff ware, with pattern in medium blue (720); outlined and filled in with blue (deep, medium and pale, 721); blue, deep red-orange and green (722). Eighteenth century, perhaps the second quarter.

Nos. 723–730: Pottery from C XIII T II 1. Old garden soil. Eighteenth century.

723. Delftware egg cup in hard finely granular buff ware, with a wide and a narrow underglaze brown stripe below the rim, the surfaces covered with white opaque tin-glaze.

Nos. 724–730: Stoneware tankards in hard grey fabric, varying from light to dark in colour, with salt-glazed surfaces mottled red-brown to brown.

724 and Fig. 136, No. 10. Medallion with stamped dolphin; two.

725 and Fig. 136, No. 9. Medallion with stamped eagle in frame.

726. Inscribed '**James Hut Canterbury 1716**' opposite the handle.

727. Inscribed]anks, below stamped **WR** with crown above. This stamp continued into the reign of Queen Anne.

728. Inscribed El[with the same stamp as No. 727.

729. Medallion fragment.

730. Medallion with a different dolphin stamp from No. 725, with inscribed letter on right.

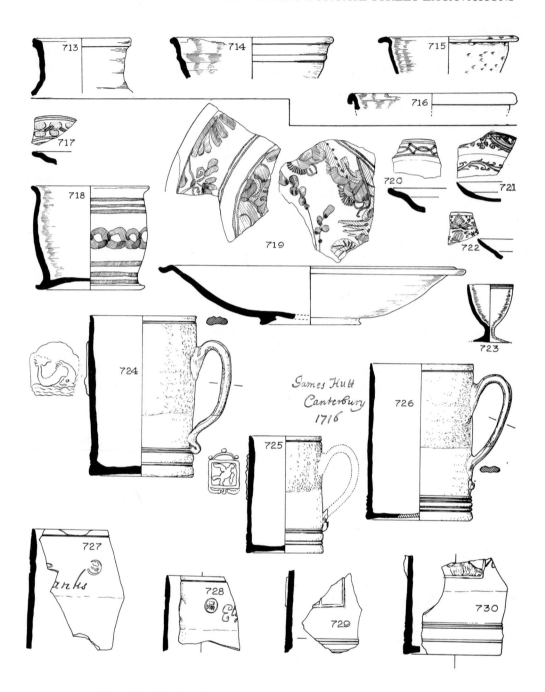

Fig. 123. Post-medieval pottery from C XIII Site T. Scale 1 : 4

VII. POTTERY FROM C XV X, BUS STATION SITE

(pp. 135-43)

A. ROMAN (Fig. 124)

731. Storage jar in coarse hard light grey ware, unevenly burnished, with graffito **ABIT**[, third or fourth century; also a Saxon cooking-pot sherd cf. No. 753, hand-made in rather finely granular dark grey ware, c. A.D. 850–950. X III 18, Pit cut through Roman levels.

732. Fine hard orange-red paste and colour-coating, with a row of stamped rosettes between rows of square demi-rosettes; Oxfordshire, of unusual form. X V Pit 9, medieval, containing other residual late Roman pottery.

733. Coarse granular dark grey-brown ware, unevenly burnished; hand-finished. X III 20. Occupation-earth, A.D. 270–350.

734. Coarse granular grey-brown ware with well-made rim but irregular surface below this, unevenly burnished, X III 16. Pebbly floor of building dated to the second half of the fourth century.

B. SAXON (Fig. 124)

Nos. 735–738: Pottery from X I Pit 6. Sixth century.

735. Hand-made jar-sherd in finely granular grey ware with lighter grey to buff surface, with vertical burnishing, decorated with a shallow groove between scored lines. Cf. Simon Langton Site[95] No. 90, Jutish, fifth century.

736. Finely granular grey ware, lighter grey-brown core, with pattern of stamped circles between regular grooves, smoothly burnished.

737. Hand-made in rather finely granular grey ware with uneven surface, partly burnished.

738. Hand-made in finely granular grey ware with a few larger grits, irregular surface, slightly smoothed.

739. Handled sherd in finely granular grey ware, hand-made, X II 13. Clean gravel above supposed Roman bank.

95. *The Archaeology of Canterbury*, v, Marlowe Car Park volume (forthcoming).

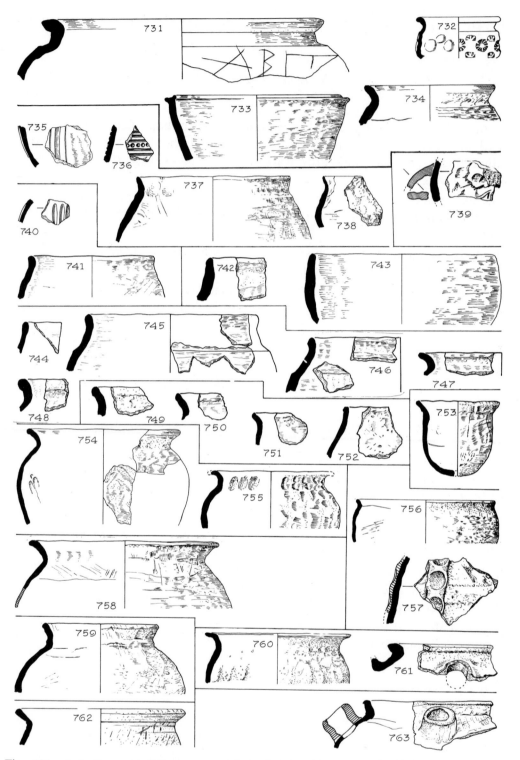

Fig. 124.   Late Roman and Saxon pottery from the Bus Station site (C XV Site X). Scale 1 : 4

Nos. 740–741: Pottery from X II 16. Dark earth over Roman Pit 3.

740. Hand-made in smooth burnished grey ware with grooved decoration; cf. East of Marlowe Theatre[96] No. 30, Jutish, fifth century.

741. Finely granular dark grey ware with uneven burnished surfaces, and a similar rim in buff ware, both hand-made. Fifth century; also grass-tempered sherds.

Nos. 742–743: Pottery from X I Pit 3. Medieval pit.

742. Ware similar to No. 740: the white quartz-sand grits are comparable with those in fifth-century ware.

743. Hand-made in granular grey-buff ware with unevenly burnished surfaces cf. Simon Langton Site[96] No. 114, perhaps sixth century. No. 762 also came from I Pit 3.

Nos. 744–748: Pottery from X I 22. Grey-brown earth cut by Pit 9. Fifth and sixth centuries.

744–746. Rather soft and finely granular grey-black and grey-brown hand-made ware, both surfaces burnished with narrow strokes, probaby fifth century; also many sherds in this ware.

747. Slightly coarser ware than No. 744, dark grey-buff, partly burnished; probably sixth century.

748. Rather coarse granular pale red-buff ware, partly burnished surfaces; cf. East of the Marlowe Theatre[96] No. 45, fifth century.

Nos. 749–752: Pottery from X I 21 (above 22). Sixth or seventh century.

749. Coarse brown shell-tempered ware, hand-made with unevenly burnished surfaces.

750, 751. Hand-made grey ware with fine quartz-sand and grog tempering, unevenly burnished.

752. Finely granular light grey ware, hand-made with irregular faceted surfaces, burnished on upper part. Very late sixth or seventh century. Cf. No. 168. X V 1. Brown medieval occupation earth with late Saxon to twelfth-century pottery and a coin of Henry II (dated 1180–89).

96. See note 95.

753.   Finely granular light grey ware, hand-made with irregular faceted surfaces, burnished on upper part. Very late sixth or seventh century. Cf. No. 168. X V I. Brown medieval occupation earth with late Saxon to twelfth-century pottery and a coin of Henry II (dated 1180–89).

Nos. 754–755: Pottery from X V 11. Medieval dark soil sealing Saxon Pits 10 and 8.

754.   Hard rather finely granular dark grey-brown ware with a high proportion of grit, uneven burnished surface, cf. No. 334 (unburnished) *c.* A.D. 850–950.

755.   As No. 754 but hand-made.

Nos. 756–757: Pottery from X VI Pit 4. Medieval, with Group III cooking-pot.
c. A.D. 1080–1150.

756.   Ware as No. 754 *c.* A.D. 850–950, and two cooking-pot rims of this date.

757.   Finely granular grey-black ware with a few large grits, lighter core, tending to flake, with thumb-impressed applied strip; Ipswich ware, second half of eighth to first half of ninth century.

758.   Hard finely granular dark grey-brown ware with uneven surfaces and finger-impressions on neck, knife-trimmed and partly burnished, probably early tenth century. X V 13. Grey loam below (11) containing a Medieval Group II cooking-pot dated *c.* A.D. 1050–1100.

759.   Hand-made in finely granular grey-black ware, brown core, with knife-trimmed irregular faceted surfaces, partly burnished. X V Pit 1, medieval.

Nos. 760–761: Pottery from X V Pit 8. Late Saxon.

760.   Hard shell-tempered grey-black ware with irregular hollowed surface, partly burnished.

761.   Spouted pitcher in hard rather finely granular grey-black ware with trace of burnishing on rim.

762.   Hard finely granular grey ware with vertical trimming, cf. Group I No. 3, *c.* A.D. 975–1025. X I Pit 3, medieval. See also Nos. 742, 743 from this pit.

763.   Spouted pitcher in fairly hard and finely granular grey ware with faceted knife-trimmed surfaces, partly burnished. Though the upper part at least seems to be hand-

made, the knife-trimming resembles Group I cooking-pots,[97] dated to *c.* A.D. 975–1025. X IV 18. Loam floor (not in section).

C. MEDIEVAL (Fig. 125)

Nos. 764–765: Pottery from X I Pit 4. c. A.D. 1080–1150+.

764.   Hard granular reddish ware, grey core.
765.   Ware as No. 764, grey throughout; the rim is more developed than typical Group III forms, and may be a little later.

Nos. 766–768: Pottery from X I Pit 1. c. A.D. 1080–1150.

766.   Hard granular light reddish ware.
767, 768.   Hard granular grey-buff ware; three similar rims.

Nos. 769–770: Pottery from X III 7. Earth and yellow loam, secondary floor,
late thirteenth century.

769.   Crucible in hard granular light grey ware (similar to cooking-pots), sooted.
770.   Coarse grey shell-tempered ware; two.

Nos. 771–772: Pottery from X III 5. Tertiary floor of gravel, fourteenth century.

771.   Granular red-brown ware with diagonal grooves on body, covered by worn glaze.
772.   Hard finely granular light reddish ware, grey core, with applied thumb-impressed strip.

97.   For reference to Group I, see Introduction, p. 24.

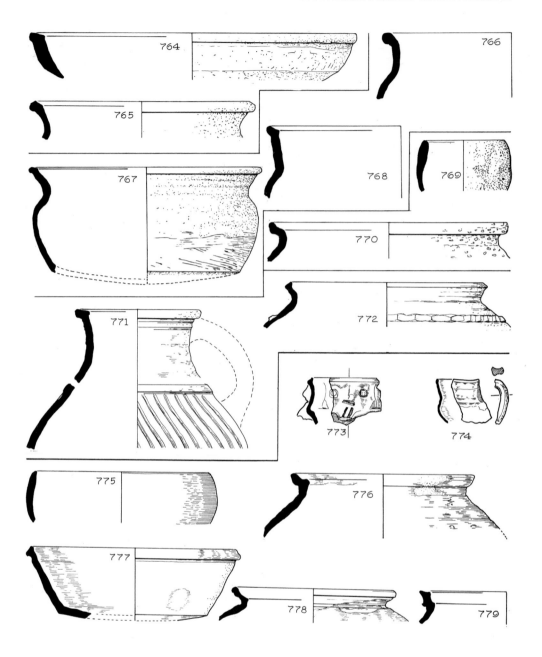

Fig. 125. Medieval and post-medieval pottery from the Bus Station site (C XV Site X). Scale 1 : 4

D. POST MEDIEVAL (Figs. 125–127)

Nos. 773 (medieval)–779: Pottery from X III 1. Dark earth, sixteenth century.

773. Face-mask from the side of a jug in hard very finely granular light reddish ware, with incised eyes and mouth, and applied nose and (broken) beard, covered with glaze, orange-green. Probably fourteenth century and from Scarborough.

774. Lobed cup and separate handle in fine buff ware, covered inside and down to shoulder outside with mottled dark and light green glaze; three. Probably fifteenth century.

775. Smooth hard burnished buff ware, similar to Nos. 777–9.

776. Hard granular red-grey ware similar to fourteenth-century cooking-pots, covered outside and on rim inside with thin (worn) glaze, orange green; two. Late fourteenth to fifteenth century.

777. Hard very finely granular red-buff ware, covered inside and on rim with good yellow and green glaze.

778. Ware similar to No. 777, with grey core, partly covered outside with glaze, orange-green.

779. Ware as No. 777, unburnished.

Nos. 780–795: Pottery from X II 4. Thick deposit of brown earth. Sixteenth century.

780. Fine hard grey stoneware, covered with light grey salt-glaze. Raeren.

781. Finely granular buff ware, roughly made.

782. Hard granular grey ware with some thin glaze, dark green, near the spout; another in light reddish ware. Both resemble Tyler Hill fourteenth-century ware, but are probably a little harder.

783. Tudor-green cup in fine hard cream ware, covered inside and on neck outside with smooth mottled apple-green glaze; two.

784. Jug-sherd in hard finely granular buff ware, with stamped applied floral decoration, partly covered with mottled apple-green glaze.

785. Hard granular red-grey ware, grey core, partly covered with thick green glaze streaked with orange; thumbed base (one handle found).

786. Fairly hard finely granular orange-buff ware, greyer core, partly covered with thin glaze, bright yellow-green.

787. Hard granular red-grey ware, red core.

788. Hard finely granular light grey ware with finger-nail impressions on rim, and set of four perforations below; some thin glaze, orange, on rim.

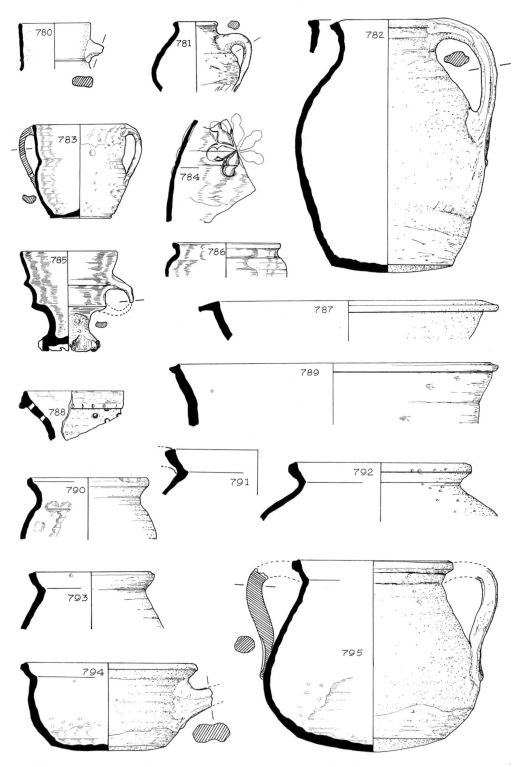

Fig. 126.   Post-medieval pottery from the Bus Station site (C XV Site X). Scale 1 : 4

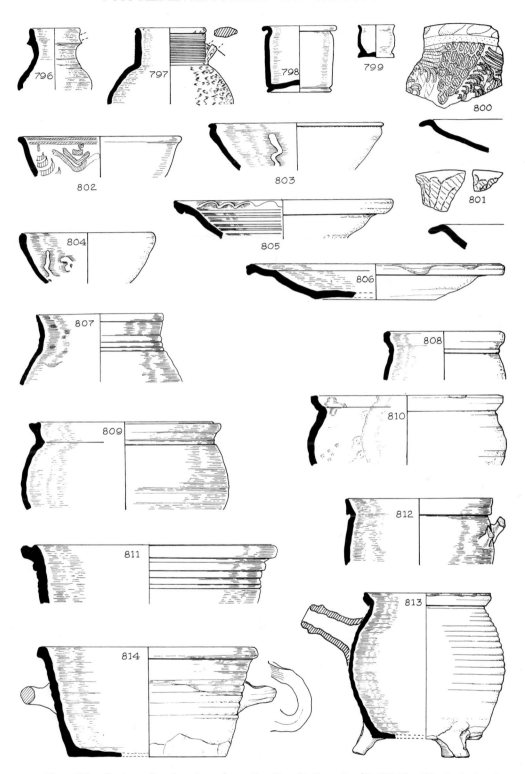

Fig. 127.   Post-medieval pottery from the Bus Station site (C XV Site X). Scale 1 : 4

789.   Hard deep reddish ware, grey core, splashed with thin glaze, orange.

790.   Hard granular reddish ware with some thin glaze, orange-green, inside; sooted.

791.   Hard finely granular yellow-buff ware, grey core, with trace of handle.

792, 793.   Hard granular red-buff ware with greyer surface, splashed with thin glaze, orange-brown.

794.   Hard rather finely granular buff ware, similar to No. 793 but coarser; inside of base covered with thin glaze, orange-green.

795.   Hard granular grey-brown ware, bright red core, covered on inside of base with thin glaze, orange-brown.

Nos. 796–814: Pottery from X I 1. Black garden soil with pottery ranging from the sixteenth to the eighteenth century.

796.   Hard light grey stoneware, covered with salt-glaze, closely-mottled yellow-buff outside, and another in grey ware with yellow-brown glaze.

797.   Hard light grey stoneware covered with salt-glaze, mottled yellow-brown outside. English.

798.   Delftware ointment jar in hard finely granular buff fabric, covered with white opaque tin-glaze. Lambeth, late seventeenth to early eighteenth century.

799.   As No. 798, eighteenth century.

800.   Maiolica plate in hard finely granular buff ware with white opaque tin-glaze inside, yellow-buff outside, with design in blue with some green background, and a yellow band on inner edge of rim. Probably early seventeenth century, London or Dutch.

801.   Ware as No. 800, with design in green outlined in brown.

802.   Maiolica dish in hard very finely granular buff ware with opaque white tin-glaze inside, white-buff outside, with design in pale blue and pale purple. Seventeenth century.

803–805.   Slipware dishes and plate in hard finely granular reddish paste with design in white slip, showing yellow against brownish-orange background under smooth internal glaze. Seventeenth century.

806.   Hard very finely granular buff ware, covered inside with apple-green glaze. Mid or early seventeenth century.

807.   Hard very finely granular bright orange-red ware, covered with thick (reduced) glaze, deep brown with darker flecks. Seventeenth century.

808.   Ware as No. 806, with grey surface, covered inside with smooth glaze, orange-brown.

809.   Hard finely granular light red-grey ware, covered with smooth glaze, orange-brown. Probably seventeenth century.

810.   Hard finely granular buff ware, some yellow glaze inside (rim incomplete). Sixteenth century.

811.   Hard finely granular reddish ware, grey core, covered with (worn) glaze, orange-brown. Probably seventeenth century.

812. Hard granular bright reddish ware, covered with smooth orange-brown glaze with dark flecks (one handle found). Seventeenth century.

813. Hard finely granular buff ware, covered inside with rather thin light green glaze (rim incomplete). Surrey, third quarter of the seventeenth century.

814. Smooth hard reddish ware, covered inside and on upper part outside with smooth glaze, orange. Probably eighteenth century.

VIII. POST-MEDIEVAL POTTERY FROM ST. GEORGE'S STREET BATHS SITE: cf. pp. 27–40 (Fig. 128)

815. Bellarmine jug with stamped medallion, in hard rather dark grey ware, salt-glazed: coarsely mottled dark and red-brown outside. The common rose, crown and heart pattern typical of the mid seventeenth century. Frechen. C IX C Post-hole 1.

816. Hard finely granular reddish ware, rouletted, covered inside and to above the base outside with rather thick glaze, orange-brown; associated with a Lowestoft porcelain saucer dated 1760–1770, and a Chinese blue and white saucer of the first half of the eighteenth century. Below the west wall of the cellar of C IX C, thus dating it.

IX. POST-MEDIEVAL POTTERY FROM MINOR EXCAVATIONS ALONG ST. GEORGE'S STREET

(Figs. 128–130)

Nos. 817–828: Pottery from C IX B II 2. Late sixteenth to seventeenth century: cf. p. 51.

817. Stoneware jug in fine hard grey ware with stamped decoration and blue underglaze colour outside, salt-glazed. Late sixteenth to early seventeenth century. Westerwald.

818. Hard rather dark grey stoneware, salt-glazed: coarsely mottled yellow-brown outside, grey inside. Second half of sixteenth century. Frechen.

819. Delftware drug jar in very finely granular pink-buff ware with pattern in medium blue, salt-glazed. Late sixteenth to early seventeenth century, probably Rotterdam.

820. North Holland Slipware bowl in hard finely granular red-buff ware with pattern in white (pale yellow) slip against deep yellow background, glazed inside and on upper half outside. Seventeenth century. See J.G. Hurst, D.S. Neal and H.J.E. van Beuningen, 'North Holland Slipwares', *Rotterdam Papers* ii (1975), 47–65.

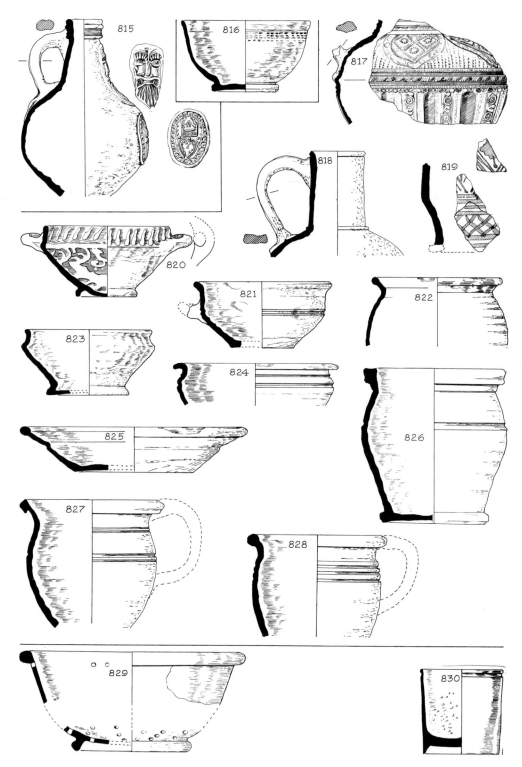

Fig. 128.   Post-medieval pottery from St. George's Street Baths (Nos. 815–816) and from C IX Site B in
St. George's Street (Nos. 817–830). Scale 1 : 4

821. Hard finely granular dark grey ware, bright red core, nearly covered with glaze, dark green, inside, and with loop handle.

822. Hard very finely granular grey-brown ware, with a little glaze, orange-green, on rim.

823. Hard finely granular reddish ware, grey core, covered inside and on upper part outside with glaze, orange-green. (No handles found on incomplete sherd).

824. Fine hard pale buff ware, covered inside with smooth glaze, yellow; slightly glazed outside.

825. Hard finely granular yellow-buff ware, covered inside with yellow-green glaze.

826. Hard finely granular red-buff ware (rim incomplete), covered inside with glaze, orange-brown.

827. Chamber-pot in reddish ware, less smooth than No. 826, with similar glaze inside.

828. Ware as No. 827, red-grey.

Nos. 829–830: Pottery from C IX B I 3: cf. p. 51 and Fig. 8.

829. Strainer in hard pale buff ware, both surfaces covered with smooth glaze, pale yellow. A.D. 1830–1850, also a willow-pattern dish of this date.

830. Druggist's mortar in hard cream ware, covered with smooth white-buff glaze, worn grits inside. Early nineteenth century.

Pottery from C XIX Z: cf. p. 57 and Fig. 16.

831. Buff delftware with mottled purple (manganese) tin-glaze on cream ground. Seventeenth century. Z I Pit 2.

Nos. 832–841: Pottery from Z II Pit 2. Seventeenth century.

832. Maiolica drug jar in buff ware with underglaze pattern in deep blue on cream ground, tin-glazed. Seventeenth century.

833. Dutch delftware plate in buff ware with pattern in deep and light blue on white, tin-glazed; the glaze outside is transparent (yellow). Chinese panel pattern with religious symbols. First half of the seventeenth century.

834. Maiolica plate, with pattern in medium blue and bright yellow; the glaze outside is slightly opaque (buff). Early seventeenth century.

835. Delftware plate in buff ware with pattern in deep and medium bright blue, including part of a central motif underneath; both surfaces covered with opaque white tin-glaze. Second half of the seventeenth century.

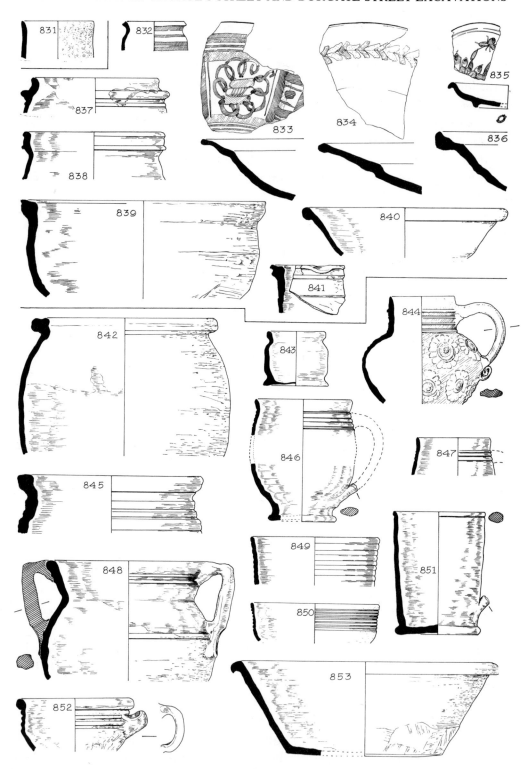

Fig. 129.   Post-medieval pottery from St. George's Street (C XIX Site Z). Scale 1 : 4

836. Hard finely granular reddish ware, covered inside with rather thin glaze, light orange-brown.

837. Hard finely granular buff ware, with some thin glaze, yellow inside.

838. Hard finely granular reddish ware, grey core, partly covered with glaze, orange-green; trace of a handle (not shown).

839. Ware as No. 838, covered inside with thin glaze, orange-brown.

840. Hard finely granular pale buff ware, thinly glazed inside, yellow.

841. Ware as No. 838, red-buff, nearly covered inside with glaze, orange; the rim top has been pressed outwards at intervals as on Nos. 862, 916.

The pit also contained sherds of a jar of the same type as No. 842, a coarse-ware plate as Rose Yard No. 19, a maiolica plate as Rose Yard No. 84 (first half of the seventeenth century) and a white delftware chamber-pot as No. 902 of the second half of the seventeenth probably to the early eighteenth century.[98]

Nos. 842–853: Pottery from C XIX Z II Pit 4. Seventeenth century.

842. Hard dull reddish ware, with smooth glaze, deep orange-brown on lower part inside.

843. White delftware drug jar with buff paste; two. Late seventeenth century.

844. Fine hard light grey stoneware with overall pattern of stamped flowers on blue underglaze background, salt-glazed. Westerwald.

845. Hard dull reddish ware, coarser than No. 842 with worn glaze, orange-brown on both surfaces. Another jar sherd of this type was found in Pit 2.

846. Hard finely granular reddish ware with rather uneven surfaces, covered with thick (reduced) glaze, dark brown and green.

847. Ware as No. 846, covered with smooth glaze, orange-brown.

848. Hard reddish ware with fairly thick glaze, orange-brown on upper part, thinner inside, sooted; elbow handles perhaps copying a metal cauldron.

849. Ware as No. 846.

850. Smooth hard finely granular reddish ware, glazed inside, orange-brown.

851. Ware as No. 846, with thick red-brown glaze with dark streaks.

852. Smooth finely granular buff ware, covered inside and on rim and handle with glaze, yellow.

853. Hard light red-buff ware, covered inside with rather uneven glaze, deep yellow.

98. The post-medieval pottery from the Rose Yard is published in the volume of this series dealing with the Marlowe Car Park area (*The Archaeology of Canterbury*, v, forthcoming).

Nos. 854–857: Pottery from C XIX Z III Pit 1.
Seventeenth century. (Fig. 130).

854. Delftware plate in buff ware with panelled pattern in deep and medium blue on white, tin-glazed; nearly transparent glaze outside (pink-buff). Second quarter of the seventeenth century. Two maiolica sherds can be dated to the seventeenth century, and perhaps to the second half respectively.

855. Hard bright reddish ware, covered with smooth glaze, red-brown with dark streaks.

856. Hard finely granular red-buff ware, covered inside with glaze, orange-yellow.
There was also a similar rim with combed wavy line decoration, the same type as Rose Yard No. 17 dated to the first half of the seventeenth century, and another plate sherd of the same date, of Rose Yard No. 19 type.

857. Hard rather coarse buff ware with some glaze, yellow, inside. There was also a jug sherd of Rose Yard No. 95 type, two stamped stoneware sherds (Fig. 136, Nos. 6–7) and a fourteenth-century patterned tile fragment (Fig. 69, No. 6).

POST-MEDIEVAL POTTERY FROM AREA R (Fig. 130)

Nos. 858–864: Pottery from C XV R II 2. Seventeenth-century cess-pit.

858. Maiolica drug jar in buff ware with pattern in pale blue and purple on white, tin-glazed; almost certainly Lambeth, seventeenth century.
Also a sherd of a Chinese blue and white porcelain cup, seventeenth or early eighteenth century.

859, 860. Slipware bowl and dish in hard finely granular reddish ware with internal pattern in white (yellow) slip on a background coloured orange-brown by the internal glaze.

861. Hard finely granular buff ware, inside and lip covered with thin glaze, yellow.

862. Hard red-buff ware, inside and lip covered with thin glaze, orange. Cf. Nos. 916, 841.

863. Hard reddish ware, nearly covered inside with glaze, orange-green.

864. Ware as No. 862, reddish.

Nos. 865–868: Pottery from C XV R IV Pit 7

865. Hard finely granular bright reddish ware, covered with thick (reduced) glaze, dark brown. First half of the seventeenth century.

866. Chamber pot in hard finely granular reddish ware, covered with thin glaze inside, orange-green.

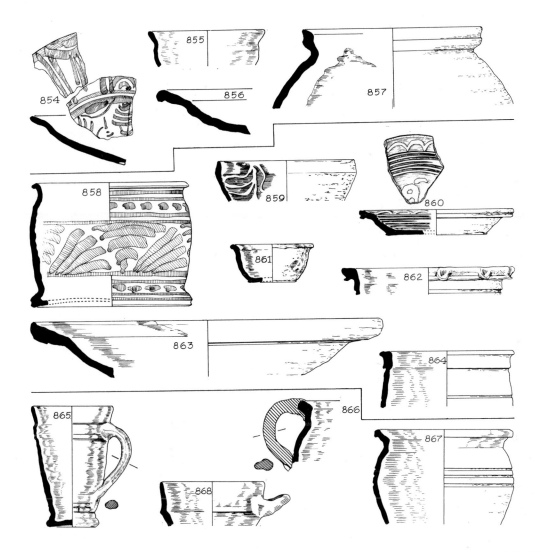

Fig. 130. Post-medieval pottery from St. George's Street (Nos. 854–857 from C XIX Site Z; Nos 858–868 from C XV Area R Trenches II and IV). Scale 1 : 4

867. Hard finely granular dark reddish ware, nearly covered with glaze, orange-green, inside and on rim and neck. Unglazed jars of this type were found in a pit dated to the first half of the seventeenth century (Rose Yard No. 111).

868. Hard finely granular red-grey ware, covered with smooth glaze, 'metallic' dark brown, with loop handle. First half of the seventeenth century. Cf. Rose Yard No. 103. Also from this pit were two stoneware medallions (Fig. 136, No. 8).

For other post-medieval pottery from Area R, see Nos. 219–44.

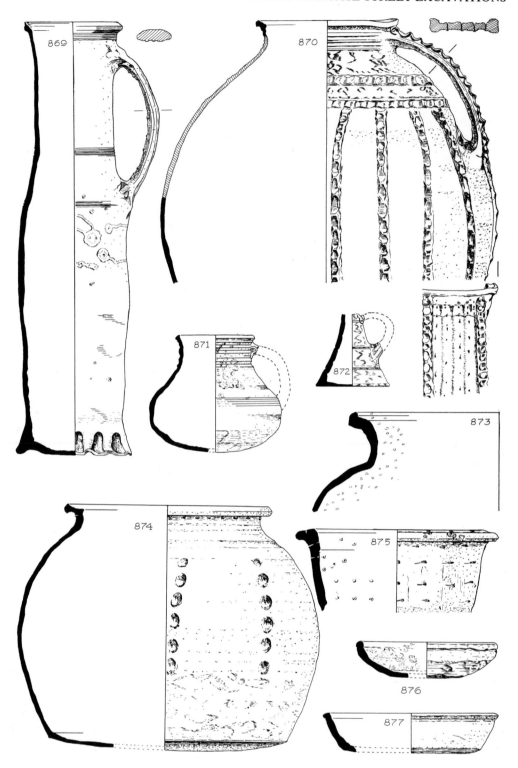

Fig. 131. Medieval pottery from the site of the Roman Theatre (C XIX Site D). Scale 1 : 4

APPENDIX I.

MEDIEVAL AND POST-MEDIEVAL POTTERY FROM THE SITE OF THE ROMAN THEATRE

Additional pits, not published in *Britannia*, i (1970), pp. 83–112.

A. MEDIEVAL (Figs. 131–132)

Nos. 869–877: Pottery from C XIX D X Pit 1. Trapezoidal pit, probably an earth-closet, along the inner edge of the inner corridor wall of the Roman theatre (*ibid.*, fig. 5) partly lined with mortared flint and medieval tile walling where it diverged from the Roman wall. Second half of the thirteenth century.

869. Baluster jug in hard granular reddish ware, smoothed on lower part; the narrow streaks of thin glaze are probably accidental.

870. Hard granular grey ware with applied thumb-impressed strips on body and handle, and glaze, dark green, on shoulder (reconstructed from two jugs).

871. Hard granular red-brown ware with patchy glaze, green, on neck and shoulder (rim incomplete, but no indication of a spout).

872. Base of handled bowl or small jug in granular buff ware, covered with glaze, yellow-green.

873. Grey shell-tempered ware.

874. Hard granular reddish ware, sooted, with vertical rows of finger-impressions on the body, pierced below the rim.

875. Hard granular grey ware splashed with glaze (orange brown) on rim, pierced on rim and body.

876. Hard granular reddish ware, with patchy glaze, green and orange, inside.

877. Ware as No. 876, unglazed.

Nos. 878–881: Pottery from C XIX D X Pit 2. Against the inner face of the outer corridor wall of the Roman theatre. Second half of the thirteenth century.

878. Hard granular reddish ware, sooted; perhaps first half of the thirteenth century.

879. Hard granular grey ware.

880. Hard granular red-brown ware; two.

881. Ware as No. 880, with four applied finger-impressed strips.

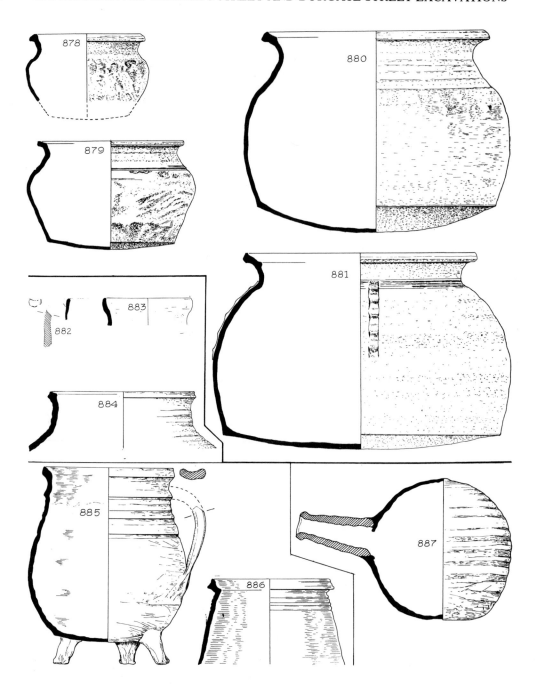

Fig. 132.   Medieval and post-medieval pottery from the site of the Roman Theatre. Scale 1 : 4

B. POST-MEDIEVAL (Figs. 132–135)

Nos. 882–884: Pottery from C XVI D I Pit 2. Cut by Pit 1.

882.   Jug in fine hard finely granular white-buff ware covered with smooth light green glaze with darker mottling. Fifteenth century, probably French, cf. No. 541. Another rim (not figured) came from I Pit 1, pre-dating the cellar (see No. 887).

883.   Hard grey ware covered with glaze, orange-green and 'metallic' brown.

884.   Hard bright reddish ware with grey-brown surface.

Nos. 885–886: Pottery from C XVI D I Pit 1. Wall-lined pit cut through Pit 2.

885.   Hard finely granular reddish ware, with some thin glaze, orange-brown inside. Probably seventeenth century.

886.   Hard finely granular bright reddish ware, covered with 'metallic' brown glaze; handle fragment. There was also a spout fragment in this ware.

887.   Hard finely granular reddish ware with pronounced wheel-marks, Martincamp type III flask. C XVII D I. Infilling of a cellar which used part of the outer corridor wall of the Roman Theatre as its floor. Seventeenth century. See J.G. Hurst, 'Martincamp flasks', in D.S. Neal. 'Excavations at the Palace of King's Langley, Hertfordshire, 1974–6', *Medieval Arch.*, xxi (1977), 156–7.

Nos. 888–925: Pottery from C XVII D III Pit 2. Seventeenth and eighteenth centuries.

Nos. 888–895 are in maiolica, with white opaque tin-glaze over a buff fabric.

888.   Cup with design in deep and medium blue, coloured blue between the panels and on the base; the design is repeated on the opposite side. There is a running motif below the rim inside, and a leaf in the centre of the base.

889.   Drug jar in finely granular yellow-buff ware with blue design.

890.   Plate in yellow-buff ware, the design outlined in blue (not filled in) and with blue leaf-veins.

890A.   Similar to No. 890 but with a different design on the rim.

891.   Design in deep and medium blue.

892.   Blue design on pinkish-white tin glaze (reconstructed from three similar plates).

Fig. 133. Post-medieval pottery from the site of the Roman Theatre. Scale 1 : 4

893. Finely granular buff ware with pinkish-white tin glaze, the design outlined and filled in with deep and medium blue.

894. Dish in yellow-buff ware, with design in deep, medium and pale blue: the central flower is outlined in blue but the infilling, in paler blue, does not coincide with the petals.

895. Finely granular buff ware, the design outlined and filled in with deep and medium blue.

896. Delftware handle and rim as No. 897 in hard buff fabric covered with opaque tin-glaze, white mottled with buff (perhaps misfired); also a sherd with the same discolouration as if from this bowl, with design in brown underglaze colour.

897–902 (eight). White delftware in buff fabric with smooth opaque white tin-glaze; No. 898 could be handled. Seventeenth century: No. 902 after A.D. 1650.

903. Hard finely granular deep buff ware, covered with smooth yellow-brown glaze.

904. Slipware bowl in hard finely granular reddish ware with regular pattern of large dots in white slip, showing yellow against an orange-brown background under internal glaze.

905. Staffordshire slipware posset-pot in hard finely granular buff ware, with pattern of large dots and combed lines in brown slip against a glazed yellow background; both surfaces glazed.
Another was found in a floor in Canterbury Lane (No. 471, not figured).

906. Slipware plate with finger impressions round the rim, in hard finely granular light buff ware, with trailed pattern in dark brown slip against a glazed yellow background. The outer surface, unglazed, has been smoothed.

907. Ware as No. 906, with stamped pattern in dark brown and deep yellow underglaze colour.

908, 909. Slipware plates in hard finely granular red-brown ware, with pattern in white slip showing yellow against an orange-brown background under internal glaze. Seventeenth century.

910. Hard grey stoneware with stamped pattern resembling rouletting over yellow-brown underglaze colour, which extends to the rim; the salt-glazed surfaces elsewhere are rather smooth, lightly flecked with yellow-brown outside.

911. Stoneware tankard in fine hard light buff ware, rather smooth golden-brown salt-glaze, finely mottled outside, plain inside. Eighteenth century. English.

912. As No. 911, in coarser grey stoneware, more unevenly mottled red-brown outside.

913. Smooth hard finely granular buff ware, reddish core, covered inside and on rim with thin glaze, yellow (upper and lower edges of rim are chipped). Spanish olive jar from Seville area. See J.H. Goggin, 'The Spanish Olive Jar', *Yale University Publications Anthropology*, lxii (1960), 1–40.

914. Hard finely granular grey ware with red core and rather granular surface, covered inside with glaze, dark green.

915. Hard finely granular bright reddish ware with smooth surface, covered inside with glaze, orange-brown.

916. Hard finely granular reddish ware with smooth grey-brown surface; the rim has been

Fig. 134.   Post-medieval pottery from the site of the Roman Theatre. Scale 1 : 4

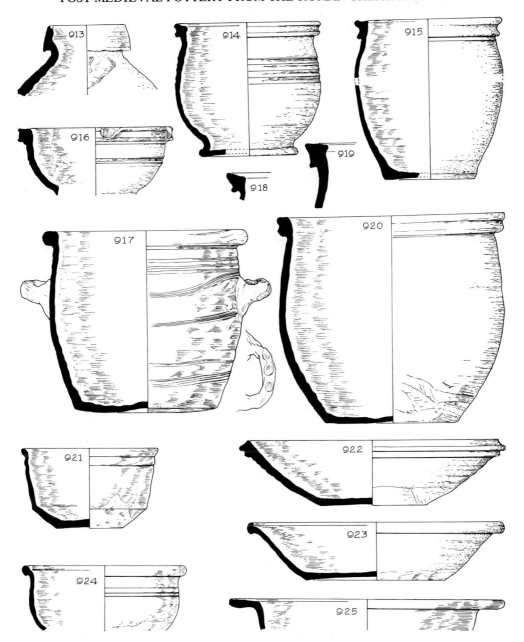

Fig. 135.   Post-medieval pottery from the site of the Roman Theatre. Scale 1 : 4

pressed down at intervals; covered inside and on lip with smooth glaze, dark green-brown. Cf. Nos. 841, 862.

917.   Hard finely granular reddish ware, grey core, with irregular scored lines on body and finger-impressions on handles; covered with glaze, orange-brown.

918–920.   Hard finely granular red-buff ware with smooth surface, covered inside with glaze, orange-brown.

921.   Hard finely granular reddish ware, covered inside and down to carination outside with smooth thick glaze, dark green-brown.

922, 923.   Hard finely granular reddish ware, covered inside with glaze, orange-brown.

924.   Hard finely granular reddish ware, covered inside and partly outside with rather thin glaze, orange-green.

925.   Hard finely granular grey ware, nearly covered with smooth (reduced) dark brown glaze, thick in places.

The pit also contained a Chinese porcelain cup of the late seventeenth to early eighteenth century, a blue and white cup and several blue and white plates of the mid eighteenth century, all of Chinese porcelain.

APPENDIX II

GRAFFITO AND STAMPS ON POTTERY (Fig. 136)

Nos. 1–4: Amphora stamps

1.   **RN.N** Not in Callender. C XI N I Pit 2, undated (p. 65).
2.   **S]EPTPR,** cf. Callender 1595. C XXII C I 31. A.D. 210–230 (p. 86).
3.   **PIAFI** (*retro.*), Callender 1329(b). C XXVIII C XX 44. A.D. 230–260.
4.   **DOM,** Callender 552, South Spanish *c.* A.D. 140–180? C XIV M II 11 (p. 117). A.D. 215–235. Fig. 116, No. 612.

5.   Graffito **NICAN**[. . . on dark poppy-head beaker from the Roman theatre. C XVII D III 11. A.D. 220–250. cf. *JRS*, xli (1951), 144, No. 26.

For a graffito **ABIT**[, see Fig. 124, No. 731.

Nos. 6–12: Stoneware

6.   Face-mask from Bellarmine jug sherd. Frechen. C XIX Z III Pit 1. Seventeenth-century pit (p. 298).

The presence of Badorf-type ware at Canterbury is to be seen against the background of the general trade relations of the Rhineland in the ninth century and later. In recent years the intensity and extent of this long-distance trade have been amply demonstrated by numerous discoveries at sites reached by sea-trade across the North Sea. From the kilns near Cologne the mass-produced Badorf-type ware was exported down the Rhine to Belgium and Holland, and it has been found in some quantity at the trading-station of Dorestad[101] on the Lek Rhine. Thence some of it was shipped to Frisia, where it is found in the terps (settlement mounds) in the provinces of Friesland and Groningen.[102] The bulk of the trade, however, passed eastwards over the North Sea to the trading-station of Haithabu[103] (Hedeby) in Schleswig-Holstein, whence it crossed the Baltic to the town of Birka[104] on Lake Mälar west of Stockholm. The distance covered by this long-distance trade from the Rhineland is over 900 miles.[105]

Discussion of Badorf-type ware in further detail here is unnecessary since a full discussion of finds in Britain and of the dating of the ware has recently been published by R. Hodges.[106] In the present report the date implied by the Badorf-type sherds is taken as c. A.D. 850–950, and they establish the chronology of a large group of local late Saxon wares. At Southampton (Hamwih) Badorf sherds were rare in comparison with wares from France, a situation no doubt attributable to geographical influences. At Canterbury Badorf-type sherds seem no more common, but Frankish wares are here equally rare. Two sherds of Pingsdorf ware (Nos. 317–318), imported from the Rhineland at a slightly later date, show a continuance of trading contacts.

Frankish wares mainly from northern France were relatively abundant at Hamwih, and were divided among various classes. At Canterbury Nos. 349 and 353 can be assigned to Hodges's Class 13, Nos. 316 and 325 to his Class 14, and No. 27 to his Class 15. Class 13 is thought to have been produced in eastern Belgium; Class 14 vessels may have come from several centres in northern or central France, and Class 15 has similarly varied sources.

101. L. Hussong, *Bericht über die Kieler Tagung 'Das Ahnenerbe'* (1944), 186–9, fig. 8.
102. P.C.J.A. Boles, *Friesland tot de elfde eeuw* (1951), 431–7.
103. H. Jankuhn, *Haithabu: Eine germanische stadt der Frühzeit* (1938), 142; Jankuhn, *Die Ausgrabungen in Haithabu 1937–1939* (1943), 176.
104. H. Arbman, *Schweden und das Karolingische Reich* (1937), 92 ff.
105. The distribution of Badorf ware and other groups of Rhenish pottery in the ninth to twelfth centuries is discussed by W. Hübener in *Archaeologia Geographica*, 2 (1951), 105.
106. See note 100.

APPENDIX IV

A NOTE ON THE SKELETAL MATERIAL FROM SITE
C XV B (p. 53)
By D.F. Roberts

The remains represent a child, a young male adult (Inhumation 2), a male adult of middle age (Inhumation 3), another male adult of middle age (Inhumation 1 and 4), with the possibility of the presence of a fifth individual. It is perhaps of interest that the three adults present were all male, were all fairly strongly muscled, and were not senile. All burials had apparently occurred with legs extended. The associated animal bones were not considered.

(a) *Scattered medieval fragments, Trench B IV*

These fragments include a small femur and a lower jaw with some deciduous teeth still in position, with first permanent molars erupted and with central incisors erupting, and therefore probably represent the remains of a child aged about 6–7.

(b) *Inhumation 2*

The practically complete skeleton was buried in the extended position, lying on its back with head turned left and right arm passed across the body so that the hand was in front of the forehead. The remains appear to be those of a male of medium size. Mandible and maxilla possess complete dentition in perfect condition, with a slight amount of wear. Skull sutures remain open, though the sagittal has begun to close. The condition of teeth and skull indicates an age in the region 23–28 though the absence of epiphyses suggest a slightly younger age. Muscle markings and morphology (especially of skull and pelvis) indicate the sex, while the occurrence of slight asymmetry suggests that the individual was right-handed.

Skull length	185	mm.	Parietal chord	114.5 mm.
breadth	144	mm.	Occipital chord	98.3 mm.
Min. frontal	98.5	mm.	Foraminal breadth	26.5 mm.
Frontal chord	114.5	mm.	Cephalic index	77.8 mm.

(c) *Inhumation 3*

The remains consist of the upper regions of the lower limbs and part of the pelvic girdle. The fragments of ilia indicate that the individual was male, the femora that he was of medium build, with stature estimated at 165–166 cm. The separation of the upper segment of the sacrum suggests an age less than 45, and an adult of age 30–40 appears likely.

Left femur, maximum length   44.50 cm.
Right femur, maximum length 45.10 cm.
Oblique length   44.25 cm.
Oblique length   44.65 cm.

(d) *Possibly part of Inhumation 3*

The fragment of temporal indicates an adult male of mature but not old age, the fragment of humerus a medium build, and the general appearance indicates no reason why these fragments should not be attributed to Inhumation 3.

(e) *Inhumation 1*

The remains consist mainly of fragments of long bones. Size and morphology indicate an individual of medium build, the piece of left ilium a male, the fragment of lower jaw containing a worn carious molar, a mature, though not senile age.

(f) *Inhumation 4*

A very disturbed burial. A number of animal bones are included. The left clavicle indicates a mature adult individual, the sacral fragments a male, the hand bones that he was of medium size. It would not seem unreasonable to suppose, and there is no evidence to the contrary, that Inhumation 4 represents the same individual as Inhumation 1, on grounds (a) of the following agreement of regions:

1	*4*
Mandible fragment	Shoulder girdle and upper
Iliac fragments and upper	thorax fragments
leg bones	Fragment of sacrum
Left lower arm bones	Hand bones

(b) that the part individuals concerned were of similar sizes and ages, (c) of a hint at articulation between sacral fragment of 4 and ilium fragment of 1.

(g) *Associated with Inhumation 1*

Included are fragments of animal bones. The inclusion of a fragment of the distal end of a femur already present in Inhumation 1 indicates that these remains should not be associated with individual 1. Possibilities are:
  (a) The fragment is not human, difficult to prove either way on account of its small size.
  (b) It belongs to Inhumation 4, in which case Inhumation 4 does not belong to Inhumation 1.
  (c) Since it belongs to neither 2 nor 3, a fifth individual is represented.

APPENDIX V

REPORT ON ANIMAL BONES FROM C XI N, TRENCH II
PIT 2 (p. 66)

By Ann Brocklebank

Species identified, and the number of recognizable specimens of each, were as follows:

Ox	Pig	Sheep or Goat	Sheep	Goat	Red Deer	Horse	Dog
37	27	30	1	1	1	1	1

Of the bones examined there were 99 determinable fragments, giving the probable number of individuals shown above. Of these the following were immature: Ox 6; Pit 7 (of which three were perhaps sucking-pigs); Sheep or goat 15, forming about 28 per cent of the whole. Ox, pig and sheep or goat are fairly evenly represented, so that it may be assumed that the proportions of the different species kept roughly corresponded. Lambs were apparently eaten as often as sheep, but there is not enough evidence from the bovine bones to suggest autumn killing of immature stock.

Only one fragment, of a skull with a vestigial horn-core, was certainly identifiable as sheep. It was of interest as suggesting the presence of a hornless breed. A single large horn-core of goat was also found.

There were several bovine horn-cores, of two different sizes. The difference may only be sexual, but there is a suggestion that a breed with longer horns and altogether larger than the Celtic Ox was kept, perhaps an improved breed, or a cross from an improved breed imported by the Romans.

The red-deer bone was a calcaneum or heel-bone, not a very edible portion, but one must assume that the animal was hunted for food. So, also, for the horse. The single metapodial is not from a meaty part of the limb and affords no evidence whether the animal was eaten.

Remains of dog suggested no more than a single individual, all parts of the skeleton being represented.

From the numerous jaw-bones of sheep and pig it might be concluded that sheep's head or boar's head frequently figured in the bill of fare. These parts, however, were relatively imperishable and have probably been differentially preserved. Even if not used, every beast slaughtered would have yielded a waste head, for which the rubbish-pit was the logical resting-place.

Twenty fragments of birds were found in addition to the mammalian remains, chiefly of legs and wings, of a size usually corresponding with that of a rather small domestic fowl. The probability is that they are, indeed, mainly of *Gallus domesticus*.

APPENDIX VI

ANIMAL BONES FROM SAXON LEVELS IN CANTERBURY LANE

By Professor B.J. Marples

Note: The measurements given are in millimetres: a single measurement indicates the total length of the bone; where seven measurements are given they give the length, the two diameters at the proximal end, and two diameters at the middle of the shaft and at the distal end.

C XX C I (8). Main late Saxon occupation-layer

(a) *Ox*

    5 skull parts, one with horn core.
    3 horn cores, oval section: bases (and convexities) 63 × 45 (160); 58 × 43 (175).
    1 base with flat side (? species) cut at base 51 × 41 (120+).
    6 loose teeth.
    8 jaw parts, 5 of them the distal half.
    5 vertebrae including atlas (3 cut).
    1 humerus, distal end.
    1 metatarsus and 1 part (204.0, 41.0, 41.0, 22.5, 24.0, 47.5, 27.5).

(b) *Sheep*

    5 skull parts, 2 with horn cores, 1 measuring 29 × 18 (92), flattened but convex both faces.
    5 other horn cores, ? species (see Ox). 3 cut at base
        (i)   convex; base (and convexities) 37 × 28 (120)
        (ii) convex, slightly flattened *c.* 42 × 39 (150)
        (iii) other 3 not measurable, but 2 very flattened.
    4 jaws.
    1 vertebra.
    2 humeri (both cut) (149.0).
    1 radius (138.0).
    1 metacarpus (133.5, 23.0, 18.0, 14.5, 11.0, 26.0, 17.0).
    1 metatarsus and 1 fragment (127.0, 19.0, 20.0, 11.5, 10.0, 23.5, 15.5)

(c) *Pig*

9 skull parts.
3 teeth.
8 jaw parts, 6 of them the distal part, 2 with large tusks.
1 vertebra.
1 pelvis fragment.
1 femur.

(d) *Red Deer*

One fragment of skull with base of antler and the bases of four shed antlers. The extreme measurements of the burrs are: 72 × 65, 71 × 64, 83 × 72, ? × 73, 73 × 65. In each an oblique upward cut had removed the brow-tine and the beam was cut through obliquely. The two cuts start just above the burr and meet at right angles.

Also present are a short length (*c.* 30) of beam, two oblique offcuts, one short tine and the tips of three tines. The saw-cuts are very smooth and three false starts show that the blade was 1 mm. thick. Antler-working probably took place on the site.

(e) *Fowl*

1 tarsal (68.5).
1 ulna.

(f) *Goose*

1 ulna (140).

(g) *Goat*

1 skull part, cut by base of horn.
Base of pair of horn cores, flattened and convex, tips missing (57 × 37).
2 horn cores, flattened and convex; base (and convexities) 56 × 35 (270).

C XXIII C V A (4A). Late Saxon occupation-layer

(a) *Ox*

8 vertebrae — 4 cut.

2 parts of pelvis.

2 scapula fragments.

9 skull parts, 7 with teeth.

8 teeth.

1 hyoid.

Horn cores — 1 on skull fragment, round section; base (and convexities) 40 × 34
(130). 4 parts, flat or concave on one side, 2 chopped at base, 3 sawn across
square.

4 jaw parts.

Humerus, 1 distal end.

Radius, 2 proximal ends.

Ulna, 2.

Metacarpus, 4 parts (2 immature).

Femur, 3 distal ends (1 immature).

Tibia, 1 part (immature).

Metatarsus, 4 parts.

12 phalanges.

1 calcaneum (immature).

(b) *Sheep*

5 fragments of skull with teeth.

3 teeth.

Part of small horn core, base 38 × 30, strongly curved. Depressions round the
middle suggest that it might have been constricted by e.g. a chain.

4 jaws (2 with last M erupting).

6 vertebrae (2 cut).

5 ribs.

1 humerus and 1 fragment.

1 radius (144.5, 29.0, 14.5, 16.5, 9.0, 26.5, 17.0).

Metacarpal, 3 parts (2 immature).

Tibia, 1 part (immature).

1 metatarsal and 1 part (142.0, 20.5, 20.0, 11.5, 11.5, 23.0, 15.0).

2 phalanges.

Pelvis, 1 part.

(c) *Pig*

1 half skull cut sagitally without snout, and 3 fragments.

6 teeth.
1 whole jaw, 2 proximal halves, 4 symphysis region.
1 vertebra.
Femur, 1 epiphysis.
Tibia, 1 part (immature).
2 metapodials.
Pelvis, 1 part.

(d) *Red Deer*

1 base of cast antler (burr 62 × 56), beam and brow tine cut off by smooth saw cuts.

(e) *Roe Deer*

1 shed antler with 2 tines.

(f) *Fowl*

Humerus, 2 (72.5).
Tibia, 2 (1 immature) (120.0).
Tarsus, 1 part with spur.
Clavicle, 1 part.
Radius, 2 immature, ? species.

(g) *Fish*

1 large jaw with sockets of many small teeth.

APPENDIX VII

DECORATED SAMIAN[107] (Fig. 137)

1. Drag. 29. S.G., probably Claudian. C XV R III 29, primary metalling of north-east to south-west street (p. 70).

2. Drag. 37, C.G., style of Austrus, *c.* A.D. 125–145. C XV S I 5, another piece in 8. Layer preceding Apsed Building (p. 43).

3. Drag. 37, E.G., late Antonine or early third century. C XIV M I 26. Roman pit (p. 113).

4. Drag. 37, C.G., style of Criciro, *c.* A.D. 140–160. C XIV N I 4. Roman pit (p. 117).

5. Drag. 37, C.G., style of Docilis, *c.* A.D. 125–145. C XV S II 22. Secondary floor of house preceding Apsed building (p. 43).

6. Drag. 37, C.G., style of Attianus, *c.* A.D. 135–160. C XV S II 25. Occupation-layer below floor earlier than Apsed Building, Room 2 (p. 43).

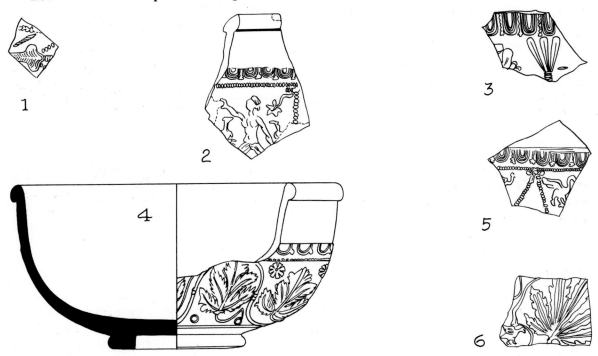

Fig. 137. Decorated samian. Scale 1 : 2

107. The samian from these excavations was examined and identified by Mr. B.R. Hartley, to whom the authors express their thanks.

APPENDIX VIII

THE BUTCHERY LANE HOUSE AND BUILDINGS BELOW THE PARADE AND ST. GEORGE'S STREET

By T. Tatton-Brown, P. Blockley and P. Bennett

The Butchery Lane Roman building was first excavated in 1945–46 by Audrey Williams and Sheppard Frere.[108] In 1958–61 the cellars in which the building was found were enlarged and converted into the 'Roman Pavement' Museum. Several more walls and other features were discovered by Dr. F. Jenkins during this work, and an updated plan was drawn by Miss Louise Millard but remained unpublished. Recently a new and more accurate plan has been drawn by Paul Blockley which also incorporates discoveries made in The Parade in 1976 and 1982 (Fig. 138).

A. THE HYPOCAUST ROOM

The small hypocaust room jutting into the courtyard was partly excavated in 1945–46. Subsequently more of this room was exposed during conversion to a museum. At this time the west wall and flue of the hypocaust room were completely uncovered, though they had been cut by a nineteenth-century well and by the old cellar wall. Dr. Jenkins suggests a possible extra flue to the south (Fig. 138) as well as a possible door in the wall to the west (not now visible). In this area a late third-century coin hoard was found (see below for details).

Period I

Before the construction of the heated room in Period 2, a door had led into the courtyard through the south wall of the corridor. This door, which survived as a course of tiles narrower than the width of the flint and mortar foundations, was presumably blocked when the heated room was added.

Period II

The small heated room was built. This room, approximately 3.7 m. square, was of flint and mortar build. It was presumably entered from the corridor, through a new door west of the earlier one. Around the room, in the courtyard, ran a tile gutter which, like the room itself, had been badly disturbed by medieval pits. Its north-east corner had subsided into a deep medieval feature, and many of the *pilae* had also been disturbed. Along the east wall,

---

108. A. Williams and S.S. Frere, *Arch. Cant.*, lxi (1948), 1–45.

fragments of the upper *opus signinum* flooring survived. Each wall was lined with a long pilaster 47 cm. high, constructed of flint and mortar with tile courses, to support the upper floor. Excavations in the flue area have shown that a small stoke-room adjoined the west wall. The flue itself is constructed of tile courses bonded in mortar and clay, as is the extension 1 m. long into the hypocaust.

A very young baby's skeleton, of Roman date, lay in the hypocaust debris in the south-east quarter of the room. The excavations in 1946 located a coin of Constantius II or Constans (A.D. 345–61) in the hypocaust debris.

An area of collapsed masonry, in the north wall of the hypocaust, may be evidence for a flue leading hot gases into further heated rooms in the corridor area to the north of the exposed room. This hypothesis requires testing by excavation which, it is hoped, may be undertaken in 1983 when the whole area may be reconstructed.

B. THE COIN HOARD

A hoard of 50 third-century radiate coins was found in the area west of the hypocaust stokehole in the Roman building in Butchery Lane. These have been identified by Mr. Ian Anderson as follows:

Regular coins

Victorinus, A.D. 268–70. Rev. *Salus*. *RIC* 71
Claudius II. *Consecratio* issue of A.D. 270. Rev. *Pietas*. *RIC* 284
Tetricus I, A.D. 270–73. Rev. *Laetitia*. *RIC* 91
Tetricus II, A.D. 270–73 (two). Rev. *Seculum*, altar. *RIC* 269 and rev. uncertain.

Irregular coins, all dated c. 270–90

Obv. Tetricus II. Rev. *Laetitia*
Obv. Tetricus I. Rev. *Pax* (four)
Obv. uncertain. Rev. *Pax* (two)
Obv. uncertain. Rev. pontifical implements (five)
Obv. uncertain. Rev. *Salus* (three)
Obv. uncertain. Rev. *Sol.* (three)
Obv. Tetricus I. Rev. *Spes*
Obv. Tetricus II. Rev. *Spes*
Obv. uncertain. Rev. *Spes* (two)
Obv. Tetricus I. Rev. *Virtus*
Obv. uncertain. Rev. *Virtus* (two)

Obv. uncertain. Rev. Stag. Copied from coin of Gallienus (260–68)
Obv. Tetricus II. Rev. uncertain (two)
Obv. and rev. uncertain (seventeen).

All the coins are now in Canterbury Museum.

C. WALLS DISCOVERED IN THE PARADE IN 1976 AND 1982

A slit-trench, *c.* 50 cm. wide and 2 m. deep, was cut by the G.P.O. in The Parade in March-April 1976 (Figs. 1 and 138). A series of Roman walls and floors was exposed and recorded very briefly by T. Tatton-Brown and P. Bennett with the help of the Contractor, J. Quinlan of Herne Bay, and are described starting at the southern end of the trench. A very thick double wall was uncovered which is clearly the same as that encountered in the 1982 sewer shaft (see below) and by Professor Frere in 1946. To the north of this was the disturbed foundation of a Roman floor (? *opus signinum*). This room was 3.6 m. wide and had a wall 55 cm. wide on the north dividing it from a large room containing a tessellated pavement. Most of the room contained large grey *tesserae*, but in the centre was a mosaic panel, similar to those found in 1945 in the room on the east side of the courtyard. The panel, only part of which was uncovered, was cleaned and photographed[109] and then unfortunately destroyed almost immediately by the new pipe-trench. The decoration of the panel was in black lozenges set in a white ground, and inside this were the remains of a guilloche pattern in red, white and black tesserae. The southern edge of this panel was 1.95 m. north of the south wall of the room; the room itself was 7.2 m. wide from north to south. Part of the north wall of the room survived (it contained some string-courses of Roman bricks), and beyond this was another room, floored in *opus signinum*. This room, *c.* 8 m. wide from north to south, was badly disturbed in its central section by the sewer-trench coming out of Butchery Lane. The north wall of the room, also 55 cm. wide and made of flints and bricks set in yellow mortar, had on its north side another room with an *opus signinum* floor; but the width of this final room could not be fully determined as the whole of its northern part had been cut away by deep pits and modern disturbances. The south wall of this final room still retained some painted wall-plaster.

D. 1982 SEWER TUNNEL IN THE PARADE
AND ST. GEORGE'S STREET

In the period June-August 1982 a tunnel was driven under part of The Parade and St. George's Street to lay a new main sewer. The western shaft giving access to the tunnel, opposite No. 16, The Parade, was cut 4.2. m. below the present road-surface, and the tunnel

---

109. See brief note by T. Tatton-Brown in *Arch. Cant.*, xcii (1976), 240 and Pl. II (opposite p. 244) which shows the mosaic panel.

itself (1.2 m. wide and 1.3 m. high) was dug on a slightly rising gradient to the east for a length of approximately 120 m. A second 'emergency' shaft was dug 83 m. east of the first when a high-pressure water main was encountered in the heading (see p. 324). A third and final shaft was sunk close to the intersection of St. George's Street and Canterbury Lane. The foundations of eight Roman walls and a drain were cut by the tunnel and are shown on Fig. 1. All the walls were located in the first 32 m. of the tunnel, and as the heading was below the level of natural brickearth in that length, only the foundations of the walls were observed high in the sides or in the roof of the tunnel. Thanks are extended to the contractors, D. Justice Limited, and to their employees for allowing the recording to take place.

The remains are described from south-west to north-east.

(a) *Wall 1* was in a position bordering the north-western edge of the narrow Roman lane running south-west from Area Y. No metalling was observed, but the tunnel lay at too great a depth; it is uncertain how far this lane extended. The wall was 0.6 m. wide with a foundation of compacted gravel. The wall was of flints in yellow-brown mortar.

(b) *Drain*, 0.7 m. wide with a foundation of flints and *tegulae* oblique to the line of the tunnel; the drain-channel itself was above the roof of the tunnel. This drain is probably a continuation of the drain found each side of Rose Lane (Fig. 1) in 1946 (*Arch. Cant.*, lxviii (1954), 118–20) where it was *c.* 1 m. wide.

(c) *Wall 2* was 0.62 m. wide with foundations of compacted gravel. A tile bonding course was noted in the roof of the tunnel. As plotted, this wall lies very close to Wall **a**, noted on p. 64, n. 38; but Wall **a** was 0.9 m. wide and was probably therefore separate; its foundations need not have been as deep as the tunnel and no doubt it represents a different period of construction.

(d) Between Walls 2 and 3 a bedding of small flints and compacted gravel was noted in the roof of the tunnel; it was perhaps the basis for an *opus signinum* floor.

(e) *Wall 3* was 0.62 m. wide with a foundation of compacted gravel; the masonry was flints in tough yellow mortar and at least one tile course was noted in the roof of the tunnel.

(f) *Wall 4* was 0.5 m. wide on a gravel foundation; it was built of 'fresh' fair-sized flints in yellow-brown mortar; a tile course was seen.

(g) *Wall 5* was 0.67 m. wide of flints in tough yellow mortar, with a shallow foundation of compacted gravel. This wall may be earlier than its neighbours.

(h) *Wall 6* was 0.6 m. wide, of fair-sized flints in yellow-brown mortar resting on a foundation of compacted gravel *c.* 0.35 m. deep.

(i) *Wall 7*, 0.62 m. wide was of fair-sized 'fresh' flints in tough yellow-brown mortar and rested on gravel foundations *c.* 0.5 m. deep. This wall with Walls 2, 3, 4 and 6 represent a single separate building parallel to and south-east of the south wing of the Butchery Lane House.

(j) *Wall 8*, 0.6 m. wide, with gravel foundations *c.* 0.4 m. deep, was built of fist-sized flints in yellow mortar; two fragments of greensand were noted in the masonry. This wall, now traced across almost the whole width of The Parade, is identical with the thick wall noted here in 1976 (above, p. 322) and in 1946, and is part of the Butchery Lane house.

APPENDIX IX

THE SOUTH-WEST SIDE OF THE ST. GEORGE'S STREET BATH-BUILDING

By Paul Bennett

The discovery and excavation of the St. George's Street bath-house has been described in Chapter I above; the south-west side of Rooms 1, 5 and 9 extended under the pavement and was inaccessible. In July 1982 a tunnel for a new sewer was dug below St. George's Street, as already mentioned in Appendix VIII D above. Approximately 82 m. from the entrance-shaft to this tunnel in The Parade a high-pressure water-main was encountered in the heading. As this constituted a threat to the workmen's safety, an escape-shaft was cut opposite Nos. 19 and 21 St. George's Street and the tunnel realigned to avoid the water-pipe. On Friday, 3 July, during the cutting of the emergency exit, the south-west corner of the St. George's Street Roman bath-house was exposed, and partly cut into. After hurried consultations with the Canterbury City Council, the Ancient Monuments Inspectorate and the contractors, a two-day (weekend) excavation was undertaken to record this part of the building before destruction continued. Despite every effort to re-route the tunnel away from the building, the presence of numerous potentially dangerous services, together with the cost and time, sealed the fate of this part of the building — one of the best-preserved Roman structures yet found in Canterbury. The south-western ends of Rooms 1, 5 and 9 (later cut into by the realigned tunnel), were sealed in part by a sequence of road-metallings dating back to a least the late Saxon period, and the walls and heating systems for all three were very well preserved. The tunnel cut away the main south-west load-bearing wall of the bath-house on a converging course with the interior of Rooms 5 and 9.

The internal arrangements within Room 1 were not exposed beyond the escape-shaft since the tunnel did not cut away the fabric of the wall completely at this point. The interior of Rooms 5 and 9 was visible in the north-east side of the tunnel (Fig. 139) and a section through the *praefurnium*, opposite Room 5 was recorded in the south-west side. Though partly obscured by wooden shuttering and despite inadequate lighting (much of the recording was done with the aid of a torch), a record of the exposed fabric both in the escape-shaft and in the tunnel was achieved.

The success of this hectic salvage operation is owed to many. Thanks are extended to the City Engineer of the Canterbury City Council, and to the contractors, D. Justice Limited, who allowed the work to take place; Messrs. J. Rady, I. Anderson, P. Barford and T. Tatton-Brown helped with the excavation of the escape-trench. Miss M. Green, Mrs. C. Simpson, Mrs. M. Taylor and Mrs. M. Lyle helped with the general public, who showed a keen interest in the work. Finally my personal thanks are extended to Mr. Simon Pratt, who worked 'from crack of dawn to sunset' to help complete the excavation and the final records.

A cross-section through three rooms and a stoke-hole were recorded during the cutting of the escape-trench and the tunnel (Rooms 1, 5 and 9).

Room 1

The south-west corner of Room 1 (at the south-west corner of the building) was excavated in the escape-trench. At least two major constructional phases were observed, but only Period II work was examined. The south-east wall of Room 1, 0.54 m. wide, was truncated by an eighteenth-century cellar (the north-west wall of Frere's cellar 'C'). The main south-west wall. 0.95 m. wide, had been cut down by a pit, which was in turn sealed by street metallings. Both walls were built almost entirely of rubble greensand blocks (from the Hythe beds), with string courses of whole and broken *tegulae* and bricks. Patches of external rendering were noted on both walls. The upper 0.28 m. of the surviving wall had been truncated by the workmen cutting the escape-trench before the commencement of the excavation and part of the floor and bridging tiles were cut through.

An area approximately 0.9 m. (NE-SW) by 1.15 m. (NW-SE) was excavated inside Room 1. The primary heating arrangement remained intact and the Period II system (standing over 1 m. high) was built over the surviving upper floor. Four *pilae*, on average 19 tiles high, were uncovered in the restricted area. A thin layer of burnt orange-red clay sealed the Period I upper floor and a large broken tile was laid over the clay bedding, supporting each *pila*. The *pila* closest to the south-west corner of the room was set on a diagonal; the remaining stacks were laid four-square to the room. A rubble pillar, made of a mixture of reused bricks, *tegulae*, box flue-tiles, mortar lumps and tufa set in orange-red clay, was located 0.94 m. from the north-west wall and 0.27 m. from the south-west wall. This pillar and the tile *pilae* supported a layer of bridging tiles (intact tiles each measured 0.55 × 0.55 × 0.06 m.). A layer of off-white *opus signinum* mortar sealed the bridging-tiles, and was sealed by a single course of *tegulae* which was possibly the bedding for the *opus signinum* Period II upper floor. The Period I box-flue system, held in place by randomly-spaced T-shaped iron hold-fasts, was largely reused, with the scar for the internal Period I wall-rendering surviving on the reused floor (Fig. 141). The early box-flues (of average internal dimension 80 × 107 × 504 mm.) were supplemented by a new system of box-flues (internally 118 × 180 × 200 mm.) and boxed *tegulae* (Fig. 141). One additional Period II feature was the insertion of a soft greensand block ledge, located opposite the rubble pillar in the main south-west wall and at the level of the course of bridging tiles. The ledge, approximately 0.6 m. long, 0.12 m. wide and 0.1 m. thick, was perforated by two holes and supported three Period II box-flue tiles.

The *pilae* had shifted position and the pair closest to the south-west wall had rotated and tilted to the south-west. Many of the tiles included in the *pilae* were probably reused from the Period I building, since mortar was found adhering to them, although clay separated each tile in the stack. A number of larger unmortared tiles were also noted. These tiles (of average dimensions 202 × 215 × 46 mm., as opposed to 192 × 199 × 42 mm. for the mortared tiles) may have been manufactured for use in the Period II building or may have been reused from another building.

Room 5

Two constructional phases were recognised in the truncated fabric of Room 5. The room may have projected into the core of the wall, creating a narrowing of the wall-width at this point. The room was 2.82 m. wide and intact walling extended from the bottom of the tunnel to above the roof of the heading, a height in excess of 1.5 m. A recent sewer cut through the centre of the room at right-angles to the tunnel, removing a section of flue and cutting away the upper levels of an external *praefurnium* attached to the centre of the south-west wall of the room.

Period I

The wall dividing Rooms 1 and 5 (approximately 0.6 m. wide), widened at the base to 1.85 m. and formed a bench standing 0.72 m. above the surface of the primary floor. This wall was rendered with a layer of *opus signinum* 1.5 cm. thick. The wall dividing Rooms 5 and 9, 0.77 m. wide, was built almost entirely of tiles and was also rendered. The primary floor, an 8 cm. layer of off-white to pink *opus signinum*, was bedded on natural brickearth. A stack of mortared bricks 0.72 m. wide abutted the bench and an 8 cm. layer of off-white *opus signinum*, probably the upper floor of the Period I hot room, sealed the bench and the tile-stack. The vertical south-east face of the tile-stack was the south-west side of a flue, underlying the Period I upper floor. The remains of a south-east stack of mortared tiles, approximately 0.4 m. wide, abutted the wall dividing Rooms 5 and 9. An area of wear in the primary floor, 0.66 m. wide, indicated the size of aperture for the stoke-flue, the wear possibly being the result of the raking of ash and debris from the stoke-hole over a long period.

The brick piers exposed in the side of the tunnel were undoubtedly supporting stacks flanking either side of the stoke-hole. The bench located in the south-west corner of the room was probably an additional support for the Period I upper floor. *Pilae* supporting the floor at the level of the bench undoubtedly existed on the other side (north-east) of the supporting piers. On the opposite side of the tunnel the remains of a *praefurnium* was recorded. Much of the structure had been truncated by the sewer and by a medieval pit. Two stacks of tiles 0.6 m. apart and bonded with clay, defined an aperture which was choked with charcoal, ash and burnt clay. The tile stacks were located on an off-white *opus signinum* floor. The floor was completely worn away between the stacks and a shallow depression cut into the underlying natural brickearth — the result of successive rakings over a considerable period. To the south-west of the stoke-hole the fabric of the south-west wall survived intact.

Period II

The Period I stoke-hole was filled with a mixture of concrete, mud and tiles, and a new stoking floor was established at a higher level (obscured by retaining planks within the tunnel).

A new support-bench was built above the old, and the main wall dividing Rooms 1 and 5 was thickened by a further 0.27 m. and rendered. A pier of mortared tiles 0.47 m. wide abutted the new dividing wall and extended up above the roof of the tunnel. Abutting this pier was a second stack of tiles creating the south-west side of the new stoke-hole, which supported the remains of the corbelled roof of the fire-box. The wall dividing Rooms 5 and 9 was also thickened (by 0.27 m.) and re-rendered. The remains of a supporting stack, cut by the sewer and bedded on clay infilling, abutted the thickened and re-rendered south-east wall. The upper floor of the Period II room was not located; this probably existed above the roof of the heading.

As Professor Frere has indicated above (p. 37), this room was a *caldarium* (the principal hot-room of the bath suite) in both Periods I and II. The location of the *praefurnium*, in a position anticipated by Frere also confirms his interpretation of the arrangement for this part of the building.

Room 9

Two construction phases were recorded in Room 9.

Period I

The room, 1.98 m. wide, had very little Period I fabric remaining. The south-east wall was 0.54 m. wide and built of rough ragstone blockwork with string courses, thickened at the base to 0.67 m., creating a narrow bench standing approximately 0.4 m. above the primary floor. The south-east and south-west walls were rendered approximately to the level of the primary lower floor.

This floor had been badly disturbed during the cutting of the tunnel and again when a new sewer was inserted along the north-east side of the tunnel. Although part of the floor was visible (an off-white *opus signinum* mortar, approximately 5–10 cm. thick, laid on a pad of fist-sized flints), an actual surface was not observed. Professor Frere discovered regularly-spaced *pila* scars on the lower floor at the north-east end of the room. *Pila* scars were not observed in the cutting, but undoubtedly existed since *pilae* must have supported an upper floor, probably at the level of the bench in the south-east wall. No traces of a box-flue system survived from Period I in the cutting, although box flues were known to have been fixed to the south-east and north-east walls of the room.

Period II

The Period I heating system was completely dismantled and the remaining lower floor (with *pila* scars) was sealed by a mixture of concrete and debris. The infill extended up to approximately the top of the bench. A thin 4 cm. layer of off-white *opus signinum* sealed the dumped debris and capped the bench. A new *pila* system was then built on the floor. The south-west wall was re-rendered with a layer of mortar 5 cm. thick and a box-flue system fixed to the south-west wall. Five *pilae* (on average 6 tiles high) standing approximately 0.35 m. tall supported a course of bridging tiles and a layer of off-white *opus signinum* 0.16 cm. thick. The surface of the *opus signinum* was very abraded and may not have been the actual floor. Frere's section C-D (Fig. 3) indicates that the floor may have been approximately 0.25 m. above the course of bridging-tiles. The abraded floor and the remains of the box-flue system were sealed by demolition debris.

Room 9 contained a hot-plunge bath in both periods.

The Levels South-East of the Bath-house in the Tunnel

The area south-east of the building was severely disturbed by pits and modern brickwork. The intact levels in the heading consisted of natural brickearth, for the bath-house had been built on a terrace cut into a gentle slope (see below). No trace of the Roman street, located approximately 9 m. south-east of the bath-house was located in the cutting.

The Area South-West of the Bath-house (Figs. 140, 142)

A sequence of courtyards and drains associated with the exterior of the bath-house were recorded during the cutting of the escape-trench.

The bath-house had been constructed on a terrace cut into a gentle slope. Natural brickearth was located at 11.08 m. O.D. in the cutting for the escape-trench, at approximately 11.70 m. O.D. south-east of Room 9, and at 12.50 m. O.D. some 26 m. south-east of the building at the end of the tunnel.

Sealing the natural brickearth in the escape-trench was a sequence of early Roman layers, 0.15 m. thick. These deposits were capped by a thick layer of tile and gravel (25) possibly indicating a courtyard metalling pre-dating the bath-house. Sealing this surfacing was a 0.4 m. deposit of grey-green clayey silt mixed with mottled brickearth (24). This thick homogeneous layer may have been levelled upcast from the cutting of the terrace for the bath-house.

The primary courtyard metalling (20), laid on a thin bed of redeposited brickearth (21), sealed the earlier deposits. Cutting the upcast deposit and associated with the primary court-yard was a masonry drain (22). This drain had been found further north in Cellar A (p. 29); it was 1.25 m. wide abutting the north-west wall of the bath-house, and was found to continue beyond the south-west corner of the building (Figs. 2 and 140).

Bath-house and drain were of contemporary build. The drain, built of ragstone lumps, and a few flints with tile string courses, had a bed of tightly-fitting *tegulae* creating a culvert 0.25 m. wide. The interior of the drain was badly eroded, indicating considerable use, and the culvert filled with a dark grey glutinous clay (23). Associated with the drain which took effluent from the bath-house (it flowed north-east to south-west), was a second metalling (18). This metalling was separated from the first by a deposit of fine-grained grey silt (19) possibly flood silt from drain overflow. The second metalling was sealed by an identical deposit of possible flood silt (17). A third metalling sealed the silt (15). The laying of this new surfacing terminated the life of the masonry drain, which was replaced by an open drain (16). This new drain was probably cut late in Period I, but continued the line of the old one. The drain had a tripartite fill, with a lens of grey 'rapid silt' at the base sealed by a deposit of dirty yellow mortar and accumulated debris from the eroded side of the earlier drain, and a final bulk infill of olive-green sandy silt. The third metalling was resurfaced at least once and was capped by a layer of sandy silt (14) similar to that infilling the open drain. A second open drain (11) cut the first, and a new courtyard metalling laid (13). This drain, with a wide shallow-sloping north-west edge no longer flowed beyond the building, but fed into a soakaway (12) located outside the south-west corner of the bath-house. The soakaway, aligned roughly north-south, was 1.50 m. long and 0.9 m. wide and was very deep. (The pit was emptied to 10.00 m. O.D. but not bottomed.) Both drain and soakaway were probably cut during Period II. Neither feature showed obvious signs of protracted use; the drain, lined with a layer of clay, was filled with a mixture of degraded mortar and sandy silt sealed by a dump of dark loam mixed with mortar and tile rubble. The soakaway had fresh, almost vertical sides and showed few signs of erosion, even on the side closest the drain. The pit was filled with domestic debris, particularly oyster shells and animal bones.

The final courtyard was resurfaced at least once and was eventually sealed by a layer of dark loam (10) similar to that infilling the final drain. This seemingly short-lived drainage-system may confirm Professor Frere's suggestion that the Period II occupation of the bath-house was of short duration. The final courtyard, the backfilled drain and the soakaway were sealed by a thick, compact deposit of degraded mortar and rubble (9), which may have accumulated during a period of abandonment and decay. The latest Roman deposits were sealed by an interesting sequence of later levels.

The later Levels

Sealing the latest Roman deposits was a layer 5–10 cm. thick of black loam (8). This deposit resembles the ubiquitous 'dark earth' commonly found sealing the latest Roman levels over much of the city, and may indicate a long period of abandonment following the end of Roman Canterbury. Sealing this layer was a very thick (c. 0.6 m.) homogeneous deposit of grey-green silty loam (7) containing many oyster shells and animal bones. Cutting this deposit in the south-west corner of the escape-trench was a shallow pit (6) with a slightly darker infilling outlined by numerous tipping oyster shells. A fragment of an eighth- or ninth-century loom-weight was recovered from the pit.

Early St. George's Street

The surface of the made ground, though unmetalled, may have been a late Saxon street. Constant use of this unmetalled thoroughfare created a wide U-shaped hollow. The upper 5 cm. of the made ground were more compact and contained more bones and oyster shells than the underlying matrix. This upper deposit (5), which may have been churned up or deposited

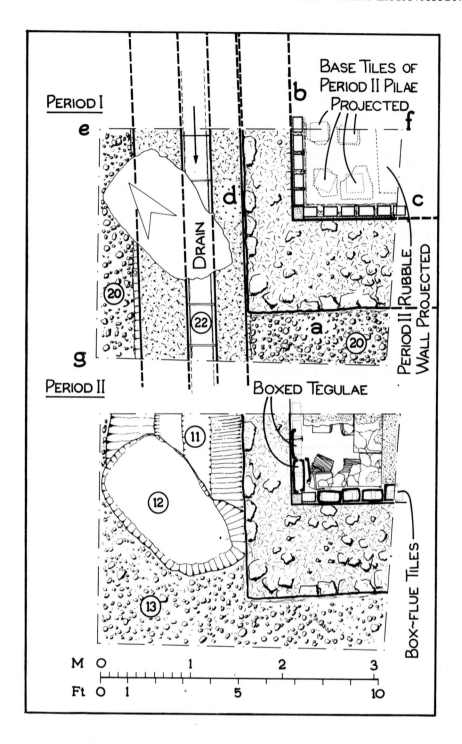

Fig. 140. St. George's Street Bath-Building. Plan of Room 1 and external drain at two levels, as exposed in escape-tunnel. Scale 1 : 40

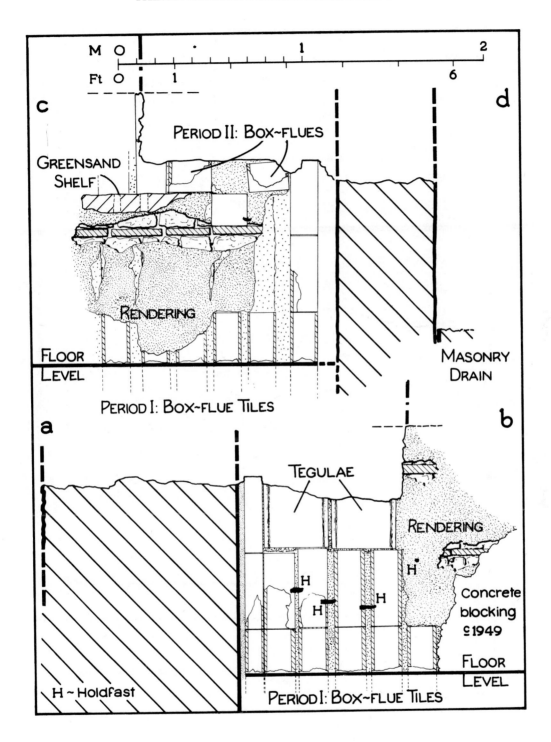

Fig. 141. St. George's Street Bath-Building. Internal wall-elevations in Room 1. Scale 1 : 20

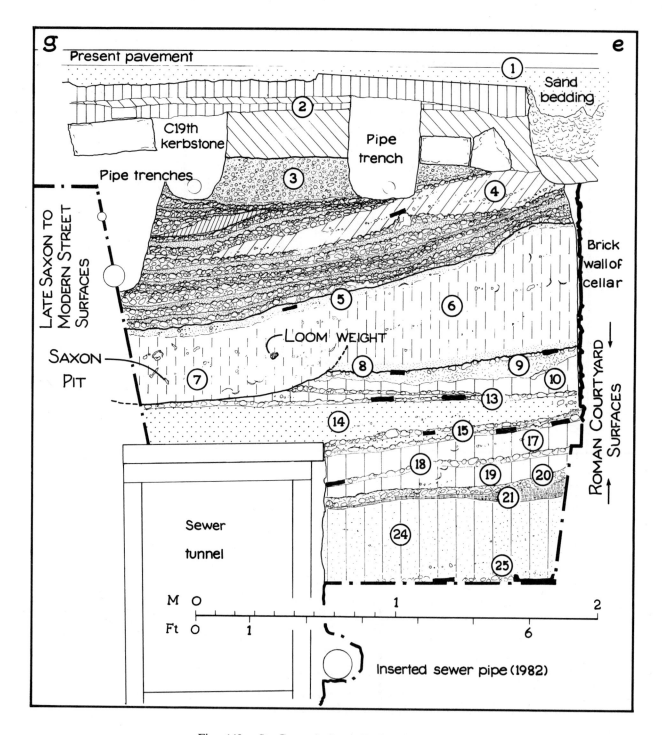

Fig. 142.   St. George's Street Bath-Building. Section G-E.

during the use of the unpaved roadway, contained a small number of late Saxon sherds (Group I, *c.* A.D. 975–1025).[110] Documentary evidence indicates that a road existed here from at least the tenth century. The hollow-way (approximately 0.5 m. deep) was eventually metalled at least eight times (4) during the later Saxon and medieval periods. A deposit 0.25 m. thick of heavily rammed gravel (3), which probably consisted of a number of individual metallings, may have been laid down in the post-medieval period.

Flanking the north-east side of the escape-trench were the south-west walls of Frere's cellars A and C (excavated in 1947). The wall of Cellar A, constructed mainly of roughly-hewn chalk blocks with a few bricks, incorporated part of the main north-west wall of the Roman bath-house in its footings. The upper levels of the cellar wall were later cut down and a coal-chute incorporated in the fabric. The wall of Cellar C cut away part of the upper floor of Room 1 of the bath-house and partly overlay the north-west wall. A sewer pipe was later inserted through the cellar wall.

Sealing the succession of gravel road-metallings and flanking the frontage represented by the walls of Cellars A and C were layers of hardcore and tarmacadam for the pavement of modern St. George's Street (2). The tarmacadam pavement and the truncated cellar walls were sealed by a deposit of sand bedding for the paving slabs of the present pedestrianised St. George's Street laid down in 1975.

APPENDIX X

A RAZOR FROM THE ST. GEORGE'S STREET BATH-HOUSE SITE

By Pan Garrard and Lyn Sellwood

A bronze-handled, iron-bladed razor was found unstratified on the St. George's Street Bath-house site in 1982 (Appendix IX). The handle (Fig. 143, Pl. XXXVII) is in the shape of a gryphon's head with stylised body which has a crescent-shaped cut-away to accommodate the iron blade. The handle appears to be considerably worn, for the creature's feathers below the plumed crown are only faintly visible. Around the neck circles are impressed above an encircling moulding probably representing a chain and collar. The iron blade, now represented by only a fragment, is fitted into a slot below the collar and secured by two iron rivets. Its shape would have been roughly triangular.

Razors of this type are rare in Britain. Three comparable examples from late Iron Age contexts were published by Stead in his account of the Welwyn burial (*Archaeologia*, ci (1967), 38 and fig. 23), although with heads of other than gryphon type. The Canterbury razor is precisely paralleled by a group of continental pieces of Mariën's class B 1 (*Helinium*, xi (1971), 213–27; cf. *ibid.*, xiii (1973), 71–8). The distribuiton of these centres upon the Maas and the Rhine with its tributaries, although there are more widely scattered examples, including one

110. For this classification, see Introduction, p. 24.

from Narona in Dalmatia (A.J. Evans, *Archaeologia*, xlviii (1885), 77 and pl. II), now in the Ashmolean Museum. Gryphon-headed razors date from approximately the end of the first century A.D. to the mid third century. It was evidently an antique when lost.

Thanks are expressed to Dr. G. Lloyd Morgan and to Dr. Martin Henig for advice, and to Rebecca Mair for drawing Fig. 143. The photographs for Pl. XXXVII were taken by Canterbury Museums.

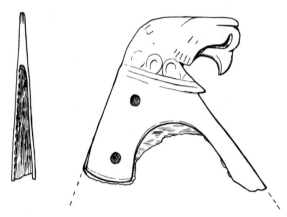

Fig. 143.   Bronze razor with iron blade from the St. George's Street Bath-Building. Scale 1 : 1

APPENDIX XI

A NOTE ON THE STREET-SYSTEM IN THE EASTERN PART OF CANTERBURY (Fig. 1)

The Roman street which runs a few metres south of Burgate Street (Fig. 1) takes a north-westwards course that aims for the West Gate, where there is some reason to suppose that a Roman gateway preceded the present medieval one.[111] That the street did extend so far was established in 1953 in a small excavation within a cellar on the north side of St. Peter's Street.[112] In the reverse direction, however, as Fig. 1 shows, the street does not aim for a gate, and must either have been cut off by the defences or have terminated before it reached their line. Nor did limited excavation on the site of the Burgate produce any evidence either for a Roman gateway or of Roman street-metalling.[113] Nevertheless, the conclusion that a Roman gate did precede the Burgate is hard to avoid, for there is good evidence that the road from

111.   Defences volume, S.S. Frere *et al.*, *The Archaeology of Canterbury* vol. ii (Maidstone, 1982), 20.
112.   Report forthcoming in a later volume of this series.
113.   S.S. Frere *et al.* (*op. cit. note 111*), 74.

Richborough aims at this point on the defensive circuit rather than for the Quenin Gate 190 m. further north. How, then, did the Richborough road connect with the street-system of the city? The probable solution to this problem is provided by a discovery of street metalling in a cellar on the south side of the modern street at No. 68 Burgate Street (Fig. 1), which is recorded by Paul Blockley below. The discovery suggested that on the east the main nucleus of the regular street–system ended at the north–south street running just west of Canterbury Lane, and that the Richborough road ran obliquely in to join it, making a slight bend southwards at or near the later line of the city wall in order to do so (Fig. 144). Although no metalling was found in either excavation, there is just room between Trenches C XX and C XXI (Fig. 1) to accommodate the course of such an oblique street.

This solution neatly solves the local problem at the Burgate, but it raises a wider difficulty. The strategic character of the Richborough-Canterbury-London road and its evident early military importance must suggest a date of construction soon after the Roman invasion, before the beginnings of urban development at Canterbury; and it would be reasonable to expect that the later network of streets would have been constructed with this road as base-line. Yet, it is the Dover-London road which runs straight through the city from the Riding to the London Gate and was evidently the line from which other streets were laid off at right-angles or parallel (Fig. 144). This fact is valuable evidence for the importance of Dover and of the road to it in the Claudian period.

The line taken by the original military road from Richborough within the city is still obscure. The bend at the site of the Burgate and the oblique course within, that leads to another and sharper bend at the junction with the street-grid, are clearly not to be thought original features. Did the road at first run straight to the vicinity of the early Roman fort recently identified near the Castle,[114] and perhaps link with the Dover road somewhere near the London Gate? Or did it continue the main alignment from the vicinity of St. Martin's Church to join the Dover road outside the Riding Gate? Or, thirdly, did it follow a straighter version of its later course through the Burgate before bending north-west parallel with the Dover road to become the forerunner of the east–west street on the south side of Burgate Street? If so, it would be easy to see how adaptations of the line could occur, when the street-system itself was laid down and the east–west street may have been extended some 130 m. eastwards to link with the north–south street that runs on the west side of Canterbury Lane. The eastern part of the east–west street has not been sectioned and cannot be proved an extension; further west, behind No. 47 Burgate Street, excavation showed that the original metalling there was of very early date.[115]

This third possibility would carry interesting implications, for the two parallel alignments of early road would suggest that the establishment of the city was already in mind.

114. P. Bennett et al., The Archaeology of Canterbury vol. i, Excavations at Canterbury Castle (Maidstone, 1982), 25–30.
115. Arch. Cant., lxiii (1950), 90 ff.

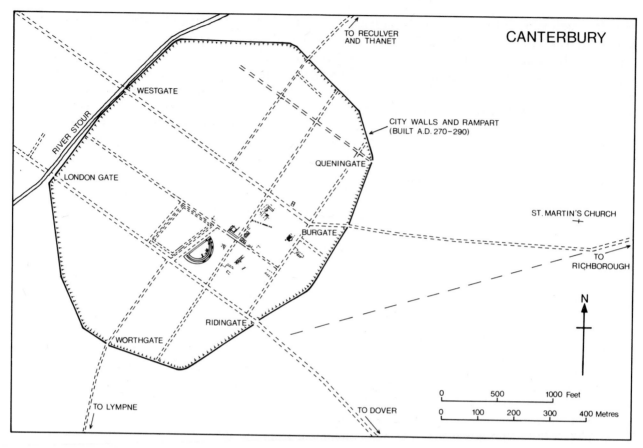

Fig. 144.   Roman Canterbury. Plan to illustrate approach roads and street-system as so far understood.

STREET-METALLING AT NO. 68 BURGATE STREET

By Paul Blockley

During the summer of 1981 opportunity arose for brief investigation of the stratification beneath the cellar floor of No. 68 Burgate Street.[116] The compact metalled surface of a Roman street was located (Fig. 1). This is interpreted as part of a street running in through the Burgate to join the main street running across the city from the West Gate.

116.   Thanks are expressed to the staff of No. 68 for allowing this work to take place.

PLATES

PLATE I

St. George's Street Bath-Building. View of Cellar A looking south, showing external wall and drain, with the cold bath in Room 3 visible below remains of cellar staircase (p. 27).

PLATE II

St. George's Street Bath-Building. Rooms 2 (right) and 3 looking south-east: second period remains (p. 27).

PLATE IV

St. George's Street Bath-Building. Room 2 showing the hypocausted apse inserted in Period 2 (p. 31).

PLATE III

St. George's Street Bath-Building. Room 3 showing the ghost of the first-period hypocaust below the second-period cold bath (p. 31).

PLATE V

St. George's Street Bath-Building. Room 1 looking west, showing second-period tile floor and wall-flues (p. 31).

PLATE VI

St. George's Street Bath-Building. Room 1, looking west, showing second-period hypocaust after removal of floor, with first-period wall-flues descending to earlier hypocaust below the lower floor and broken above it to allow admission of gases at the new level (p. 31).

PLATE VIII

CENTIMETRES
INCHES

Bossed tile (*tubulus mammatus*) from St. George's Street Bath-Building, Room 2, rubble packing behind second-period apse (p. 31).

PLATE VII

St. George's Street Bath-Building. Room 1 showing first-period hypocaust and floor *in situ* below second-period hypocaust (p. 31).

PLATE IX

St. George's Street Bath-Building. Room 7, looking west, showing second-period floor and doorway to Room 6 (p. 32).

PLATE X

St. George's Street Bath-Building. Room 7, looking west showing remains of the first-period flue from Room 6 and ghosts of hypocaust *pilae* below the level of the second-period unheated floor (p. 32).

PLATE XI

St. George's Street Bath-Building. Room 7 looking south-west, showing remains of the arched flue from Room 6 below the door, and ghosts of the first-period hypocaust below the make-up for the second-period unheated floor. On the left is the nineteenth-century drain-tunnel (p. 32).

PLATE XII

St. George's Street Bath-Building. Remains of first hypocaust in Room 5, below the floor of Cellar C, looking south (p. 37).

PLATE XIII

St. George's Street Bath-Building. Room 9, looking west, showing second-period hypocaust and bath floor used as the floor of Cellar D; the *pilae* rest on rubble sealing the ghosts of the first-period hypocaust (p. 35).

PLATE XIV

St. George's Street Bath-Building. Room 9 looking ESE, showing remains of the first-period hypocaust (p. 35).

PLATE XV

St. George's Street, Apsed Building. Rooms 1 (right) and 2 (left), looking south (p. 44).

PLATE XVI

St. George's Street, C XIV Site Q Trench I Pit 2 showing lining (p. 60).

PLATE XVII

Area R, Trench III, Section through Roman north–south street, looking east (p. 70).

PLATE XVIII

Area R, Trench I, sixteenth-century cellar, looking north-east (p. 76).

PLATE XX

PLATE XIX

Canterbury Lane, Trench C II looking south-east, with the fourteenth-century well in the background and the late Saxon cobbled floor in the foreground (p. 92).

Canterbury Lane, Cellar C I, late Saxon cobbled floor, looking south-west (pp. 81, 88).

PLATE XXI

Burgate Street, C XIV Site M Trench I. Fourteenth-century bread-ovens
of period 1, Phases 1 and 3, looking north (pp. 114–5).

PLATE XXII

Burgate Street, Site M. Fourteenth-century bread-oven of Phase iii, looking north-west (p. 115).

PLATE XXIII

Burgate Street, Site M, looking north. Bread-oven of Period 1, Phase 4 overlying oven of Phase 3 (p. 115).

PLATE XXIV

Burgate Street, Site M. Bread-oven of Phase 4, looking south (p. 115).

PLATE XXV

Burgate Street, C XIV M Trench I. Fifteenth-century tile wall of Period II at the south end of Room 2, looking south, with later brick refacing removed (pp. 115–6).

PLATE XXVI

Burgate Street, C XIV M Trench I. Brick fire-place of Period II at the south end of Room 3, looking south-east (p. 115).

PLATE XXVII

Burgate Street, C XIV M Trench III, looking south-east. Roman timber-framed partition of the early fourth century below cellar floor (p. 117).

PLATE XXVIII

Burgate Street, Area Y Trench III 4. Fourteenth-century tiled fire-back in Room 1, looking north-west (p. 124).

PLATE XXIX

Burgate Street, Area Y, Trench III 4, looking north-east. North-west wall of Room 1 (Wall B) showing tiled fire-back and second-period repair (p. 124).

PLATE XXX

Burgate Street, Area Y, Trench III 3, looking south-east; the first-period south-east wall of Room 1 (Wall C) enters the right of the picture and was reconstructed in Period III (seventeenth century) (p. 125).

PLATE XXXI

Burgate Street, Area Y. Post-medieval rain-water cistern looking east (p. 127).

PLATE XXXIIB

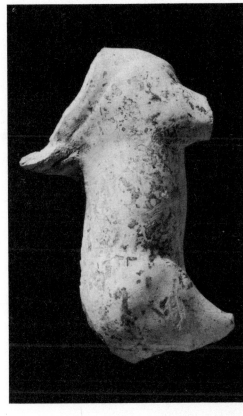

Pipe-clay figurine of a horse from Burgate Street, C X Site L (p. 175).
Scale 1 : 1.

PLATE XXXIIA

Pipe-clay figurine of Mother-goddess from
Burgate Street, Area Y (p. 175). Scale 1 : 1.

PLATE XXXIIC

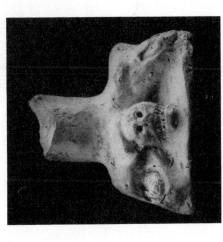

Base of pipe-clay figurine, probably
part of a medieval crucifix, from Area
R (p. 177). Scale 1 : 1.

Early medieval crucible from St. George's Street, C XI Site P (p. 177).

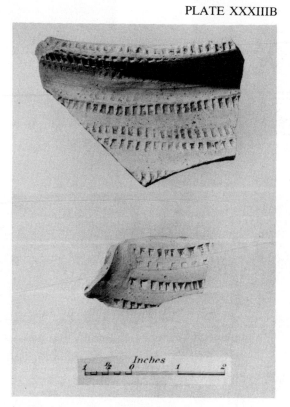

Two sherds of Badorf-type ware from Canterbury Lane (p. 232).
Scale 1 : 2.

Canterbury Lane, fourteenth-century well. Timber from layer 13, probably from the well-head (p. 93). Length 13 in. (0.33 m.).

Canterbury Lane, fourteenth-century well. Fallen timbers in layer 13, probably from the well-head (p. 93). Greatest length 17.6 in. (0.45 m.).

PLATE XXXVB

Canterbury Lane, fourteenth-century wooden dish from the well (pp. 93, and 177). Long axis, 5.8 in. (14.7 cm.).

PLATE XXXVA

Canterbury Lane, fourteenth-century well. Fallen timbers in layer 13, probably from the well-head (p. 93). Length 22 in. (0.56 m.).

Fragment of Purbeck marble pilaster capital from Area R (p. 186,
No. 10). Scale 1 : 2.

PLATE XXXVIC

Fragment of finial from Area R (p. 186, No. 11).
Scale 1 : 2.

Fragment of colonnette from Area R (p. 186, No. 12).
Scale 1 : 2.

PLATE XXXVII

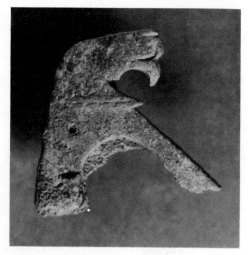

Bronze razor with iron blade from the St. George's Street Bath-House (p. 333). Scale 1 : 1.

INDEX

INDEX I : GENERAL

INDEX II: THE POTTERY

D. ROMAN POTTERY FROM DATED CONTEXTS
(dates in bold type, with page numbers)

E. SAXON